LOOKING BACK

LOOKING BACK

A Panoramic View of a Literary Age by the Grandes Dames of European Letters

by Shusha Guppy

Paris Review Editions
British American Publishing

Also by Shusha Guppy:
The Blindfold Horse

Published by British American Publishing
19B British American Boulevard
Latham, New York 12110

Manufactured in the United States of America

95 94 93 92 91 5 4 3 2 1

Library of Congress Cataloging-in-Publication Data

Guppy, Shusha.
    Looking back / by Shusha Guppy.
        p.   cm.
    ISBN 0-945167-30-X
    1. Mosley, Diana, Lacy, 1910-   —Interviews. 2. Blanch, Lesley—
Interviews. 3. Authors, English—20th century—Interviews.
4. Europe—Intellectual life—20th century. 5. Authors, English—
Homes and haunts—France. 6. Mosley, Oswald, Sir, 1896-   —
Friends and associates. 7. Upper classes—Great Britain—
History—20th century.   I. title
CT788.M66G86   1990
941.082'0922—dc20
    [B]   89-29773
                                                                 CIP

Acknowledgements

Many friends helped me during the writing of this book, to all of whom I wish to express my thanks: in particular George Plimpton, who gave me the original idea and much subsequent guidance, Jeanne McCulloch for her transatlantic support, and Yannick Belon for her kind hospitality in Paris. Above all I am deeply grateful to my interviewees for their generosity in giving me their time, educating me in various aspects of their work, and finally correcting my manuscript.

Table of Contents

Illustrations   ix

Introduction   xi

Lesley Blanch   1

Lady Diana Cooper   35

Joan Haslip   55

Juliette Huxley   87

Molly Keane   107

Rosamond Lehmann   143

Diana Mosley   173

Frances Partridge   219

Kathleen Raine   253

P.L. Travers   279

Illustrations

Lesley Blanch   *xvi*
(USED BY ARRANGEMENT WITH JOHN MURRAY
  PUBLISHERS, LTD.)

Romain Gary   13
(© JACQUES ROBERT)

Lady Diana Cooper   34
(© THE SUNDAY TIMES, LONDON 1981)

Cecil Beaton portrait of Diana Cooper   39
(CECIL BEATON PHOTOGRAPH COURTESY
  SOTHEBY'S LONDON)

Joan Haslip   54

Joan Haslip   59

Juliette Huxley   86
(© W. SUSCHITZKY)

Julian and Juliette Huxley circa 1940   95
(HUXLEY FAMILY PHOTOGRAPHS FROM LEAVES OF
  THE TULIP TREE BY JULIETTE HUXLEY, USED BY
  ARRANGEMENT WITH JOHN MURRAY PUBLISHERS, LTD.)

Julian and Aldous Huxley   96

Julian and Juliette Huxley looking for gorillas
  in Uganda, 1960   97

Molly Keane   106

Molly Keane   114

Rosamond Lehmann   142

Rosamond Lehmann   149

Diana Mosley   172
(© ALISTAIR MORRISON)

Bryan Guiness and Diana Mosley   187
(PHOTOGRAPH COURTESY FRANCES PARTRIDGE)

Frances Partridge   218
(© FAY GODWIN)

Frances Partridge at age eighteen   224
(FRANCES PARTRIDGE PHOTOGRAPHS COURTESY
   FRANCES PARTRIDGE)

Frances and Ralph Partridge, 1929   237

Kathleen Raine   252
(© TARA HEINEMANN)

P.L. Travers   278
(© JERRY BAUER)

Introduction

The absent but tutelary genius of this book is Virginia
Woolf, who said that a woman needed a room of her own
and an income of five thousand pounds a year in order
to be a writer. Many women today would also claim these
necessities, even if they had no intention of writing; indeed
the writing of novels, poems and memoirs might seem to
be a softer option than many of the callings in which
contemporary women are active: medicine, law, politics,
education, journalism and business. The desire for what
is now known as one's own space has become one of the
most fervent utterances of the feminist movement, yet few
of today's women would use that space—that essential
interval for reflection—as modestly and productively as did
the notable women interviewed in this book in their later
years, a position which allows them to reflect most marvelously on their lives. Known in their heyday as wives,
mothers, hostesses, all seem to have nourished secret gifts
and to have accomplished the impossible: eminence allied
to domesticity, in a manner which defeats many women
today. Yet all were influenced, consciously or uncon-
sciously, by Virginia Woolf's example.

There are professional writers, and there are unpro-
fessional writers. One of the difficulties experienced by

Virginia Woolf, in the course of a career which was by
any standards remarkably successful, was the ordeal she
felt she had to undergo at the hands of male critics. The
exhaustion she experienced when she had completed a
novel was compounded by the acute anxiety caused by
the anticipation of the reviews—and all the major reviewers
of the time were men, most of whom were known to her
personally. Her very real difficulty lay in perceiving the
difficulty which they did not perceive: how could a male
writer understand the intensity of a woman's desire to be
taken as seriously as her male counterparts? How could a
woman not be seen as an amateur? To be sure, Virginia
Woolf may have estimated her novels in far too indulgent
a light, yet however glowing the reviews, she still felt she
had to fight intimations of frivolousness, fantasy, insignif-
icance. One might say that although her novels are the
work of an amateur, she desired most ardently to be taken
for a professional, turning out a daily volume of words
that many another writer might envy. Still she longed for
confirmation of her genius, sought it daily, converted her
longing for certainty into the projection of that room of
one's own, that financial security, that seemed an audacious
clarion call to women of the younger generation. Yet no
good work was ever done purely on the basis of comfortable
physical conditions. And as if to prove the point, Virginia
Woolf's anxiety grew even when her own conditions were
met, when she had her writing room and her income, and
eventually the anxiety was to kill her. Thus a subtext to
her own famous statement might be this: creativity is a
mystery. It comes from within, and cannot be guaranteed
even if physical want is banished and comfort assured. To
write is to obey the work of the unconscious, and this

involves adventure, self-exploration, and even a certain amount of danger.

The women interviewed in this book are distinguished by high creativity, a quality which no doubt made them the most interesting of companions. Certainly their conversation has a liveliness which bears witness to wide experience recollected in the tranquility of great age. They seem to have been spontaneous and unselfconscious in a way that Virginia Woolf never was, yet two of them— Rosamond Lehmann and Frances Partridge—knew her personally. Neither, however, thought to follow her exacting example. If writing was incidental to their lives it was also entirely natural: it was what women did. It was, in a sense, what women did instinctively, with the minimum of fuss and effort. Rosamond Lehmann simply waited for a novel to "tap her on the shoulder." Frances Partridge found it useful to publish reminiscences of a traumatic life. Both ladies were amazed to find themselves newly popular at an age when they expected to be regarded as back numbers. Similarly, Molly Keane, who started writing as a very young woman in order to provide herself with pocket money, was content to wait several years before producing her masterpiece, *Good Behaviour*, which shows her powers mysteriously improved by her long silence. P.L. Travers, the creator of Mary Poppins, uses mystical terms to explain how these stories were "given" to her; Kathleen Raine places her faith in higher wisdom as a guide to her writing. This may argue that creativity is nourished by forms of belief, however subjective these may seem. But it is also true to say that the serenity of the women interviewed is variously nourished and inspired. Lesley Blanch, a beauty, a traveller, and an adventuress, says that she owes her entire career to a mysterious Russian who appeared in her room from time to time when she was a young child, and this too might serve as chance, as inspiration, even as guidance. From the standpoint of their great age these women would seem to underline the importance of the spiritual, the impalpable, the conditions not mentioned in Virginia Woolf's famous programme. Only the unrepentant Diana Mosley seems to be completely devoid of grace.

The problem, therefore, would seem to be that there is no problem. None of the women interviewed seems to have experienced that sense of marginality that afflicted Virginia Woolf. They seem too well-bred to divulge the extent of their own hard work: writing was an accomplishment to which they laid no special claim but which they unhesitatingly embraced as their own. This was an elegance that was perhaps connected with their amateur status; although all are now accepted as professional writers—and Joan Haslip, to cite but one instance, is the most professional of biographers—they have no personal programme to offer, are not aggressive, not beleaguered, not in pain, as so many younger women seem to be today. It might be said that literature as an essentially female calling owes much to the example and the good manners of women like these, all of whom have much to teach their successors.

There has been talk recently of the new feminism. Women, it is said, burdened with career choices, will opt for traditional roles, deserting the creative writing class for the home. One can see the pioneers shaking their heads in disappointment and dismay. Yet paradoxically this may enable a whole generation to experience literature and the ways in which literature is produced. The lives of women are exemplary from nearly every point of view; they have something to teach the young. The many lessons to be learned from the women interviewed with great sympathy and understanding by Shusha Guppy include those of age, love, marriage, bereavement, faith, and finally the business of writing, all of which constitutes material of profound importance, and a revelation to younger women starting out on the same road.

The women in this volume are as old as the century, a century which has seen enormous changes in the status of the female sex. Much has been learned, something perhaps forgotten. If there is to be a new synthesis—and it is difficult to see how there can not be—it will have to contain the best of the new and the best of the old. The extraordinary youthfulness of these exemplary women is perhaps their most inspiring legacy, proving that a natural hope or faith will survive many shocks, and that a natural gift, however modestly regarded by its owner, will contain a message to the world.

Anita Brookner

LOOKING BACK

Lesley Blanch

Lesley Blanch was already a distinguished traveller and journalist when her first book, The Wilder Shores of Love, was published in 1954. It was immediately acclaimed as a classic, and became a worldwide best-seller. It told of four nineteenth-century women of contrasting backgrounds and temperaments who sought in the East the adventures and emotions which were rapidly disappearing from the industrialized West.

Her following book, The Sabres of Paradise, which took six years to complete, with research in Russia and Turkey, was the biography of the Imam Shamyl, the religious leader of the Caucasian tribes who fought the invading Russian armies in 1834 to 1859. It combines biography and history with beautiful descriptions of the Caucasus and the campaigns in which both the young Tolstoy and Lermontov participated. Four years later she published Under a Lilac Bleeding Star, a selection of her travel pieces, in which she discussed some of her predecessors, compulsive romantic travellers whose ground she too had sometimes covered. Pavilions of the Heart, "a light book," is about the houses or rooms where great loves have been lived: George Sand and Chopin at Nohant, Liszt at Woronince, et cetera. Round the World in 80 Dishes, a cookbook containing some of the dishes she

1

savored on her travels, preceded Journey Into the Mind's
Eye: Fragments of an Autobiography *published in 1968. It
tells how she was visited in her nursery by a mysterious
Russian whom she simply calls "The Traveller," a friend of
her family who periodically appeared laden with gifts—
Fabergé eggs, icons, etcetera. Later he became her lover.
One day he vanished, never to return. The Traveller is the
origin of Lesley Blanch's passionate and life-long involvement
with Russia and Russian literature.*

In 1983 her biography of Pierre Loti *revived an interest
in the "unjustly neglected" French writer and launched a
number of reprintings of his books in France. Her most
recent book which was published last year is* From Wilder
Shores: Tables of My Travels, *in which she describes her
experiences of food through a life of travel, whether with
bedouins in the desert or the President of the United States
at the White House.*

*Lesley Blanch was born in London in 1907, the only child
of upper middle-class parents, and was educated at St. Paul's
School, "but above all at home." She studied art at The
Slade before becoming a journalist and later the Features
Editor of* Vogue, *"something generally dubbed chi-chi, something you never live down!" An early marriage was short-
lived and soon forgotten; then in 1946 she married French
diplomat and Goncourt Prize-winning author Romain Gary,
a naturalized Russian, with whom she travelled in various
parts of the world where they were en poste. The marriage
was dissolved in 1962.*

*At eighty-three Lesley Blanch is still extremely attractive
and vivacious. Though she describes her home as "a peasant
dwelling set in a bamboo grove," it is in fact a beautiful
small house on the hills beside the Italian border in Southern
France. The tiny station of Garavan, nearby, built by Queen*

Victoria, is the last stop before Italy, and sometimes from her garden you can see frontier patrols along the rock heights that separate the two countries. A keen gardener, she has created a very personal enclosed garden, with fig and citrus trees, jacarandas and mimosas, as well as lesser shrubs and bushes. It is a green bower screened by tall cypresses and bamboos: "Annihilating all that's made to a green thought in a green shade," she quotes Andrew Marvell.

Inside, the house is filled with the mementos of her travels and adventures: Russian icons, samovars, Qajar paintings, and rugs from Persia and Turkey, exotica from India. Divans and the scent of incense and jasmine further enhance the exotic and relaxing atmosphere. During the day Ms. Blanch dresses in shirt and trousers, but in the evening she changes into long kaftans and robes, brought back from her travels. She works at a desk strewn with books, papers and household bills in the livingroom. All other rooms, including her own bathroom, are also lined with bookshelves. Ms. Blanch is visited by a stream of friends and admirers, but her much-loved constant companions are her two cats, Smiley ("because he smiles all the time") and Kucuk (Turkish for "little"). This interview took place in September of 1988 at Lesley Blanch's home in Garavan, before and after a delicious lunch that she had cooked and which we consumed in the shade of a fig tree in her garden.

INTERVIEWER

You were born into an upper middle-class family. Were your parents wealthy?

LESLEY BLANCH

No. They were always broke. My father was a very clever and cultivated man, but he didn't *do* anything. He spent

his time in museums and galleries, discussing things like
Chinese porcelain and early oak furniture, about which
he knew a great deal. They had been quite well-off, especially my mother, but the money trickled away gradually.
My mother was not strictly beautiful, but seemed so. She
was extremely elegant and artistic, and extremely frustrated
too. Having married she had decided to become a devoted
wife, and everything she touched she made lovely—houses,
plants, food; she had magical hands.

INTERVIEWER

As an only child you must have been much cherished.

LESLEY BLANCH

I suppose I was, but I was also smacked every day as a
matter of course: "Has she had her smacking today? No?
There!" Whack! I was frightfully naughty and a great tease.
I did everything to annoy people, and I still do!

INTERVIEWER

*You went to St. Paul's Girls' School, which is considered
the best in England, but in your autobiography you say that
you were educated by reading and listening to your "elders
and betters." Who were they? Who instilled the love of
literature in you?*

LESLEY BLANCH

My parents, The Traveller, and anybody who came into
the house. My parents didn't suffer fools gladly, so our
visitors were interesting, and I always was surrounded with
books and pictures. I fell in love with Russia through The
Traveller, and learned a bit of Russian. I don't know it
well, but I'm not lost when I go to Russia. I used to go

to London University when it was at Somerset House and listen to Prince Mirsky's lectures on Russian literature.

INTERVIEWER
Presumably you were not expected to work, so how did you start? Did you know you wanted to write?

LESLEY BLANCH
I was certainly given the idea that I had to earn my living double quick! I went to The Slade and studied painting. Among my contemporaries were Oliver Messel, Rex Whistler and others who became famous later. I picked a living doing book jackets and private commissions before I started journalism. For example I knew something of Pushkin's life and times, so I would write an article on that, a subject not generally known. My father fell ill and there was no money left, so I worked very hard. All the Fabergés the Traveller had given me were sold. Eventually I became Features Editor of British *Vogue* and had to write about everything *except* fashion—books, people, plays, travel. That was in the late thirties. During the war, I wrote propaganda stuff for the Women's Services.

INTERVIEWER
You met Romain Gary during the war. Where?

LESLEY BLANCH
In London. He had joined de Gaulle and become an airman, a navigator with the Lorraine Squadron. He had no money and no home, but I had a charming old house in Chelsea and some beautiful things in it. It was all new to him and he was amused by it on leave. He used to lie in bed—a Louis XVI piece saved from the bombing of an

earlier house—and say: "You mean that Staffordshire rabbit was in your nursery when you were *six*? *Quelle continuité!*" He was Russian by birth and I fell in love with him partly because I found again The Traveller in him. I would recite old rhymes in Russian, or give him cucumber pickle and endless glasses of tea, and he felt at home, somehow he found his Slav roots again.

INTERVIEWER

You are very much in the tradition of the romantic English woman traveller who falls in love with the East and goes off, enduring all sorts of hardships. It started with Lady Hester Stanhope, didn't it?

LESLEY BLANCH

No. She was not a really romantic figure, any more than Isabella Bird Bishop, the travel writer. Perhaps Hester Stanhope had a romantic *life*, but she was not really a romantic in *herself*. England has always had a tradition of such involvements with the Middle East and the Arab/ Islamic world. It was a superb setting for heroic and romantic living. Unfortunately it has been marred now by the Israeli-Arab conflict. I am probably one of the last of a breed who knew something of those lands as they once were.

INTERVIEWER

What made you choose those particular four women in The Wilder Shores of Love?

LESLEY BLANCH

They were essentially romantic and adventurous creatures who fled the early nineteenth-century menace of machinery

and industry, and I felt at one with them. Jane Digby—
Lady Ellenborough—was wildly romantic, had endless love
affairs, and ended by marrying a sheikh and living beside
him in the desert. Isabel Burton married Richard Burton,
the great Arabist who translated *The Arabian Nights*. He
was her Oriental landscape. These women sensed the
whirring wheels of industrialization approaching, and es-
caped to find fulfillment, as *women*, in the East.

INTERVIEWER

*Isabel Burton is chiefly famous for her final act of burning
her husband's writing on Eastern eroticism, for which she
will be blamed by posterity.*

LESLEY BLANCH

It is silly to blame her. She burned a bit of what the
West sees as pornography, but what does it matter? There
is no shortage of Western pornography available today,
and as she thought she was saving his soul, being an ardent
Roman Catholic, rather than a prude, why blame her?

INTERVIEWER

*Isabelle Eberhardt was a curious case: highly promiscuous,
dressing as a man and dying of her excesses—physical and
perhaps spiritual. In the book you say that like her you could
"live and die in the Sahara." For most people the Sahara
is just an infinite expanse of hot sand, rather monotonous
and dangerous.*

LESLEY BLANCH

If they say that, it means they have not understood! I
can't explain the attraction of the desert except to say that
it is wild and mysterious and magical as my garden here

is on rather greener terms. I don't like a tame countryside. In England only Cornwall and Scotland have a few wild places left, which I love. You can keep Surrey and the good-style Cotswolds! But then I don't belong in England. I don't belong anywhere—it is rather restful!

INTERVIEWER

After The Wilder Shores of Love *you wrote a long preface to* Harriette Wilson's memoirs, The Game of Hearts. *She was a famous courtesan—the great Duke of Wellington was one of her clients. She tried to blackmail him, which elicited the famous reply: "Publish and be damned!" What interested you in her?*

LESLEY BLANCH

Her delightful immorality. For the first edition I wrote a long preface of some fifty pages in which I spoke about prostitutes and their place in society, which I think very necessary. It was stupid to close down the brothels, because prostitution goes on but now it can't be controlled, whereas if brothels were permitted, and properly supervised from the point of view of health and hygiene, they would be agreeable places, free of blackmail and scandal. Homosexuality has now become perfectly acceptable—about time too—though I think that demanding women, particularly in the United States, have made it so impossible for men that they have to turn to each other.

INTERVIEWER

It took some six years to write your next book, which you told me you consider your best: The Sabres of Paradise, *the story of the Imam Shamyl. Your husband Romain Gary admired it greatly, and called it a masterpiece, didn't he?*

LESLEY BLANCH
Yes. Praise from him was praise indeed!

INTERVIEWER
*It has a very rich texture and is beautifully written, and
it was a great success everywhere—France, Germany,
Russia. . . .*

LESLEY BLANCH
And I have just heard that a Daghestani man, an officer
in the Soviet Army, has translated it into Daghestani
language, which is interesting. Well, there had been nothing else on this splendid subject, except in Russia. I wrote
it in Los Angeles in the late fifties. My husband was then
the French *Consul Genéral* there. I used to get up at three
or four in the morning and write, and my research often
took me away, sometimes to Turkey and the Caucasus.
But when I finished it there seemed to be something
missing, a gap, and I decided I must go back to Istanbul,
where Shamyl had lived briefly in exile after his defeat.
My husband thought I was mad, and discouraged me. We
always had to give a huge party on July 14th for the
French citizens of Los Angeles—there were about eleven
thousand of them there. Hundreds used to come to this
annual affair. It kept me busy twenty-four hours, but I
left the next day. I had a feeling that I *had* to go and
find Shamyl's family. I arrived in Paris and went straight
to the Turkish Embassy, but they could tell me nothing.
I came down to our house in the Midi, but there was no
boat leaving, and the Orient Express was not running,
while the planes were all full. Eventually a seat was found
for me on a plane leaving from Rome the next day. I

stood up all night in a crowded train laden with suitcases,
cardboard boxes, nuns and sailors, in suffocating heat. From
Rome, where I only just caught the plane, I reached
Istanbul. I went to the old Park Hotel: "Oh Madame Gary,
why didn't you let us know you coming? We have no
room!" But they knew me well, and turned someone out
to give me a bed. I threw myself down, exhausted, but
could not rest. I *had* to go to Besiktas, along the Bosporus
(where Shamyl had once lived). The area was different
then—old dilapidated houses and beggars, a most desolate
place. Today it has been tidied up and rebuilt. I asked
the beggars, Shamyl? Shamyl Imam? One of them finally
pointed to a dead-end alley. I went down it and found a
broken-down door and pushed it open. A woman looking
very Caucasian with slanted eyes and dark hair came out,
tight-lipped. She spoke French and I asked her if it was
possible that Shamyl had ever lived there? She gave me a
look like a steel dagger and said: "Why do you want to
know?" I said I was writing a book about him. She looked
me up and down and said: "He died in Mecca." "I know,"
I said. Then she said something which I contradicted, and
she responded by saying: "I see you know your subject—
you can come in."

She was Shamyl's great-granddaughter, and she was leaving that very night for Jakarta where her husband was the
Egyptian Ambassador. She had only come over for her
sister's burial. So you see, another couple of hours and I
would have missed her! Hence my premonition that I *had*
to leave immediately after that exhausting party in Los
Angeles. She said: "I'll stay," and did. We became great
friends. She gave me all sorts of papers and letters and
unknown material. I became a friend of the whole family.
My husband had been so discouraging about ever finding

any more material that I couldn't resist sending a telegram:
"Floating on the Bosporus with Shamyl's great-great-grand-
son." Apparently he showed it to his secretary: "*Ma femme!
Quel numéro, ma femme!*"

INTERVIEWER

*When you left England in 1946 after your marriage, you
were en poste in Bulgaria for two years, I think. And later
you wrote* Under a Lilac Bleeding Star, *which is a Bulgarian
saying, isn't it?*

LESLEY BLANCH

Yes. There they say that a compulsive traveller is "born
under a lilac bleeding star." I have travelled all my life,
so it fits. Of course that meant leaving my husband often—
you might say far too often. He had other women of
course, all men do. They are so proud of their. . . apti-
tudes!

INTERVIEWER

*What about you? As a very attractive, and they say, sexy
woman, you must have had lots of offers on your travels?*

LESLEY BLANCH

Naturally. And I liked having adventures in far away, wild
countries. Everywhere I travelled I collected lots of friends,
and yes, I did have lovers too.

INTERVIEWER

*You went to Bulgaria after the war, when the country was
in turmoil. Were you happy there?*

LESLEY BLANCH

Yes, very, although there were problems: practically no food and many dramas. There were three armies of occupation—American, British and Russian. I learned to speak Bulgarian of a kind, pretty quickly. We made many friends. Best of all I got to know the gypsies. We had no money and I had no chic clothes, but I remember I had some scarlet damask curtains which I had brought from England to brighten a leased apartment; so I took them down, and the gypsies came and made me some *chalvaris* (wide Turkish trousers) which I still have, and still wear at home. They would crouch on the floor and sew. They would not take any money: "Oh no, not from you! You are one of us!" they would say. "Will you come to my daughter's birthday feast, christening? Will you dance at my son's wedding?" Of course, I would and did. I remember they were always sitting on the ground in their *mahallahs* or camps, picking nits from their heads and putting them in a saucer! But the sun shone, then, and I adored their seducing music.

INTERVIEWER

When you went back to Paris from Bulgaria, your husband worked at the Foreign Office, Le Quai d'Orsay. Did you get to know the intellectuals? It was the heyday of the Existentialists—Sartre, Simone de Beauvoir, Camus, et cetera. . . .

LESLEY BLANCH

Romain knew them all. I knew Camus, but not very well. I spoke French rather badly. I am not an intellectual in their way. I *loved* Malraux—he was a really romantic figure. Nancy Mitford was a great friend, just settling there, and

Romain Gary

becoming a part of the Paris scene. Both Romain and I revered de Gaulle, though I never met him. He wrote me a lovely letter about *The Sabres of Paradise*, and I have heard he said that it was remarkable that a woman should be able to understand the battles so well and describe them so vividly. True, I used to have my bed covered with maps, working out the campaigns.

INTERVIEWER

It is sometimes difficult for two writers to live together. Apart from practicalities, there is the question of professional

*jealousy and competitiveness. Was Romain Gary jealous of
the success of your first book?*

LESLEY BLANCH

He didn't like it at all. His friends couldn't believe it
because they thought him such a great man, but he was
jealous all the same.

INTERVIEWER

What about you? Were you jealous when he won the Goncourt for The Roots of Heaven?

LESLEY BLANCH

Oh no! I wanted him to be successful and fulfilled. It
never entered my head, never! Sometimes I got fed up
with his implacable selfishness, but we had a lot of laughs
together, and I took on all the chores while he, convinced
of his genius, devoted himself to his writing.

INTERVIEWER

*Considering the modus vivendi you had achieved with Romain Gary, were you surprised when he wanted to divorce
you and marry Jean Seberg?*

LESLEY BLANCH

Yes. And I said I would not give him a divorce for a year,
to see how it went. But finally they married, and had a
son, whom I sometimes see. He is a very handsome boy.

INTERVIEWER

Did you feel bitter about the split?

LESLEY BLANCH

Only in the sense that we had become very great friends, and had worked out a way of living together in which I took on all the chores and complications and mechanics of life. We understood each other perfectly about work and had the same sense of humor, and we both *loved* animals. He used to say "Lesley doesn't mind my infidelities, she is very eighteenth-century!" And then we had just begun to have some money, which we never had before.

INTERVIEWER

What did you do after your divorce?

LESLEY BLANCH

We both continued to live in Paris and not overlap. But fifteen years later I came down here and bought this place and made this garden. At the end of his life Romain wanted to buy a house in this area. He always loved the Midi. He said to a friend: "I played my cards wrong, I should have stayed with Lesley—she let me do what I liked."

INTERVIEWER

Were you surprised when he committed suicide?

LESLEY BLANCH

No, I wasn't surprised. We both believed in euthanasia and the right to choose one's death in dignity. He didn't want to grow old: "Oh you are so young and enthusiastic! You don't mind anybody knowing you are sixty!" he would shout down the dinner table, advertising the fact! He spoke English perfectly, with only the faintest Russian accent.

But knowing how the English-speaking people find a French
accent irresistible—rather like darling Charles Boyer's—he
would turn on a strong French accent for any attractive
woman next to him at a dinner table. It made me laugh,
and he would catch my eye and laugh too.

INTERVIEWER

Journey Into The Mind's Eye, *which you subtitled* Fragments of an Autobiography, *and which includes an account
of your travels in Russia, notably your trip to Siberia on
the trans-Siberian train, was written partly in memory of
The Traveller. When did you first go to Russia?*

LESLEY BLANCH

In the early thirties. I went to Moscow and Leningrad
because of my interest in Pushkin. By the way, I have just
heard from a friend that there is now a metro station near
where he fought his fatal duel, and it is faced entirely
with *black* marble. Isn't that wonderful? When I first went
there Stalin was starting his purges. There were few tourists, and as I spoke a little Russian the authorities didn't
bother with me much. I wasn't aware of the persecutions,
but one saw it was a grim and harsh life all round. There
were still children hunting in packs, the *Bezprezoni*, looking
for food. There were still some *droshkies*, and I would
take one and go to museums or the *traktirs*—cafés. I saw
Shostakhovich's *Lady Macbeth of Mtsensk* at the Bolshoi—
or was it the Mariinsky?—and met the composer on the
stairs. I recognized him from his photos and introduced
myself. He invited me to a party in the Green Room after
the performance. There was a samovar and cakes, and
several of the performers and people I didn't know who
were all very welcoming.

In the fifties, after Stalin's death, I went back and travelled in the Caucasus. Things were easier there, and under Khrushchev too, just as now everything is changing with Gorbachev. I think he is wonderful! The capitalist world is stupid not to hold out a hand to him—to give him a chance.

INTERVIEWER
Was your husband ever with you on those journeys?

LESLEY BLANCH
No. He didn't feel the same interest in Russia as I did, although he was Russian, Russian-Jewish, but I thought of him as just Russian, and that is what he liked in me: making a Russian home for us, with cabbage soup and samovar and piroshkis. Later he passionately wanted to be French, because he was grateful to France and de Gaulle was his hero. But you can never *become* French, can you? I can't, anyway.

INTERVIEWER
People like you who are passionate about Russia and Russian literature are usually disappointed by the Soviet Union. But in your book you seem to approve of it. In the passage relating to your trip to Siberia you write most poignantly and vividly about the plight of the convicts in the nineteenth century with their chains and fetters dragging through the frozen steppes, yet hardly mention the millions and millions who perished in Stalin's concentration camps, in worse conditions. How come?

LESLEY BLANCH
I think the Russian Revolution was an inevitable move in the context of the twentieth century, just as Khomeini's

Islamic revivalism is today. It is something, a phase, to be
gone through. I don't think it will kill Persia, and it hasn't
killed Russia. You might remember what the Tzarina Al-
exandra said: "Russia can only be ruled by the *knout*"—
the whip. Yes, that very English, rather silly stubborn lady
who was killed in Ekaterinburg in 1918, said that. I don't
know what conclusions to draw from that.

INTERVIEWER

*You had travelled in Persia in the past and in 1974 went
back to write the biography of Queen Farah. Did you get
the impression that a revolution was inevitable?*

LESLEY BLANCH

Yes. That book was a commission—the only one of my
books I have written on that basis; otherwise I have always
chosen what I wanted to write. But I loved the Shahbanou.
She was a most charming woman, and she did an enormous
amount for Persian culture and the arts, such as the
Museum of Carpet, which she created, and the Museum
of Qajar Paintings. She used to buy old houses to save
them from demolition—because of course they were all
being pulled down to be replaced by hideous modern
buildings. She once said to me: "Look at this photograph
of the Gates of Qazvin—I was only a few years too late
to save them!" I got to know her rather well, and we
often talked very freely, but then she would be called away
to some duty, and my time was up. She was—and is—a
remarkable human being.

The destruction that followed the fall of the monarchy
was in a sense inevitable. However, the world's treatment
of the Shah is one of the most ignoble episodes of modern
history. Only Sadat was loyal. The craven attitude of the
French, the Americans, and the British. . . When you

think that some African leaders who are reported to have cut up children and made chops and steaks out of them still live in great comfort in Europe, one realizes how political maneuvers stink.

INTERVIEWER

You told me that you alternate long, serious books with short, light ones. After The Wilder Shores of Love *you wrote the Harriette Wilson introduction and a cookbook,* Round the World in 80 Dishes. *I know what an accomplished cook you are, having sampled your cuisine, but what made you write a book about it?*

LESLEY BLANCH

I wrote it for a child in America. He was the son of the friends with whom I was staying in Long Island, and one evening he disappeared for a while and came back with a very good omelette he had made. So I wrote a little book for him, and did the illustrations myself. I enlarged it for England, where people still lived on rations and couldn't travel to taste exotic cooking. Nowadays cookery books are serious business, but I can't be serious about it. Sometimes when I'm writing I start cooking to relax, but usually I forget about it until the smell of burning tells me it is ruined. There goes another saucepan and my dinner, I say.

INTERVIEWER

The "light" book that came after The Sabres of Paradise *was* Pavilions of the Heart. *What gave you the idea?*

LESLEY BLANCH

I thought that houses in which people have lived and loved were interesting. I put in certain things people already

knew about, for example Liszt's life in Woronince, a
château in Poland, and lesser known ones such as the
Portuguese nuns. The book ran into trouble: the editor,
Tony Godwin, who was a wonderful man left the firm
for the States, then the art editor got pregnant and left,
and the girl who replaced her had never heard of Delacroix,
and one illustration was printed upside down! It was a
mess. I tore into the editorial director, who being a gentle-
man had to stand and take it, while I being no lady just
let fly! I insisted on a brief Errata, saying that a proper
one would be as long as a lavatory roll. But the writing
is nice, so I'm not ashamed of it.

INTERVIEWER

*Your biography of Pierre Loti, which was published in 1983,
has led to a revival of interest in him and his work. What
made you choose him, since there are other biographies of
him done by Frenchmen?*

LESLEY BLANCH

Yes, but not good ones in English. He was an interesting
character, and I shared his deep love of Turkey. He was
not just a mawkish and sentimental writer as some think.
Remember, people like Henry James and Marcel Proust
admired him greatly. He wrote beautifully and had very
sensuous rhythms. The French say, "Oh yes I read him
at school, the book about his love affair with the Turkish
woman, *Aziyadé*, and so on." But his travel books are
marvelous; and the one he wrote on China, reporting on
the Boxer Rebellion is terrifying. It took me three years
to write this biography. I always read all I can about my
subject to get a balanced view before I begin, and I always
try to find the families concerned. I had the luck to meet

his daughter-in-law. She had lived beside Loti in the same house and didn't like him. In fact she skinned him alive for me! Anyway, the book was a great success in France, although at first the French were dubious about my enterprise, because they thought that an English woman, speaking French in a rather careless way as I do, writing about *their* author, couldn't possibly get it right. But *La Revue des Deux Mondes* gave it six pages, it won a prize and it set off a whole new interest in him. I get many fan letters: *Figaro* asked me to write about his mother, and *Match* wanted me to write about his house; *Figaro* invited me to a cruise they were having in Turkish waters to give a lecture on Loti, but I declined that. I like to travel alone.

INTERVIEWER

One of the things I enjoyed about The Wilder Shores of Love *and* Loti *was their brevity. Today biographies are so very long and contain a great deal of unimportant information, don't you think?*

LESLEY BLANCH

Oh yes, typical American style! I hope I'm more succinct. Lately there have been endless full-length books about each of the four women of *The Wilder Shores*. I keep getting asked to review them! The other day I was sent one about Isabelle Eberhardt. It is very worthy and well-researched, but rather pedestrian and redundant. But when you get a man like Paul Bowles, who has lived in North Africa and has lately translated some of Isabelle's short stories, and knows what he's talking about, then it is very interesting. He knows what the Sahara means, the magic of it, the feel of it, and what *she* felt.

INTERVIEWER

There was an error of attribution in Loti *about a poem by Auden which you had said was by Eliot, and I remember how every reviewer picked it out—irresistibly!*

LESLEY BLANCH

Yes, it makes them feel superior. I suppose I forgot to check it at the last minute. Editors don't check things any more, and typesetters are worse. It also often happens when you are your own proofreader. You know your rhythm, you've been writing it for years, so you're skipping along and don't catch a fault. The proofreaders today are hardly any better than the typesetters, who don't care what they're printing. I remember a secretary I had once— I wrote a review of the ballet *Swan Lake* and she typed *Swan Cake!* I said, "But Miss Jones 'the elaborate convulsions of Swan Cake' doesn't make sense!" She was very pretty and pert, and said: "No, Mrs. Blanch, nothing you write makes any sense to me!" I cherished that.

INTERVIEWER

You have written only one novel, The Nine Tiger Man, *which was very well received when it appeared. Your autobiography,* Journey into the Mind's Eye, *reads like a novel too, especially the story of* The Traveller. *Were you not tempted to write more fiction?*

LESLEY BLANCH

No, because I can't invent. For biography I have to remember, and then work round a character. In biography you don't invent anything, but you interpret. However, that doesn't mean that you don't use your imagination.

That novel was a landscape—the landscape of Rajput India which I adored. I had pulled a ligament in my leg and had to stay on an island in Jaipur. The Indians were very kind; they used to heave me about in a boat and take me round the island. You could hear the leopards coughing at dusk in the far hills, and the parakeets flew round turning the sky green. The whole thing was extraordinary. One day I saw what I thought was a log, but it was a crocodile. I had heard the story of a group of English women being put on that island during the Mutiny and not daring to escape because of the crocodiles—just stuck there, with no news and fearing the worst. From that I imagined the whole novel. That story evolved, but no other ever has.

INTERVIEWER

It is interesting that your husband was the opposite: he only wrote fiction, and won the Goncourt twice, the second time under a pseudonym. What do you think of his work now?

LESLEY BLANCH

I don't read novels. Few last. Romain was not a disciplined writer, but he had wonderful ideas, and sometimes wrote wonderful stories. The one about the strolling players, for example. I thought *The Roots of Heaven* was fine. It had a momentous theme, like his autobiography, *Promise at Dawn*, which he wrote in Hollywood and gave me to read in installments as he went along. Of course he invented a certain amount of that, but basically it was true.

INTERVIEWER

Speaking of Hollywood, did you enjoy living there? Who were your friends? Did you mix with the film world?

LESLEY BLANCH

Yes. We both loved it. And we knew everybody: Aldous and Maria Huxley, Stravinsky and his wife Vera, George Cukor, who became a great friend, Gary Cooper, Charles Boyer—everyone. James Mason, Sophia Loren, David Selznick . . . Later I worked for George Cukor at M.G.M., which was fascinating. I wrote *The Sabres of Paradise* while based in Hollywood. At the time Cecil Beaton was there too, for *My Fair Lady*. We used to escape up to the hills for a picnic sometimes: "Where are we all going to dinner tonight?" Cecil would ask wearily, and I would say to so-and-so's—usually some filmstar. "Oh Jesus! She'll be wearing a tiara!" he would say. In Hollywood you have to know the failures as well as the successful people. The failures were especially interesting; they knew all the seamy side of Hollywood. They lived downtown where nobody chic would dream of being seen. The snobbery was enormous there, but as I didn't mind being seen at the wrong address, I would drive down beyond Hollywood and Vine and find a sort of synthesis of the past. People sitting in their verandas, in rocking chairs: an old cowboy in boots would say: "Yes, Ma'am, I used to round up the cattle for so-and-so," naming a star like John Wayne or Hoot Gibson. I knew John Wayne, and liked him very much, despite his ghastly politics.

INTERVIEWER

What about failed women?

LESLEY BLANCH

They wore baby dresses and heavy make-up, and looked like wrecks. They had been lovely and were often full of good stories. Few grew old well.

INTERVIEWER

It is amazing that living there and having an entrée *into
the film world, you didn't have your books made into movies.
They seem made for it, especially* The Wilder Shores of
Love *and* The Sabres of Paradise.

LESLEY BLANCH

M.G.M. bought one story from The Wilder Shores, but
nothing came of it. Cukor bought The Nine Tiger Man,
and I believe Fox has it now. Periodically people buy
options for radio, television, films, but they never come
to fruition. It is one of those things.

INTERVIEWER

*Your prose is very poetic and graceful. Did you read, or
still read, a lot of poetry?*

LESLEY BLANCH

No. I'm not very keen on poetry. I had a grounding in
English poetry because it was part of my home life, and
I still read Byron, some Browning, and of course Blake,
and always Donne. I also like Stevie Smith. When I was
very young I was plunged most unsuitably into the Restoration playwrights. I was introduced to Russian authors
by The Traveller and read them a great deal, first of all
Pushkin. I was very fond of some of the minor Russians
nobody else reads: Aksakov, Saltykov, Shchedrin, etcetera.
I was brought up on Herzen. I have two sets of his work:
Constance Garnett's translation in small volumes, published in 1925, which I take with me everywhere. Now
he has been discovered and is properly lauded by the
Oxford intellectuals.

INTERVIEWER

Herzen was a liberal. Are you, politically speaking, a liberal?

LESLEY BLANCH

Of course. I should say I'm rather pink. I know great
wealth produced industry and patronage of the arts and
all that, but that was a different world. Today when I see
the prices of houses and clothes and food I wonder how
the young are going to live, and in what surroundings.
Greed is destroying the planet through over-exploitation
of natural resources. Look what we are doing to the seas,
the forests, the animals! Here in the summer people throw
their dogs out on the roads and go off on holiday. The
late Duchess of Windsor knew that, and the cruelty of
it, and she used to send people to collect them and give
them shelter or find them homes. She is still a very much-
maligned woman. I knew the Windsors in Paris and remember them with affection.

INTERVIEWER

What about French literature? Who do you read and like?

LESLEY BLANCH

I read the classics. I love Gérard de Nerval, Merimée,
Stendhal, Barbey d'Aurevilly, Gobineau's *Contes Asiatiques*,
et cetera. In English I also read nineteenth-century writers,
Kilvert's *Diary*, Queen Victoria's *Letters*, and such. I love
The Babur Nameh [memoirs of the Emperor Babur]; Dean
Stanley's book on the Eastern Church is superb. I par-
ticularly enjoy Lampedusa's writing—not only *The Leopard*
but all his shorter pieces. These are some of my favorites.

INTERVIEWER

*You also have read American writers, and were—still are—
friends with some of them. I remember you telling me once*

about Carson McCullers, a favorite of mine. Can you tell me about her?

LESLEY BLANCH

I knew her very well in New York. She liked my books and I had not read hers, but I caught up and read them then. She is marvelous about the Deep South, and gave me a taste for books of that region. So I read Eudora Welty, Tennesee Williams, William Faulkner. I enjoyed the society of Truman Capote as I loved his books. I remember a party given by Leo Lerman at his house in the east Eighties, and I was sitting between Edith Sitwell and Marlene Dietrich, and Truman was lying across my lap with his head on one hand and his feet on the other! And I thought if this is American literary life, I'm enjoying it!

I also *love* American folk music—just as I love the folk or traditional music of the Middle East, Persia, Asia, or elsewhere I travel. I *write* to music: it isolates me, but my tastes are catholic: Bach, Wagner, reggae or pop—if good.

INTERVIEWER

Did you ever witness Carson McCullers' drinking bouts?

LESLEY BLANCH

She was very fragile. I remember one day taking a friend from England to see Carson. She was living up the Hudson, and we arrived for lunch. She said: "I guess you're thirsty? Would y'all like something to drink?" She produced a large teapot and we thought it was rather odd to serve tea at that hour, but out of the teapot came neat gin, served in teacups *before lunch!* She was a very sick woman, and extremely neurotic too.

INTERVIEWER

What about older American authors—Henry James, Edith Wharton, et cetera?

LESLEY BLANCH

I have read them, and admire them greatly. By the way, a contemporary American writer I think supremely good is Gore Vidal. For his irony, wit, style, and the way he tears through American institutions. I am by nature an iconoclast myself and enjoy his bombshells. He is an old friend I cherish particularly.

INTERVIEWER

Do you have a routine for work? When do you work?

LESLEY BLANCH

I used to write early in the morning—I was rather *matinale.* When I was writing *The Sabres* in Hollywood and I was running a house and doing lots of entertaining, I used to write when I came back from a party, then have two or three hours sleep, get up at five and write till eight. Alternatively I would get up at three and work till seven, then get into the car and go up into the hills around Los Angeles to have breakfast in some cowboy café. But it was irregular work—Romain and the house came first.

INTERVIEWER

Nowadays you can write any time you wish, do you write more slowly?

LESLEY BLANCH

Sometimes it rattles off quickly. But there are certain types of work over which I get *le trac* [stage fright]: journalism and reviewing books. I hate the time limit and the clock. It is no good just skimming a book, you are *reviewing*. I read it carefully and write about it with care, whether panning or praising.

INTERVIEWER

Do you like writing? I mean the actual process—you write so beautifully and it reads so easy.

LESLEY BLANCH

Oh no! It's hard! *Painful!* I sometimes write a page fifteen times. I use children's exercise books with lines. There are twenty lines on a page, and I can see that each page represents about 220 words, so I know how I'm going. I throw out the notebooks after the first draft is typed. The pleasure is when you feel you have done something good. I will "die with my eyes closed," as the old Oriental saying goes, for having written *The Sabres of Paradise*, because by so doing I've fulfilled a true desire.

INTERVIEWER

What about travelling? Did you like travelling rough or in comfort?

LESLEY BLANCH

I like impromptu travelling, roughing it one moment and the next going to dinner at an embassy. They usually know I'm there, and I take a stylish sort of dress with me and turn up looking terribly *mondaine*, having perhaps slept in the bus the night before. Then everybody asks one to endless lunches and dinners which if one accepted one would stop doing anything else. I have always particularly enjoyed going to the British Embassy in Turkey. It is such

a historic place: it's where Lord Stratford de Redcliffe gave
a ball after the Crimean War and the Sultan, to mark his
gratitude, left his palace for the first time and watched the
dancers with great interest. Travelling, I like not to know
what's going to happen next, when you don't know when
and where you are going to sleep or what or who you
will encounter.

INTERVIEWER

*I know that for the moment you don't undertake long,
difficult journeys because of a broken knee, which luckily
has healed almost completely. But where would you like to
go next, if possible?*

LESLEY BLANCH

I love Afghanistan more than anywhere else, perhaps, but
how to go back now? I long for the Middle East too.
Afghanistan is so unspoiled, so savage still, and the men
are so handsome. You go over those appalling mountain
passes and suddenly come across a little *Chai-Khaneh* [tea
house] with a samovar, and a few grubby cushions, and
you want to stay there forever. I never wanted to leave.
I wanted to take a little house and live there, but they
said I would never stand the winter; it gets to forty degrees
below zero. I would have caught pneumonia and died,
uncomfortably.

INTERVIEWER

Who are your favorite travel writers, past and present?

LESLEY BLANCH

Lucie Duff-Gordon's *Letters from Egypt* is one of my *livres
de chevet*. She lived and died there, and she adored the

Egyptians. She became consumptive in 1850, and went to
Luxor where later she died. But her understanding of the
country and its people, and her description of the cama-
raderie she shared with them are marvelous. I feel a special
affinity with her—I too feel very close to Egypt.

Tolstoy's description of the Caucasus in *The Cossacks*
is superb, as are Lermontov's, though he is more cynical.
I love Robert Byron—another cynic. He sent everything
up, but he is supremely good. Lord Curzon is marvelous
on Persia and Central Asia. Of today's writers I think
Peter Levi writes of his travels very well. He is a poet and
an Oxford don. Some travel books are full of information,
worthy, but I wish they combined it with fine writing,
which is what you enjoy in Gérard de Nerval on Turkey,
for example, or Flaubert on Egypt, or Loti everywhere.
All these young travel writers nowadays give you masses
of information, historical research and so on, but not much
style. Dervla Murphy is so intrepid that one forgets she
has first done her homework. Recently I read a curious
book, Philip Glazebrook's *Journey to Kars*; it is like no
other, and records the sort of haphazard travelling which
I myself like to do.

INTERVIEWER

*Life is so precarious today that even the young, like my
children and their friends, frequently have intimations of
mortality. Do you think of death? It seems an incongruous
question, not to say crass, to ask one so youthful and lively.
Do you believe in an after-life? Or indeed in God?*

LESLEY BLANCH

I don't know. God is within us, if He is anywhere.
Something like conscience. Sometimes I feel that heaven

would be where I could meet all my animals again. People might be too complicated. For example, suppose a man has had two wives, one after another, and has loved them both deeply. Will he meet them *both* again? What would he do?

INTERVIEWER

En effet, *the logistics of heaven don't bear thinking about!*

LESLEY BLANCH

I don't want to die as long as I am well in my body and my mind. There are too many things I like doing. Life is a present; one can't have enough of it, can one?

Lady Diana Cooper

Lady Diana Cooper was born in 1892, daughter of the 7th Duke of Rutland. Her mother, Violet Lindsay, was a Pre-Raphaelite artist and beauty, and the granddaughter of the 24th Earl of Crawford. Her pale, iridescent beauty— her skin which Winston Churchill described as being "the texture of Chinese silk," her acute intelligence and iconoclastic wit, her innocent sense of fun, frank enjoyment of privilege and total lack of snobbery, made her "The Idol of the Golden Generation" before the First World War—a generation in which aristocracy and Bohemia met and mingled, and in which she became one of the most remarkable and famous women of her time. She was loved by some of its greatest men: Prime Minister Asquith, the great bass Chaliapin, the newspaper magnate Lord Beaverbrook, and many others. Considered a suitable bride for the Prince of Wales (later King Edward VIII, and after his abdication the Duke of Windsor), instead she fell in love and married Duff Cooper, a junior diplomat without a private income.

In the twenties, partly to improve their finances and partly because she "could never say no," she starred in two silent movies (the first British technicolor films) and later enthralled America and Europe in Reinhardt's The Miracle. She later gave up her career to become a "full-time wife" when her husband left the Foreign Office for a career in politics and literature. After several ministerial posts, including Minister of Information in Churchill's War Cabinet, Duff Cooper became British Ambassador in Algiers, and then in Paris at the end of the war.

Throughout her life, Lady Diana Cooper was befriended and admired by many of the famous writers and literary figures of her time: Evelyn Waugh immortalized her in Scoop as Mrs. Stitch; D.H. Lawrence portrayed her in Aaron's Rod as Lady Artemis Hooper; she was Arnold Bennett's Lady Queenie Paulle in The Pretty Ladies; her friend the playwright and novelist Enid Bagnold gave a touching and accurate picture of her old age in The Loved and the Envied.

Her own three-volume autobiography was published in the sixties and became a best-seller, revealing a writer of considerable talent and originality. With her son Viscount Norwich (author John Julius Norwich), she founded the Duff Cooper Literary Prize.

Lady Diana Cooper lived in a large house in Little Venice, London, full of the mementos of her long and exceptional life. At the time of our interview she still looked beautiful despite her extreme frailty; deep blue eyes and porcelain skin still shone with a radiance that age had not impaired. Her bedroom overlooked a quiet garden; at home she spent most of her day there, sitting up in a large, lace-draped bed, surrounded by books and periodicals, and usually accompanied by her tiny Chihuahua called "Doggie," which she took everywhere with her—even to the Royal Opera House where dogs are strictly forbidden: she hid him in her sleeve until she got to her box. A stream of friends and relatives visited her in her bedroom, and it was there that the following *interview about some of the literary personalities in her past took place in 1983. Lady Diana Cooper died June 16, 1988.*

INTERVIEWER

When did your connection with the literary world begin?

LADY DIANA COOPER

I was born into it. My mother was a "Soul." Ah, you don't know about the "Souls?" They were a group of friends, people like Lord Curzon, no less, Lord Balfour, no less, and a few Pre-Raphaelites. It didn't mean much then, but it did later, because they all became *great*. So when I came out at eighteen I was called by the newspapers "the soulful daughter of a Soul." The funny thing was that my mother didn't like being called a "Soul": she was too individual and didn't want to be part of a group, but I thought she ought to be proud of it. Then at a party one of my young men told me that I wasn't my father's daughter but Harry Cust's. He said everybody knew it. All I could say was: Oh really? It didn't seem to matter— I was devoted to my father and I liked Harry Cust too. Well *he* was a "*Soul*," very literary, and very handsome. He had a magazine called *The Pall Mall Gazette* where he published all the famous writers—Rudyard Kipling, H.G. Wells, and so on. My mother was very literary too: She liked all these *advanced* poets—Browning and Meredith; and I was named after Meredith's *Diana of the Crossways*. Now Meredith is an awfully complicated poet, but because of this Diana complex I had to learn his famous *Modern Love*, which is something like fifty sixteen-line poems, by heart. In those days you learned *everything* by heart—so different from today when children don't even learn nursery rhymes. And you don't write letters

either, because of the telephone; we used to write letters
all the time and there were five or six deliveries a day. I
wrote to my father when he went off shooting.

The first poem I learnt was Marlowe's "Passionate Shep-
herd to his Love":

> Come live with me and be my love
> And we will all the pleasures prove. . .

When I was seven my Nanny taught me Kipling's "The
Road to Mandalay":

> On the Road to Mandalay,
> Where the flyin' fishes play,
> And the dawn comes up like thunder. . .

something and something . . . I can't remember now. My
memory is not what it used to be—I think I am losing
my marbles!

There is this nice young man who is writing the biography of Cecil Beaton who sent me a bottle of marbles
for Christmas! But I have this theory that the more marbles
you lose the better it is: my old friend Enid Bagnold had
lost *all* her marbles and was very happy, while I have
always been a prey to melancholia. It comes over you like
a wave, engulfs you, and then subsides. . . .

Anyway, my mother's favorite author was Shakespeare,
naturally, because we were brought up with the Trees: Sir
Herbert Tree was Mr. Daddy to all of us, and his daughter
Iris Tree, who became a wonderfully talented artist and
poet, was my best friend. We used to go into his dressing
room, try on his costumes, put on his Richard III ring,
go on the stage in the crowd scenes—I don't know how
he bore us! Lady Tree was my mother's best friend, but
we never knew, until much later, that he had a whole

Cecil Beaton portrait of Diana Cooper

other family: somebody called Mrs. Reed, with whom he
had five other children.

Anyway, Shakespeare was part of our lives. But as a
child I got a disease called Erb's—I don't know if you
spell it with an H or without—it is a form of paralysis of
the arms. The doctors forbade lessons—*too wonderful!* As
a result I grew up illiterate, and I still can't spell: my
nephew Rupert Hart-Davis (author and publisher) had a
lot to do with the punctuation and spelling when he
published my autobiography.

INTERVIEWER

As a debutante you had a great number of admirers—
including your future husband—who were literary. Who
were they?

LADY DIANA COOPER

We were a group of friends called "The Coterie," and
they were all literary, but they were *all* killed in the war.
Some left nothing but letters, but some did write other
things before they got killed, like Rupert Brooke. I didn't
take to him much, I don't know why. I think he didn't
approve of us—we were too free and too drunk. I knew
the Sitwells very well; though I was very thick with the
brothers I never met *her*, Edith. I didn't like her poetry—
it was too modern for my taste, which is rather old-
fashioned. Then after the First World War, I married Duff
who became a very good writer. His biography of Talleyrand made his name as a writer, but his best book is
his autobiography—*Old Men Forget*. And now my granddaughter Artemis is editing our letters.

INTERVIEWER

Your parents wanted you to marry the Prince of Wales,
and the Duke of Connaught wrote that you were the only
woman who could keep him on the throne. What happened?

LADY DIANA COOPER

We met, naturally, but he used to say: "I'm quite a good
Prince of Wales but I shall be a hopeless king." Do you
know this poem:

And were you pleased, they asked of Helen in Hell.
Pleased? Answered she, when all Troy's towers fell

and dead were Priam's sons and lost his throne—
And such a war was fought as none had known
And even the gods took part; and all because
of me alone? Pleased?
                              I should say I was!

Lord Dunsany wrote this poem about *her*, Mrs. Simpson,
not about Helen. Everybody was, of course, against her,
but I thought she was all right. Did you see the television
series about them, "Edward VIII"? They made her look
dull but tender. She was far from dull and *very* far from
tender.

Duff wanted to be a politician and a writer; the Foreign
Office had become very boring, as it is today—it's just
cocktail parties, isn't it? So I accepted to appear in two
films. They were awful! *Awful!* But I enjoyed *The Miracle*,
and touring America. Then Duff gave up the F.O. and
became an M.P. and later a minister. People asked me if
I minded giving up my career. I didn't in the least; I
adored my husband and hated being parted from him. At
the time of Munich he was one of the few who sided
with Churchill and actually resigned. I remember getting
thousands of letters thanking him for protesting against
the invasion of Czechoslovakia. John Julius, a secretary,
and I spent days forging his signature on answers.

INTERVIEWER

*Did you meet any American writers when you were in
America?*

LADY DIANA COOPER

No. A great many journalists and stage people, not writers.
I met Noël Coward, though, who was living there and we
became great friends.

INTERVIEWER

*There is a story about your first meeting with Noel Coward.
Allegedly you said to him: "Mr. Coward I saw your play
last night and I didn't think it was at all funny," to which
he is supposed to have answered: "Madam, I on the other
hand saw you in* The Miracle *and I just laughed and
laughed."*

LADY DIANA COOPER

Totally untrue. I always *adored* Noel. You see we both
had mothers, and our two mothers got together and en-
tertained each other, thank God, which made us free to
go out and have fun. Then Noël took to horseriding.
Well, I can't ride at all, but my friend Iris Tree, who was
with me in *The Miracle*, was very good at it and loved
it. So we all three went to a riding school and Noel was
terrified! They had little things for jumping over and Noel
said: "I can't bear it because every time I want to jump
the horse turns round and says 'Bet you can't!' "

Alas, Noël got old and died. . . . I used to go to
Switzerland and stay with him, but he was ill and couldn't
go up the mountains. Now his memoirs have been published and are full of accounts of the diseases homosexuals
get. . . . Yes, I loved Noël dearly, very dearly, till the
end.

INTERVIEWER

What about Hemingway? Did you meet him?

LADY DIANA COOPER

Only years later, in Paris after the war. He came to the
Embassy and his former wife Martha Gellhorn who was
a great friend of mine—and still is—wrote to ask me to

receive him. The day he came I was in bed with a bad cold, so he came and sat by my bedside. It was cocktail time and I asked him to go next door and help himself to a drink from the drink table, which he did. Then every few minutes he went back to fill his glass and became more and more drunk. By eight o'clock he was talking utter nonsense. He started reciting a long poem, and it turned out to be his own. It was *awful!* Well I didn't know how to get rid of him—he just sat there and sozzled! So I'm afraid the meeting was not a great success and I never saw him again. But I liked his books: the one about the Spanish Civil War. . . what was it called? There goes a marble! Oh yes, *For Whom the Bell Tolls,* and the other one about the war. . . *A Farewell to Arms.*

INTERVIEWER

You met Evelyn Waugh in the twenties and became lifelong friends. Where did you meet him?

LADY DIANA COOPER

When I was in *The Miracle* in London. It is awful to admit, but I liked him because he liked me. Also, he was a challenge: everybody hated him because he was so rude and so snobbish, so I thought I would like him. We remained best friends till two years before he died. Then he became too melancholic. I used to do *everything* to cheer him up. He lived in the country, because he wanted to be a *grand seigneur,* and I would buy—very much against the grain I might add—caviar and champagne and take him to the theater: "Oh no, not the Stalls! A Box!" He wasn't exactly a drunk, but he drank a lot; I didn't mind that—I was brought up with drunks. He could be dreadfully rude: once we invited Huxley to lunch at the

Embassy in Paris—not the novelist, his brother, the one
who had run the Zoo in London, Julian Huxley. Evelyn
took a delight in nagging him and hurting him. Now Julian
had become something much grander than the Zoo, head
of UNESCO, and didn't want to talk about the Zoo. But
Evelyn *would* mention monkeys and parrots all the time
and Julian got crosser and crosser; it was very embarrassing.
We had another rough passage with Somerset Maugham,
Evelyn and I. I loved Willie Maugham, but he was very
difficult, too. I took Evelyn to stay with him in his beautiful
villa in the south of France and it was a ghastly failure,
because Evelyn got on the wrong tack. He had his portmanteau which he got out of the car hoping that he would
be asked to stay. But the silly ass said something so tactless
about stammering and deafness, and the portmanteau was
put back in the car by a servant and he was asked to
leave—because, of course, Willie Maugham stammered and
was deaf.

INTERVIEWER

*You wrote once that you thought "Graham Greene is a
good man possessed of a devil, and Evelyn Waugh is a bad
man for whom an angel is struggling." When did you meet
Graham Greene?*

LADY DIANA COOPER

He came to Chantilly where I had kept a house after we
left the Embassy in 1947. There was a cottage in the
garden, very derelict and hopeless—it didn't have a bathroom or anything. Graham Greene said: "Would you mind
if I come and live there, to write?" I said it would be
wonderful and he said: "Would there be room for a
woman?" I said yes, but she won't like it—it has no comfort.

He had a mistress called . . . you must know? I can't
remember her name—there goes another marble! Well
anybody could tell you. One day Enid Bagnold and I went
to lunch with him at the Ritz—he had got some money
for his book and taken a suite at the Ritz where he was
living with this Mrs. Thing. At lunch the talk was on
Catholicism—they were both Catholics—and G.G. said:
"You Protestants are so lucky not to have things like
Purgatory to face." Whereupon she turned on him fu-
riously and said, "How dare you say they are lucky? They
are *unlucky!*" So we went on with this very highbrow,
moral talk. After lunch Enid and I went through the
bathroom to the bedroom and there on the bed, folded
neatly, was a pair of pyjamas on one side and a nightdress
on the other! They were living together in *open sin*, with
all that high moral talk, and she was married and had five
children. He still sends me a book a year. I loved *The
Heart of the Matter*, and the one after, but I was bored
by the last one.

INTERVIEWER

In the thirties did you get involved with the Bloomsbury set?

LADY DIANA COOPER

Not really. They came after the First World War, and we
were the generation before, most of whom had been killed.
But I had a great friend, Desmond MacCarthy, who was
very thick with them, and through him I met Lytton
Strachey whom I liked very much. Desmond was a famous
journalist who wrote for all the top papers. We all loved
Desmond, but he didn't have the drive that is needed to
become really famous—he was too charming and too lazy.
Although he was queer, Lytton Strachey had a mistress

called Carrington. She went to The Slade as an art student
and so did my friend, Iris Tree. I had no talent, but I
went also for fun and to be with Iris. My mother and
sisters were very good painters and draughtswomen, but
I wasn't. My eldest sister, Marjorie, was a genius—she
could do anything. She fell in love with a young man
who was penniless and my mother didn't want her to
marry him. Then suddenly someone died and the penniless
young man became the very rich Marquess of Anglesey,
so everyone agreed to the marriage. But then *he* had second
thoughts and went away for a while. So my sister was
heartbroken, and began to go out with Prince Felix Yus-
soupov, who had murdered Rasputin. Well that was all
right by me. But then the Marquess got wind of it, rushed
back and married my sister. I wasn't pleased—I preferred
the assassin.

Anyway, The Slade was frightfully cold and frightfully
boring. You drew lots of plaster casts and then the great
moment came when you graduated to the "life class." That
was even colder, with these poor nude models trembling
and freezing to death. One evening I went to Strachey
and Carrington's house and there was Virginia Woolf. I
was staggered: I had been told she was beautiful, but I
didn't think she was at all. Then she asked me a succession
of questions, like a machine gun, and I couldn't get over
it. I can't say I liked her—all those questions! You would
have thought she was interested, but I read much later
that she did this to *everybody*.

And I knew Vita Sackville-West very well. My parents
wanted her to marry my brother John (later the 8th Duke
of Rutland), but she married Harold Nicolson. In those
days you no longer arranged marriages in England the way
you do to this day in France. Vita had rather a moustache

early on—very masculine. Then a few years ago this *extraordinary* book came out which was about her affair with Violet Trefusis. [The book was called *Portrait of a Marriage* and was written by Nigel Nicolson]. I knew Violet Trefusis very well, but I had no notion of her lesbianism. The funny thing is that her letters are much better than Vita's, who was the literary one of the two. Nowadays there is a movement that wants to liberate male homosexuals, but female homosexuals don't have to be liberated—they always have been.

INTERVIEWER

D.H. Lawrence portrayed you in Aaron's Rod *as Lady Artemis Hooper. Did you meet him?*

LADY DIANA COOPER

Only once—but I didn't take to him much. *Lady Chatterly* shocked society, but it didn't shock me. I thought Lawrence just used words which nobody else was using. I don't judge books; I have no critical faculty, I just like them or don't. But I was very friendly with Arnold Bennett who also put me in a book, which I didn't mind. Like Evelyn he was a challenge: nobody liked him, so I thought I had to. Through Bennett I met H.G. Wells whom I became very fond of. Before the First World War he had invented a game called "The War Game," with tin soldiers and guns, which we all played. We didn't know how soon afterwards we would be playing the real thing, and that most of the players would be killed. Then later I became friends with Moura Budberg, who was Wells's mistress for a long time. She was a wonderful Russian woman who had been Maxim Gorky's mistress, and then married a Baron Budberg. Anyway, we stayed friends till the end.

INTERVIEWER

At the end of the Second World War your husband was
sent to Paris as Ambassador. Your term of office has become
legendary. Did you meet many French literary figures?

LADY DIANA COOPER

In fact, we were first sent to Algiers as a stepping stone
to the Paris post. Our great friend was Gaston Palewski,
who had come to England as John the Baptist to announce
the arrival of the Saviour—de Gaulle. So in Algiers, de
Gaulle came to dinner. We were absolutely awe-stricken
and I didn't know what to talk about. Well, when people
are in despair about conversation the best thing is to talk
about childhood because then you become equals. So that
went wonderfully well—"*Mon père était très dur, ma mère*
était très douce"—that sort of thing. He had heard that
for a while, when my husband was out of office, I had
kept a small farm and when the conversation sagged he
said, "*Comment va la vache?*" But he spoke an exquisite
French and wrote it too. I think de Gaulle and Churchill
would have survived through their writing even if they
hadn't become great as statesmen. Anyway, Gaston Palewski became a Minister and brought *everybody* to the
Embassy. Through him we met Louise de Vilmorin whom
I adored. She became my husband's mistress for a while
and my best friend. One day Louise produced Malraux,
with whom she had had an affair in youth. I found him
alarming, very serious, and I knew I could never get close
to him. We used to call him "Monsieur de," with reference
to Vilmorin's famous novel, *Madame de*. . . . Do you
know that at the end, they got back together and lived
with each other till they died?

Did you read his books?

LADY DIANA COOPER

Good Lord no! I shouldn't have understood them, should I? Have you read them? Anyway, I had less time to read than before. I had read a great deal in youth.

Nancy Mitford was living in Paris too and was a great friend. She used to come to the Embassy a lot and later to Chantilly to write. She wrote a book called *Don't Tell Alfred* which made fun of me, but I didn't mind at all, I thought it was funny. Gaston Palewski was the love of her life—"The Colonel" we all called him. "Oh yes, I adore him, I adore him," she used to say, but there was never any question of marriage between them. In the end he broke her heart by marrying someone else—a fabulously rich woman who had a palace like Versailles, with a heated lake—not a swimming pool, a *lake*, heated! And the whole place was full of Talleyrand things because she was descended from him.

INTERVIEWER
Did you establish a circle of friends there like "The Coterie"?

LADY DIANA COOPER

Oh yes, *la bande*. The leaders were Louise de Vilmorin and Cocteau. Cocteau was very bright and sweet. He talked constantly and used to raise his hands so that nobody else could speak while he monologued. There was "Bébé" Bérard [Christian, a famous stage designer], whom I adored, and many others. Everybody came to the Embassy—I can't remember them all—Gertrude Stein and her girl friend,

Eluard, Aragon . . . everybody. I had met Aragon years
before with Nancy Cunard, with whom he had an affair.
Then on the rebound he married this Russian woman
[novelist Elsa Triolet] and became a communist. Nancy's
mother, Emerald Cunard, was a great friend of mine. She
had married someone quite unsuitable for her called Sir
Bache Cunard, who was a Master of the Hounds and that
sort of thing, and Emerald proceeded to take lovers immediately. One of them was George Moore who was
devoted to her and whom they said was Nancy's *real* father
because Nancy looked exactly like him. But as George
Moore looked exactly like Sir Bache Cunard it was hard
to tell. I always say it doesn't matter. People make too
much fuss about infidelity nowadays.

INTERVIEWER

*You also met Karen Blixen through Cecil Beaton at this
time. What did you think of her?*

LADY DIANA COOPER

A friend in Paris called Dolly Radziwill had married a
Dane and Karen Blixen used to come and stay with them
and I saw her often. She was not at all the *grande dame
de lettres* that you might imagine—the opposite, very simple
and interested in everything. I think she had developed
a kind of sixth sense on account of having lived so long
in Africa. Cecil Beaton was going to photograph her shortly
before she died. He rang her up to say would she mind
if he postponed it for a while. She told him that if he
didn't go then, he would never see her again. So Cecil
canceled everything and went. Then she died—she knew.
    Then a great many stage people came to the Embassy.
You see, hotels were scarce after the war. At the same

time there was a tremendous atmosphere of good will and
euphoria as a result of the Liberation and a great *va-et-
vient*. So we put up everybody—everybody who was anybody, that is—at the Embassy. Laurence Olivier and Vivien
Leigh came. I loved her—she was very beautiful and intelligent and she could talk about other things than the
stage, which he didn't. Stage people always speak about
the theater, but I don't mind that—I can take it.

INTERVIEWER

*After the war, Churchill's Conservative government fell and
Labor won the elections. You left the Embassy in 1947, but
kept the house in Chantilly. What happened next?*

LADY DIANA COOPER

Well, Churchill had won the war and couldn't believe
that they would get rid of him so soon. But they did and
he was very cross. He said, "They say it is a blessing in
disguise. Well, it is very well disguised!" Ernie Bevin became
Foreign Secretary and came to Paris. I liked him very
much and he liked us. When he called us back to London
he said, "Duff must go to the 'ouse O'Lords." But in fact
it was the Conservatives, when they came back in 1951,
who gave Duff his peerage.

Lots of friends came and stayed in Chantilly: Nancy
[Mitford] came and wrote there, Paddy [Patrick Leigh-
Fermor], Evelyn [Waugh] and many more.

INTERVIEWER

*After your husband's death you set up the Duff Cooper
Memorial Prize which last year was given to Richard Ell-
mann for his biography of James Joyce. Did you ever meet
Joyce?*

LADY DIANA COOPER

Never could read *him!* Too modern for me. I always dread
the prize-giving ceremony. This year Stephen Spender is
doing it. One year I remember it was the American poet
Robert Lowell. But he had a nervous breakdown and was
sent to a loony bin—not for the first time I might add.
So we looked frantically for a replacement and John Julius
found someone distinguished and we thought all was well.
On the prize-giving day I was standing next to a tall man
who seemed quite drunk and I started telling him the
story of how the man who was to award the prize had
gone bonkers and was taken to a loony bin. At that point
my son came forward and said to him: "Mr. Lowell will
you come with me?" I didn't know what to do—evidently
he had decided to come at the last minute. Fortunately
he seemed too drunk to take it in.

INTERVIEWER

Is there anybody you have wished to meet and haven't?

LADY DIANA COOPER

Not really. I never liked people because they were famous.
Whenever I met someone I liked them or didn't, but I
didn't care about their fame. Where I was lucky was getting
involved with the stage for a while, because it was such
fun. But not because of fame. Perhaps because I have
always been famous and took it for granted; I didn't
consider it important. Even now I keep getting letters
from all over the world asking me about all sorts of things,
even the Crimean War—as if I had been there! I don't
really want to meet any more people—I am too, too old.

Yes, I have always been famous, and I shall never know
why.

Joan Haslip

Joan Haslip is the doyenne of English biographers. Over the years she has written a dozen biographies of historical figures such as Maximilian of Mexico, the Empress Elizabeth of Austria, Marie Antoinette, etcetera that have won her worldwide acclaim. Many have received international prizes and have become best-sellers in various countries.

Joan Haslip was born in 1912 in London. Her father, a doctor, was the architect of the first scheme for a comprehensive state-supported health service. Her half-Austrian mother was a keen traveller and lover of the arts. Joan was thirteen when her father died, and her mother took her and her sister to live in Florence. Largely self-taught, Joan began to write poetry in her teens, and at seventeen returned to London to work on The London Mercury, a leading literary magazine. She published her first novel, Out of Focus, when she was nineteen and won immediate recognition as a new and original talent. Two years later she wrote her second novel, Grandfather Steps, then she turned to biography. Her first book was a life of Lady Hester Stanhope, the nineteenth-century traveller who went to live in the Levant and set the example for a whole line of romantic women-travellers that continues to this day. The popular and critical success of this first biography encouraged her to continue in this genre.

55

During World War II Miss Haslip worked as an editor for the Italian Section of the BBC, but returned to full-time writing immediately afterwards. The Crown of Mexico, *her biography of Maximilian, which was first published in 1971 under the title* Imperial Adventurer, *became a best-seller on both sides of the Atlantic and was Book of the Month club selection in the United States. She left England soon after to settle in Florence, where she has been living ever since. Although she describes her home as "a peasant house," in fact it is an attractive and comfortable house made of two cottages. It stands on a high hill above Florence overlooking on one side the city, and on the other, fields stretching far into the Tuscan countryside. Inside, it is simply furnished and has the warmth and comfort of an English country house. She is at the center of a wide circle of friends, and famous for her hospitality. Italian academics and nobility, English and American scholars, European expatriate artists and writers, and passing friends often gather around her dinner table and enjoy the delicious meals she provides, the lively conversation and the conviviality she generates.*

Tall and handsome, Miss Haslip has a keen sense of humor and strong views, yet so kind that often she "suffers fools gladly," only to regret it afterwards! She speaks in a deep expressive voice, and sometimes uses Italian expressions and quotations. This interview took place on two occasions in December 1989, at her house in Florence.

INTERVIEWER

One of the pleasant aspects of life in England is the National Health Service, the fact that we don't have to pay astronomical sums for medical treatment. Yet I for one didn't know that it was your father's brainchild. Are you proud of that?

JOAN HASLIP

Of course. My father was a doctor and worked for the Department of Health. He couldn't bear all those hospitals in the country going around "making collections": begging for money. He was in favor of state medicine and the architect of the National Health Service. In those days it would have cost one *penny a week* to contributors, yet it was rejected. When he died the plan was shelved, but later Lord Beveridge revived it and finally it was set up.

INTERVIEWER

What about your mother? What did she do? One thinks of you as very English, in fact you are only half-English, and your lineage on your mother's side is very colourful, with roots in the Balkans.

JOAN HASLIP

My mother was half-Austrian and half-Serbian. My Austrian grandfather had gone to Serbia as an expert agriculturalist. On arrival he had seen my grandmother sitting on a plum tree eating fruit and had fallen in love with her there and then. Later she was sent to Vienna to be "finished," he followed her, and they got married. I was born in a rather grand house in St. James's Square, London. My father died when I was thirteen and we couldn't keep up our way of life. My mother, who loved travelling and knew Florence well, brought my sister and me to live here. I learnt Italian but not very well; I never had lessons and couldn't write in the language, but I knew French well. You say I'm English, but in fact my father also was half-foreign: Irish.

INTERVIEWER

Were you educated at home, like most women of your time and class?

JOAN HASLIP

Yes, mostly, but for a while I did go to the classes of a remarkable woman called Miss Wolff, who had started life as a governess. Among previous alumni were Diana Cooper and Nancy Cunard and many others, and if I earn my living today writing biographies it is thanks to what I learnt before I was thirteen with Miss Wolff. She believed that women, who didn't have to earn a living in those days, had to learn history and literature, with only one hour of mathematics per week. She thought that if someone showed a particular aptitude for that subject she could have extra lessons, otherwise the average woman only needed to know how to do her own accounts, and that all that algebra and geometry was useless to her. Now of course it is the other way round—you hardly learn history, or indeed English at school. Michael Arlen wrote a novel in which the heroine goes to a school in South Audley Street— Mayfair, "where all the girls go to!" and depicted Miss Wolff as the headmistress. She recognized herself and was furious!

INTERVIEWER

After you moved to Florence, how did you pursue your studies?

JOAN HASLIP

At home. Later I went to England in winter, and went to some classes at London University. When I was sev-

enteen I went to work with John Squire, the editor of *The London Mercury*. I had written some poems, as adolescents are wont to do, and a friend of my father's showed them to him. He said: "Whoever wrote this, ask *him* to come and work with me." He expected a young man, not a seventeen-year-old girl with red curls and freckles. Jack Squire was the only man in England who made five thousand pounds a year from *belles lettres*, which is the equivalent of fifty thousand today. He was a sort of genius, and working with him was a wonderful training.

Another young recruit a few years older than me was Alan Pryce-Jones.

I was a sub-editor and learnt much from other people's mistakes: for example to avoid purple passages, and to be concise. Squire said that anybody ought to be able to write a short article of three-hundred words on any subject. He published some of my poems, as did *The Sunday Times*, but he told me: "You'll never be a very good poet but if you try you might become a good writer." I said but if I can say everything in three-hundred words why should I try and say it in three-hundred pages? He said: "Try." I did.

INTERVIEWER

Your first novel, Out of Focus, *was epistolary. It is a rather difficult genre, and there are few successful ones, the most notable being* Les Liaisons Dangereuses. *Yours was very successful; how did you do it?*

JOAN HASLIP

Because I was used to writing three-hundred-word pieces! It is about a young girl who falls in love with a Hungarian. She writes letters to him and goes out to Hungary to marry him. Then she writes about her disillusion in Hungary to a friend of her father's back home, and gradually realizes that she is really in love with this man. The last letter in the novel is written turning her down. This letter was written by Jack Squire. I was nineteen when it was published. A friend I met in the street told me that I was in the headlines in *The News Chronicle*. It was a review of the book by Norman Collins, who later started commercial television in Britain and made himself a millionaire.

INTERVIEWER

Was it autobiographical? I mean first novels often are.

JOAN HASLIP

People thought it was, but it wasn't. I had invented the whole thing.

INTERVIEWER

With the success of the book, could you leave your job at the London Mercury?

JOAN HASLIP

Yes. And I did. I became a full-time writer, and wrote my second novel: *Grandfather Steps*. It is about an upper-class Italian girl of mixed parentage, with a Polish grandmother, who falls in love with an American film producer of Polish/Jewish origin. She travels to Poland to see her grandmother's family, and visits some Jewish villages. She is horrified to find out where her lover comes from, and she can't face marrying him. She offers to live with him without marriage, but he refuses. She ends up making a conventional marriage with an Italian friend of her childhood.

INTERVIEWER

By then you were all of twenty-one, with two successful novels, both very sad, about unfulfilled love. Did you have sad experiences yourself?

JOAN HASLIP

Not at all! I was flirtatious, but I didn't have proper love affairs. I was very ambitious, and I was totally concentrated on my writing, because I had wanted to be a writer all my life and it seemed to be working. Anyway in those days you remained a virgin till you married, and love-affairs didn't go very far, you know. . . . In my crowd only one girl had a proper affair, with a married man, all others were virgins. So when later on I did have an affair I thought I was being fearfully advanced! I liked admiration more than anything else, which is an awful thing to admit, but true.

INTERVIEWER

Both novels being successful, they should have encouraged you to go on, yet you suddenly switched to biography, and for good. Why?

JOAN HASLIP

Because of the reviews of the second novel. J. B. Priestly wrote about it saying something like: "a very clever study of most unpleasant people." V. S. Pritchett wrote that I was "a pretty, witty, spendthrift writer who wastes people, themes and time." I think it was because I wrote about the cosmopolitan Europeans who travel, which was the only world I knew. It wasn't very English and they didn't like it. So I thought I would write a book they could take seriously, and once I started I realized I preferred biography to novel as a genre, at least for me.

INTERVIEWER

Why did you choose Lady Hester Stanhope? She was the first of the great Romantic travellers who went to the Middle East and started the whole tradition. How did you find her?

JOAN HASLIP

I came across her in Lytton Strachey's *Eminent Victorians.* There was a short paragraph about her of which the last

line was: "Lady Hester Stanhope died with her nose in
the air!" No publisher was willing to give me enough
money to go over her tracks in the Lebanon and the
Levant. So I never went, but you can write anything about
any country if you do enough research. In the end the
book was a success, and a very pompous man reviewed it
in *The Central Asian Review* saying that it was obvious
that I knew every inch of the country! Years later I met
him with friends in Florence and told him the truth, that
I had never set foot in Lebanon. Fatal! He was furious!

But you know Hester Stanhope is still remembered in
the Middle East. There are still legends about "the English
Sytt" told around the Arab tents, although she was half
mad by the end.

INTERVIEWER

*Why do you suppose those English women who followed in
her steps went East—and still do? The last of the breed is
I suppose Freya Stark, and very remarkable she is too.*

JOAN HASLIP

I think that the deep, underlying motive was that they
couldn't play the part they wanted in Europe. Hester
Stanhope was Prime Minister Pitt's niece, and since he
wasn't married she lived with him at Downing Street and
acted as the hostess. Well, where do you go after that?
When Pitt died she found herself a spinster without much
money, and took her young lover, Michael Bruce and a
large retinue, and went to live in the Middle East in grand
style. In those days you could take your doctor and servants
and live grandly on much less than in Europe. Take Freya
Stark, who is, as you say, the last of the breed. She too
was plain, had no money, and worked as companion to

old people. So she learnt Arabic and Persian, went travelling in the Middle East and writing about it, most ad-
mirably I might add. So I think it was basically a romantic
longing for a better, more gracious life. But I may be
wrong. Anyway, Hester Stanhope's biography has recently
been republished by Penguin, and Kenneth Rose wrote
in his review: "The evergreen Ms. Haslip wrote this book
so many years ago!" Wasn't that nice of him?

INTERVIEWER

*If you couldn't go over her tracks, how did you set about
researching her life? I mean the Oriental part?*

JOAN HASLIP

First through travel books. There is a wonderful portrait
of her in one of the best travel books of all times: *Eöthen*,
by Kinglake, who went and visited her in the Lebanon.
By the way, Lamartine and Byron visited her too. She
lived in a fortress on the mountains above Beyrouth. It
is now a ruin, as is the whole city. She led a very strange
life there; when her lover left her, she developed a very
curious relationship with a French man. But she was getting
on and her love life was at an end. She fought against
Ibrahim Pasha of Egypt when he invaded Syria. Indeed
her fortress was the only place that resisted him.

INTERVIEWER

*Do you enjoy the elaborate process of researching for a book,
which might take years before you can actually see a pattern
developing?*

JOAN HASLIP

Yes I do. I love the London Library. As you know you
pay a subscription of £70 a year and can take out as many

books as you wish. I think it is worth every penny. Then each book leads to others, and in the case of a historical character there are the official archives and documents you can look through. Personal letters, memoirs, etcetera. . . . everything helps.

INTERVIEWER

Lady Hester Stanhope was published when you were twenty-two, and it was a success with the critics and the public. As you said from then on you decided to write biography. I am interested in the mechanism of changing literary genres. What is the difference for you, as regards the process of creation, between novel and biography?

JOAN HASLIP

The chief thing that interests me in writing generally is to find out what makes people behave the way they do. In fiction you have to invent people's motives, in biography you have to stick to facts and find out the motive behind them. I must also admit that publishers were willing to give me reasonable advances for biographies but not for novels, and I needed the money. So practical matters come into what you decide to write as well.

INTERVIEWER

I feel that if you are willing to spend years working on somebody's life, you must be a little in love with them. What I find extraordinary about Michael Holroyd, for example, is that he has spent twelve years on Shaw without being in love with him!

JOAN HASLIP

You are absolutely right. The whole venture follows the pattern of a love affair: initial infatuation, experience, dis-

illusion, friendship, in that order! When I started on Hester
Stanhope, I liked the life, the ambience in the Middle
East, the romantic adventures. When I finished the book
I didn't like her at all; I thought she was an arrogant,
conceited English woman. On the other hand I was in
love with Parnell all along while I wrote his biography.
Someone said I was jealous of Mrs. O'Shea, Parnell's
mistress for whose sake he lost everything. It is true, I
couldn't bear her!

INTERVIEWER

*You told me why you decided upon Hester Stanhope, but
what made you pick Parnell for your second biography?*

JOAN HASLIP

Because of an extraordinary dream I had three nights
running. You know that my generation learnt English
history from William the Conquerer to the Corn Laws.
I knew nothing about Irish history. In my dreams I learnt
the name of Mrs. O'Shea, which I didn't know before,
and I remember thinking that she should be wearing a
bustle not a crinoline, because it was historically wrong.
In my dream I saw the whole Parnell story like a film. I
took the idea to my agent who was very discouraging,
saying: "Publishers would want a middle-aged politician to
do Parnell, not a young girl." Undaunted, I went to my
publisher, Dicky Cobden-Sanderson of the Doves Press,
and he said the same thing. But I told him that I had
had this strange dream for three nights and that I *had* to
do it. He relented and said: "Well if you must you must,
and here is a contract," and he gave me an advance. Can
you imagine any publisher doing that now? Because Lady
Hester Stanhope had not been published yet, and he didn't
know it would be a success—he just trusted me. As it

happened Parnell was a best-seller on both sides of the
Atlantic, and you know why? Because it was published at
the time of King Edward VIII's abdication and his marriage
to Wallis Simpson, and the American press was full of
the theme: "All lost for love!"

INTERVIEWER

*How did you research Parnell? It was easier because there
were still a number of people who had known him and
been involved in his downfall, at the same time it was a
sensitive subject.*

JOAN HASLIP

I am very stubborn and always do the opposite of what
I am told! Lord Russell, whose father had been the judge
at Parnell's trial said to my mother: "Tell that child not
to try Parnell, no one will take her seriously." But I went
on, and in the end he relented and gave me all his father's
papers. Other people discouraged me too, saying, "Write
a novel about Parnell, not a biography." I suppose I just
didn't look the part. J.S. Garvin, the famous editor of *The
Observer* said: "How absurd that you should be doing
Parnell, *I* should be doing him!" But he was fair, and
when the book came out he gave it to review to Stephen
Gwynn, the Provost of Trinity College, Dublin, and he
gave me a wonderful review. I wrote and thanked him,
and he later told me: "Frankly when I met you I never
thought you would write anything of the slightest interest!"

INTERVIEWER

*Another interesting aspect of your biographical work is that
your subjects are so varied, they do not belong to one
profession or one social group or activity.*

JOAN HASLIP

I did stay in Ireland for a while, I mean as locale, and
wrote a novel just before the war. It was called *Portrait
of Pamela*, and was about Pamela Fitzgerald, the so-called
daughter of Madame de Genlis and Philippe Egalité. It was
a historical novel and I was commissioned to write it. The
publishers had just had a huge success with another novel
called *All This and Heaven Too*, and they wanted me to
produce another, similar best-seller. Unfortunately it came
out at the time of Dunkirk and flopped abysmally. It was
a dreadful moment.

INTERVIEWER

What did you do during the war?

JOAN HASLIP

I set my work aside and went back to England to help
the war effort. I was sent to the reference section of the
Ministry of Information. God how I loathed it! It was full
of women who wanted the war to go on forever, because
for the first time in their lives they felt important. My job
was to make resumés of people and places for politicians
to use in their speeches. I stayed a month and was kicked
out. Then I went to the Italian section of the BBC. I
arrived in the central newsroom the day Singapore fell,
and the atmosphere was ghastly. They thought I was a
typist and showed me a rickety typewriter. I confessed I
couldn't type. I heard one man say to another: "Christ!
They've sent us a highbrow young writer to train." Luckily
a wonderful man took the trouble to train me, and I
became an editor. He didn't allow me to write, saying,
"You're talking to people listening in cellars. You must

dictate your text to a secretary, talking in short sentences and repeating the important news items halfway through." It was very hard at the beginning, and after three years it took me a long time to write normally again.

The translators and news readers were Italian-Jewish refugees. I once had a dreadful row with one of them, a very conceited young man called Mr. Cohen. He was always chosen to read Churchill's speeches, and he thought he had a wonderful voice, which was true. It was about midnight and we were all very tired, and he said that I gave him too much work to do. I replied that if I managed to write the piece despite fatigue surely he could translate it. He made a fuss, I lost control and burst into tears, saying: "How right Mussolini was to get rid of you!" It was unforgivable! I thought I would be sacked. Years later I was walking down the street in a residential part of London, and I saw someone getting out of a very grand Rolls Royce. It was Mr. Cohen. "*Tesoro! Che gioia di vederti!*" (Treasure, what a pleasure to see you.) He embraced me and we might have been great friends.

INTERVIEWER

What did you do when the war ended?

JOAN HASLIP

I remember my boss at the BBC saying: "What a pity, you have the makings of a first-class journalist and you are going back to being a high-brow writer!" Because one did become a journalist during those years. One's whole mentality changed: I would have walked over corpses to get a story put on the air *before* the German section did. I remember running down the stairs four at a time to get the story first. Anyway, I left the BBC and started to work on *Lucrezia Borgia*.

INTERVIEWER

Now that was a wicked woman, apparently. What made you pick her for a subject?

JOAN HASLIP

I liked her! My whole theme was that the Borgias were no more wicked than all the others. Half of those Cardinals the Borgias were supposed to have killed died of *over-eating!* Think of all those heavy clothes they wore, and there was no refrigeration, so many of them died of food-poisoning. But the Borgias were hated because they were foreigners and came from Spain. They were the hated *mareano*. Lucrezia herself didn't kill anyone, her brother Cesare did. She married the Duke of Ferrara and became an estimable character; it is pure legend that she was evil. Cesare was an extraordinary man who nearly made a united Italy, centuries before Garibaldi, and he probably would have succeeded had he not died at thirty-two. Lucrezia was in love with her brother and totally dominated by him. Their real father, who was the Pope, was thoroughly wicked but very clever. He cut South America in half, dividing it between Spain and Portugal. His children who were supposed to be his nieces and nephews, were called *i principi nipoti*, hence the word nepotism.

INTERVIEWER

After the Borgias you went back to the Middle East and wrote about Sultan Abdul-Hamid, the Ottoman Emperor. Was that a commission?

JOAN HASLIP

I suggested the Sultan because I have always been interested
in the end of Empire and I love the Middle East, and I
think it is my best book, although it sold less than the
others. It had the best reviews I've ever had. I went and
lived in Istambul when I was working on it, and I loved
the town.

INTERVIEWER

*Presumably you didn't know Turkish—or Arabic, the reli-
gious language of the Ottoman Empire. So how did you
research the Oriental side of the story?*

JOAN HASLIP

Many documents were in French, which was the language
of the Court and of diplomacy. Then I learnt a lot from
reading Ambassadors' reports and Foreign Office papers,
the Public Record Office documents, etcetera. . . .

INTERVIEWER

*He was the man who ordered the massacre of the Armenians
in 1903, how could you like him?*

JOAN HASLIP

There were mitigating circumstances. There was a war with
Russia and the Armenians opened the doors to the enemy,
so that they were considered traitors. Not that I condone
what the Turks did, but despite that I became fond of
him. You do when you live with someone for years. I was
very lucky because I found his last surviving wife, Khadive
as they were called, aged ninety, living in a little pavilion
in Yildiz Park. The house was delapidated, the silk hangings

were in tatters, and she was wearing an old plush coat
and looked ancient. But she still had lovely hands and a
beautiful voice. A slave opened the door and bowed to
the ground, and we were offered coffee in little jewel-
encrusted cups on a silver tray. It was like a scene in a
movie. We talked about the Sultan, and as I was leaving
she said to me: "Be kind to him, for he loved no one,
least of all himself." And you know who took me there?
The Sultan's Austrian-Jewish dentist, Sonny Gunzberg who
was still the best dentist in Istambul, utterly loyal to the
Sultan's family, supporting them out of his earnings. He
was also Ataturk's dentist, who admired him for his loyalty.

INTERVIEWER

*So would it be correct to say that you choose the subject of
your biographies at random, or come across them by chance?*

JOAN HASLIP

Yes. Sometimes somebody else gives me an idea. Patrick
Kinross, who wrote the biography of Ataturk and the
history of the Ottoman Empire, suggested Sultan Abdul-
Hamid to me.

INTERVIEWER

*Having tackled characters from so many different areas, I
wonder why you have never done the biography of a literary
figure, a writer or a poet, or indeed an artist of any kind?*

JOAN HASLIP

The only one who tempted me was Sheridan. He fascinates
me as a character, and I like his writing and his background,
eighteenth-century London. In fact after I finished *Marie
Antoinette*, my latest book, I wanted to write about some-

thing English. I thought the permissive society of the eighteenth century provided a good parallel with today's social mores. Our permissiveness started in the 1960s and has led to terrible problems. But my publisher was not interested.

INTERVIEWER

Is biography art or craft? I mean if we define art as creating something out of nothing and craft as creating something out of something else? Is it like being a poet or a painter, or like being a potter or cabinet maker?

JOAN HASLIP

It is both art and craft. Or rather it is a craft that can be artistic. The most important quality is psychological insight. Imagination is important, but not in the inventive sense. You imagine a scene that has actually happened, as if you were at the theater. A spectator needs imagination to fully appreciate the scene that is going on in front of him, on the stage or on the screen. When I am writing someone's biography I read nothing except what relates to him or her: memoirs, letters, documents, etcetera. . . . Then I dream about him or her, imagine the various events and scenes, and I get in the habit of living in his or her world. So yes, I think biography is art in so far as you use your imagination to create, but you don't create *out* of your imagination.

INTERVIEWER

You mean that the function of the imagination varies according to whether you are writing fiction or biography? But isn't it tempting to give complete freedom to it and invent as you go along?

JOAN HASLIP

I don't think that this is the age of novels. Yes, I know, everybody writes them, and they have invented all these prizes to tempt authors, publishers and readers, but look how mediocre the majority of prize-winning novels are. For me the last really good Booker Prize-winner was *The Raj Quartet*, by Paul Scott. That was excellent. But today? Another reason for my not writing novels is that I am not interested in the current fads and fashions and know nothing about them. I mean I don't know about middle-class couples in Hampstead, or feminism. I was asked to write a novel about Laclos, because I wrote an article on him and know a lot about him. He is marvelous, but would it have sold?

INTERVIEWER

After the Sultan you wrote one of your most successful and popular books: the life of Elizabeth of Austria, The Lonely Empress. *Was she your idea?*

JOAN HASLIP

I am half-Austrian and knew quite a lot about her. So when a publisher suggested her I said yes. It was translated into eleven languages and was a success everywhere. Then I wrote *Maximilian*, about her brother-in-law, who became Emperor of Mexico. I researched him in Vienna, Mexico and Trieste, where he was once Governor and much loved. He was a tragic figure in every way. His elder brother Franz Josef, the Emperor of Austria was jealous of him because of his good looks and popularity. He had married a Belgian princess who was extremely ambitious and wanted to be an empress, and who encouraged him in favour of

the Mexican venture. But the whole thing was a cata-
strophic mistake, due partly to Napoleon III's *folie de
grandeur*. He too encouraged Maximilian by giving him
French money and arms, because Mexico was in a fearful
mess. But he should never have gone, as the Mexican
people never accepted him, and in the end he lost to
Juárez and was shot in 1867. If the Mexicans had been
intelligent they would have sent him back to be utterly
ridiculous, instead of making him a hero in killing him,
and disgracing themselves. Franz Josef remained the Emperor of Austria until the First World War.

INTERVIEWER

Did you write The Emperor and the Actress, *about Franz
Josef, because of the success of* The Lonely Empress?

JOAN HASLIP

I didn't want to do it, but my American publishers offered
me a large advance. As they say, they made me an offer
I could not refuse! The book was a great success in France,
but not in England. The English don't like Franz Josef,
they prefer his wife, Sissy [Elizabeth of Austria], because
she used to go to England and Ireland and ride horses,
and they adored her. Franz Josef fell in love with Katharina
Schratt, an actress, and the English readers don't find her
sympathetic. But she gave him what he didn't have with
Sissy, whom he loved. Katharina made him human, brought
him in contact with the people of Vienna.

INTERVIEWER

The Imperial Adventurer—*the life of Maximilian*—*was
published in America under the title of* The Crown of
Mexico *and was a huge success. It brought you nice financial*

rewards. Is that why you came back to live in Florence? To avoid crippling British taxes?

JOAN HASLIP

It was in 1972 and we had a Labour Government in England under Harold Wilson as Prime Minister. I was going to be taxed over 83%! I didn't mind paying heavy taxes but not to that extent, especially when one doesn't know when the next book will be published and whether it will be a success or not. My next book was the biography of Catherine the Great. It sold quite well but nothing to compare with Maximilian.

INTERVIEWER

After that you went back, historically speaking, and wrote Marie Antoinette, which is your latest book. There are already hundreds of biographies of her, what made you want to produce another one? Do you think that the life of important historical figures have to be reexamined every few decades in the light of new discoveries? For example with the breakthrough in psychology and the advent of psycho-analysis we look at people and their motives in a different way from our predecessors.

JOAN HASLIP

My publisher, George Weidenfeld, suggested Marie An-toinette, and my reaction was rather like yours, that there were already hundreds of books about her. But he said: "Every generation needs a new Marie Antoinette!" It is true that we look at people differently. Victorian biogra-phers gave you facts, while we go in for psychological insight: why did X behave as he/she did? And how would they have acted in different circumstances? Lytton Strachey was one of the first who took this approach. The book I'm working on now is a biography of Madame du Barry. She was the illegitimate daughter of a seamstress and a monk, and she had nothing but her beauty. It is a long story, but somehow she managed to meet the King, Louis XV, and according to an apocryphal anecdote she went right up to him at their first meeting and kissed him on the mouth. He fell head over heels in love with her there and then, and till the end of his life. She was really a tart, but exquisite. After the King died she was exiled for two years, and then she got hold of the Duc de Brissac, the richest man in France, who adored her. Marie Antoinette loathed her at the beginning but later forgave her. Evidently Madame du Barry was irresistible to me.

INTERVIEWER

She had brains too, because a wealthy woman had taken her under her wing when she was a child and sent her to a convent to be educated. She stayed there nine years. So I think she captivated men with a combination of beauty and intelligence, rather rare in those days.

JOAN HASLIP

That is true, because men may fall in love with a beautiful woman but it wears off unless something else backs it up. She had artistic and intellectual admirers too. I hope to finish the book sometime next year.

INTERVIEWER

Do you ever get hunches as you go along?

JOAN HASLIP

Sometimes. But more important than hunches is chance. Unexpected events can occur which lead to a break-

through. For example I was in Corfu to visit the Achilleon,
Elizabeth of Austria's house. I ran out of money and rang
up the British Consul for help. He wasn't very forthcoming,
but when I said I had just been staying with the Greek
Foreign Minister he was suitably impressed, and he asked
me to go and see him. I borrowed the money and told
him that I was in Corfu because I was writing a book on
Elizabeth of Austria and wanted to see her house there.
"I can help you there," he said. And he told me that
there used to be an Englishman on the island who was
Elizabeth's last reader. During the war he couldn't get any
money from home and the local grocer had kept him with
food and other necessities, and in gratitude he had left
him all his papers, which the grocer had kept. So I went
and saw this man, and indeed he had two volumes of
diaries, all concerning Elizabeth's last years. He wanted to
sell them for a huge sum, but I said I didn't want to buy
them, only to read them. I paid him some money and he
allowed me to see them and take notes. So you see, chance
plays an enormous part. If I had not run out of money
and gone to see the Consul, I would never have known
of the existence of the diaries and the invaluable information they contained.

INTERVIEWER

*Eliot said that if we knew about Shakespeare's laundry list,
we would learn a lot more about him. Do you agree with
what is known as "the laundry-list" approach to biography?*

JOAN HASLIP

No, I don't. But if we knew what happened the first time
Shakespeare met Southampton, that would be interesting.
This is why the academics don't like my biographies. They
blame me for not giving any notes, but I don't like notes,

as they break the flow of narrative. It is showing off erudition to other academics at the expense of the reader's enjoyment. I write for people like myself: the semi-educated. But I think "the laundry list" approach is more fashionable. I recently read Richard Ellmann's *Oscar Wilde*, which is extremely good but full of superfluous information and *longueurs*. As it happens I know a good deal about Wilde, and I didn't find anything new in Ellmann's book. But Wilde is a fascinating character and the book, as I said, is very well done.

INTERVIEWER

Biography as a literary genre has never been more flourishing, at least in England, where it has become almost an epidemic. There are those who maintain that most biographies are just extended gossip columns. Do you agree?

JOAN HASLIP

I wish they were! They might be less dull! But no, I don't agree, because a really good biography, like Boswell's life of Dr. Johnson is marvelous. A whole vanished world is brought back to life. It has more validity than most novels. A great novel, like *War and Peace*, does the same thing, but how many modern novels measure up to that standard, or have any validity at all?

INTERVIEWER

Have you identified with any of your subjects? As some biographers say that one must, to some extent, in order to understand them?

JOAN HASLIP

Funnily enough not with any of the women whose lives I have written. But as I said, I fell in love with Parnell.

INTERVIEWER

You have now produced a large body of work. Earlier you said that you were very ambitious from the start, and of course you have now fulfilled your ambitions. Was it the reason for your never marrying?

JOAN HASLIP

I didn't want to be tied down. I have had two very satisfactory love affairs in my life. The first one was with a man much older than myself who died, the other is still a cherished devoted friend. On the whole I prefer the company of men and have more men friends than women. Here in Florence, Harold Acton and John Pope-Hennessy are wonderful friends.

INTERVIEWER

Who were the authors and books that most influenced you when you left school at thirteen, came to live here, and began to educate yourself, as you put it?

JOAN HASLIP

I loved and admired Aldous Huxley. He was a great friend of my mother's, and he used to come and stay with us here for weeks. Another writer I saw a lot of was Norman Douglas. He was extremely kind to me and used to take me out to lunch and tell me stories of the myths of the Arno Valley. He got into trouble by becoming involved with minors, of *both* sexes, sometimes, but to me he was wonderfully kind. I once asked him what an aphrodisiac was: "Well, it's a sort of cocktail," he replied, "but there's only one worth having—variety!" Between them those two men taught me a lot about life. My mother never did; she

didn't even tell me what is known as the-facts-of-life.
Norman Douglas was a magical writer. Did you ever read
his novels: *They Went* and *South Wind?* And his travel
books: *Old Calabria* and others? They are marvelous. He
wrote so beautifully, and yet no one reads him today. Very
sad really, more for readers than for him.

INTERVIEWER

*Apart from those two writers, who did you read before you
started writing yourself, and who influenced you?*

JOAN HASLIP

Somerset Maugham, who also came to Florence. Everybody
came here, and one was terribly spoilt by being surrounded
not only by beautiful things but also interesting people.
D.H. Lawrence lived in Florence at the time, and like all
my generation I was very influenced by his novels. But
he himself was disappointing. He had a high falseto voice
and a weak mouth hidden by a beard, and he painted
rather obscure pictures of huge naked women. But most
of all I read the classics, and still do. *War and Peace* and
Vanity Fair were, and still are, my favorite novels.

Another very interesting man was Carlo Loeser, who
was a great critic and art collector. He was the first man
to buy a Paul Cézanne, and he had six or seven of his
paintings in his house, as well as a number of other pictures.
He founded the *Lener Quartet*, which became the most
famous quartet in the world in the 1930s. Their impresario
had abandoned them and they were left penniless on the
streets of Florence where Loeser found them. He became
their new impresario and launched them and had great
success with them. They used to give private concerts in
Loeser's villa, in his magnificent music room with seven

Cézanne's on the walls. To my mind Carlo Loeser was a
more worthwhile man than Berenson.

INTERVIEWER

*What about biographers? Who did you read and admire—
apart from Boswell and Lytton Strachey whom you have
already mentioned?*

JOAN HASLIP

To me one of the best of modern biographies was Harold
Nicholson's biography of his father. It makes one under-
stand how the First World War began. Another is David
Cecil's *The Stricken Deer*, a biography of William Cowper.
It is a wonderful book. I was seventeen when I read it
and it was the first book I ever reviewed.

INTERVIEWER

*Traveling has been an important part of your life; did you
ever think of writing a travel book yourself?*

JOAN HASLIP

To write a travel book I feel one must either have made
oneself a part of the country and its people, and spent
almost a lifetime in that country, or otherwise be captured
by one's first enthusiasm and write under one's first impression of a country. Some of the best travel books, for
instance *Eöthen* which I have already mentioned, belong
to that category. I have often been asked to write about
Florence. But I feel I know at once too much and too
little about my town. When I was young I loved traveling
alone. When one travels alone one feels free as air, and
people are sweet to one. But if you travel with a man, or
a woman friend, you have to be with them and never
meet anyone else. I once went down the Danube alone,

and to the Middle East which I loved. I crossed the United States by myself, which is quite common these days but wasn't when I was young. Nowadays I go where I know people, or for the publication of my books, in which case there are people at the other end to meet me and take care of me if need be. For the rest of my life I shall be content to continue my journeys in Italy, Austria, England and France—the places where I feel most at home.

INTERVIEWER

How do you work and where? Do you have a routine? Do you write long hand, or type?

JOAN HASLIP

I write with a little block on my knees. Arthur Bryant once told me: "I would never have given you such a good review if I hadn't seen the ghastly way you write, curled up in a chair with bits of paper all over the place and no proper notes!" I don't know how to type, so I write long-hand, reading each sentence aloud. Then I correct and send the chapters to a wonderful girl in London who has typed my manuscripts for years. I seldom change the typed manuscript when it comes back. I can't bear sitting at a desk, and although I have a sort of routine and work during the day, I do break it when I am traveling or have visitors.

INTERVIEWER

Is writing easy for you? You started very young, have pro-duced over fourteen books, and clearly have a facility.

JOAN HASLIP

It is fairly easy, but I do a fair amount of correcting and changing, looking things up and making sure that the information is correct. But the actual process of writing is fairly easy. I don't do articles and book reviews nowadays, because they are much harder to do, and more time-consuming. Books are easier for me.

INTERVIEWER

Apart from finishing your book on Madame du Barry, what are your plans for the future?

JOAN HASLIP

Oh I never plan! Anyway, what future?

Juliette Huxley

Juliette Huxley was born in Neuchâtel, Switzerland, in 1896. In 1915, at the age of nineteen, she came to England to work as a French teacher. By chance her first employer was Lady Ottoline Morrell—patroness of the arts and artists, Bloomsbury hostess, and one of the most celebrated women of her time. She was successfully interviewed in the first-class waiting room at Oxford Station, and later Lady Ottoline wrote in her memoirs, "Mademoiselle Juliette Baillot came to us to be a companion and soi-disant governess to Julian. The first time I saw her was at Oxford Station where we sat together on a bench—a tall, slim, very pretty, shy, severe and composed Swiss girl, with plaits of fair hair done into two buns on her ears, she seemed almost absurdly young, but she herself seemed quite confident and I wanted someone young and cheerful and active for Julian. She came and was perfect. . . she took part in all our life and with her lovely simplicity and intelligence wound her way in and out of the various visitors, much liked by everybody. . . I can never forget her lovely slim figure as she dived into the pond, her long yellow hair making her look like a water nymph or a picture of a silvery saint by Crivelli."

Today, in her nineties, Juliette Huxley is still tall and slim, very charming, and looks uncannily youthful. Her *blond hair has inevitably turned silver and frames her face in soft natural waves, but her innocent blue eyes are undimmed by age and shine with humor and wonderment. She speaks in a gentle, clear voice, with a touch of an accent, and uses the occasional French word or expression.*

Her autobiography, Leaves From the Tulip Tree, chronicles her remarkable life from her Swiss childhood, her stay at Garsington Manor, the country home of Lady Ottoline Morrell, her meeting there with Aldous and Julian Huxley, her subsequent marriage to Julian, their travels around the world—meeting with some of the most famous men and women of our times—to her becoming the doyenne of one of Britain's most distinguished intellectual families.

Lady Huxley lives in a pretty, late-Georgian house in Hampstead, London. It is full of the mementos of a long and fascinating life, of works of art by friends such as Henry Moore, Georges Braque, John Piper, Henry Lamb, Duncan Grant, and Julian Trevelyan. At the back of the house is the garden Juliette tends herself, where evergreen Eleagnus trees lead to a lawn bordered with rose bushes and camilias, exotic shrubs and flowers, and where one finds pieces of Juliette's own sculpture. Her two sons—Anthony Huxley, a botanist and author of some twenty-five books on plants, and Francis Huxley, a social-anthropologist and writer— and her brother-in-law Sir Andrew Huxley, a physiologist, Nobel Prize winner and President of the Royal Society and Master of Trinity College, Cambridge, are frequent visitors, as are old and new friends. They are all received with warmth, and regaled with delicious meals and lavish high-teas.

The following interview took place in the large library of her house, a room lined with books, photographs and Huxley memorabilia.

INTERVIEWER

*You were born and brought up in Neuchâtel, Switzerland,
and at an early age became interested in literature. Did
you think of pursuing a literary career?*

JULIETTE HUXLEY

Yes. After the *Ecole Supérieure* I very much wanted to go
to the University of Geneva and study literature, but I
couldn't because I had to earn my living. My father was
a young lawyer, but one day his partner absconded with
all the contents of the safe and suddenly we became poor.
Instead of declaring himself bankrupt, my father insisted
on paying back every penny of the debts. And he did.
He was broken by the ordeal and died young. My mother,
undaunted, turned our house into a *Pensionnat*, and took
in young girls from German-Swiss and Russian families to
"finish" them and teach them French. She ran our lives
with Calvinistic severity and Swiss frugality. Her sister was
married to a very handsome Englishman, King George V's
wardrobe superintendent, and they lived at St. James's
palace in London. So when I was nineteen I was sent to
London to stay with them and look for a job. My aunt
had been a fashionable designer and had a *salon,* where
society women bought their clothes. Her husband had a
staff of valets who looked after the King's wardrobe. He
had to choose the various outfits for official engagements,
even the jewels that the King had to give as presents to
visiting foreign dignitaries. They were both very kind to
me; I learned English and read a great deal.

INTERVIEWER

What books did you read in Switzerland?

JULIETTE HUXLEY

The French classics, especially the Romantics: Racine, Molière, Victor Hugo, Alfred de Musset, Georges Sand, Rousseau, Jules Verne, and the later poets, especially Rimbaud, for whom I developed a passion, and Marceline Desbordes-Valmore, and of course lesser authors who have now been completely forgotten.

INTERVIEWER

You struck gold with your first job interview. Did you know who Lady Ottoline Morrell was?

JULIETTE HUXLEY

Not at all. But I was struck by her unusual beauty—dark blue eyes, Titian red hair, tall statuesque figure and regal manners. I never saw her flustered or rushed. She wore lovely Grecian cream crèpe-de-Chine dresses, with high waists and gold lace round the neck. I adored her completely and thought her the most perfect of women.

INTERVIEWER

What was Garsington Manor like?

JULIETTE HUXLEY

It was a Tudor house, with beautiful original panelings which Ottoline chose to paint: the large sitting-room in Byzantine red and gold, the adjoining room in soft turquoise green. Samarkand carpets of gold and orange hues covered the floors, and the silk taffeta curtains bordered with lace and silver bindings were works of art. I have never seen a more beautiful house. Life there was like a fairy tale, and often reminded me of *Le Grand*

Meaulnes. On winter evenings we would sit by the crackling fire, embroidering a large counterpane, while Ottoline read to us aloud, and in summer there would be music and dancing on the lawn which swept down to a large pond. A magnificent old Ilex tree stood sentinel over the festivities. There was another French-speaking girl there, a Belgian war refugee whom Ottoline had taken under her powerful wings. Her name was Maria. She was very beautiful, with huge grey-green eyes and black hair. We became friends and later she married Aldous.

INTERVIEWER
Ottoline Morrell was the most famous literary hostess of her day. Who were the visitors to the house while you were there?

JULIETTE HUXLEY
A stream of visitors came and stayed, some for long periods to write their books or paint their pictures: Bertrand Russell, Lytton Strachey, Dora Camyher Carrington, Virginia and Leonard Woolf, Katherine Mansfield and John Middleton Murry, Dorothy Brett, the D.H. Lawrences and Mark Gertler. . . . The house filled up on weekends. Unlike some social hostesses, who entertain artists and writers *after* they have become famous, Ottoline had a genuine appreciation of talent and spotted it long before it bore fruit. She helped to cultivate it. There was a very intelligent atmosphere—people didn't gossip much, but they spoke about the books they had read, and discussed politics, as Philip Morrell was a Member of Parliament. Bertrand Russell was the most impressive; he lived and worked in a cottage set aside from the house. In the evenings he read to us: the whole of Sainte-Beuve's *Les*

Causeries du Lundi in French, which he spoke beautifully.
Lytton Strachey stayed for long periods too. He read to
us Pope's *The Rape of the Lock*. He gave me tuition in
English literature, from Shakespeare and Donne to the
Romantics. He suggested that I learn poems by heart and
I started with Keats's *Ode to a Nightingale*.

> *Thou wast not born for death, immortal Bird!*
> *No hungry generations tread thee down;*
> *The voice I hear this passing night was heard*
> *In ancient days by emperor and clown . . .*

and so on. Then I began to write my own poems which
I had the temerity to show him! He was very kind and
patient, and tried to teach me rhythm, because of course
my rhythm was French. Unlike Ethel Merman, I definitely
hadn't got rhythm!

INTERVIEWER

*Bertrand Russell had a love affair with Ottoline. Was it
going on while he lived there?*

JULIETTE HUXLEY

No, it was over, but they remained devoted friends all
their lives. When Russell was ninety I visited him at his
house in Wales, and he showed me a large wooden trunk
saying, "*Voilà!* That is Ottoline!" It contained all her letters,
which he later disposed of to McMaster University in
Ontario.

INTERVIEWER

*There were many other love affairs going on which were
later recounted in novels and memoirs: Mark Gertler and*

Carrington, Vanessa Bell and Duncan Grant, Clive Bell and Mary Hutchinson. Were you aware of them?

JULIETTE HUXLEY

No. You see I was very young and very naive. My aunt, on the other hand, had heard that there were people who were not married but living together at Garsington. She wrote me a stern letter suggesting that I leave. I wrote back an equally forceful letter asking her to mind her own business! She took it very well and never mentioned the subject again.

INTERVIEWER

Despite her kindness and generosity, Ottoline Morrell provoked mixed feelings in her friends and protégés, some of whom wrote very unkind things about her. Is there an explanation for it?

JULIETTE HUXLEY

Perhaps she had what Cardinal Retz called "the deadly gift of intimacy"—she talked to people in such a way that they would open their hearts to her. Perhaps some of their secrets were divulged? Or they resented having exposed themselves? It was also partly jealousy. She was the sister of a Duke, she was rich and beautiful. I was very sad to learn later that many of those who had accepted her hospitality mocked and sneered at her behind her back. Virginia Woolf and Lytton Strachey would write effusive letters to her after a stay, and write the most malicious, bitchy gossip about her to each other or, in their diaries, on the same day. But she forgave them. When D.H. Lawrence caricatured her in *Women in Love* their friendship broke up. Several years later, in 1928, we spent

Julian and Juliette Huxley circa 1940

a winter with the Lawrences in Switzerland and I asked
him to write to Ottoline and make it up with her. He
did, and they made peace. To me she was perfect, and
when she died it was as if a light had gone out of my
life.

INTERVIEWER

When did the Huxleys come into your life?

JULIETTE HUXLEY

Aldous was finishing his degree at Oxford and came to Garsington for weekends. He was everybody's favorite. After he left Oxford with a brilliant double first, he worked on the farm at Garsington, as he was not eligible for active war service. We used to bicycle together and became close friends. We discussed books, in particular William James's *Varieties of Religious Experience*. On summer evenings we would sit on the roof and watch the moon rise over the surrounding countryside. He told me about his brothers: Trev who had committed suicide, and Julian who was a scientist and a professor at Rice University in Texas. Then in 1916 Julian came back to England to go to war, and came to Garsington. Later he wrote to me from the front asking me for help. He told me that despite his apparent ebullience and gaiety he suffered from severe bouts of depression which made him helpless. I was flattered and responded. After the war we married and Aldous married Maria. Ottoline was very pleased and helped and guided us in every way.

INTERVIEWER

Were you conscious at the time of the privileged circle you were marrying into?

JULIETTE HUXLEY

Very much so. On his mother's side Julian was an Arnold— Matthew Arnold was a great-uncle, and somehow the Huxleys were related to other famous intellectual families— the Darwins, the Peases, the Trevelyans—and of course they were the grandsons of the great Victorian scientist

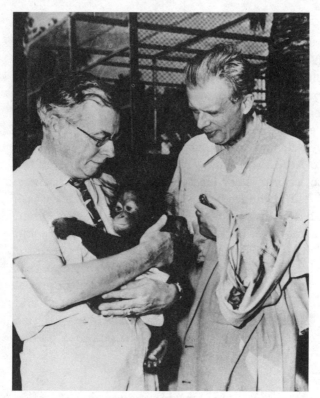

Julian and Aldous Huxley

T.H. Huxley. I was overwhelmed, but as I said, Ottoline encouraged and sustained me all along. The family was upset that *both* their golden boys should marry "foreigners" but in the end they accepted us. Julian's first breakdown came just after our honeymoon and devastated me. Somehow I thought it was my fault. We spent some time in Switzerland and when we came back he had recovered—for the next twenty-five years there was no relapse, and he wrote some of his important scientific books.

Julian and Juliette Huxley looking for gorillas in Uganda, 1960

INTERVIEWER
After your wedding you went to live at Oxford where Julian became a don of New College and taught. Did you make a whole new set of friends?

JULIETTE HUXLEY
At first I didn't know anyone, except for Julian's students and fellow dons, all interesting and bright. In those days people called on each other, wearing white gloves and

leaving visiting cards. Married women had to chaperone
young girls at balls and tea parties. I had to do all those
kinds of things. We became friends with Jack Haldane,
the famous geneticist. He was well-known for his work
on Mendelism and because he was a communist. He was
a gentle and kind man, though he appeared uncouth and
gruff. He would drop in for tea and start reciting reams
of poetry, the whole of Shelley's *Prometheus Unbound*. If
ever he dried on a word, he would beat his brow and
say: "Oh my God! What have you done with my poor
memory!" Or he would telephone the house and our maid
Mary would answer. The short conversation would go as
follows:

> *Haldane*—Who is that?
> *Mary*—I am Mary, sir.
> *Haldane*—Which one? Bloody or Virgin?

We also saw a good deal of the warden of New College,
the famous Reverend Spooner, inventor of Spoonerisms.
He had a thin, sharp voice and would say: "Mrs. Spooner
and I went to Egypt and saw the Minx by Spoonlight"
(The Sphinx by moonlight); or to a naughty student: "You
will go down by town drain!" (go to town by train), "erotic
blacks" (erratic blocks), and endless other examples like
those, mostly invented by other people. Our other friends,
those days in London, were the novelist Rosamond Lehmann, and later Sybille Bedford, who wrote the two-volume
biography of Aldous after his death. Both are still dear
friends.

INTERVIEWER

*In 1924 you came back to London and Julian became
Professor of Zoology at King's College. Is that when you met
H. G. Wells and Julian began working with him?*

JULIETTE HUXLEY

Yes. Wells had just published his *Outline of History* and was basking in a radiant reputation. We often stayed with him and his patient, sweet wife Jane at their house in Kent. He and Julian gave full rein to their intellectual fencing and collaborated on the very popular *Science of Life* series, which was designed to bring science to the ordinary man. Later they were collected in three large volumes. We also stayed at his house in the south of France where he lived with his mistress Odette Keun, for all the world as if his wife didn't exist. At the same time he kept a couple of affairs going in London for good measure! Odette Keun was a very interesting woman. She had been a nun and expelled from the convent because she had frightened the Father Confessor with accounts of her sexual fantasies! She and H. G. often quarreled and she would call him *"Sale petit calico,"* the dirty little draper, because H. G. had started life in a draper's shop; later they would make up as though nothing had ever happened! I'm afraid H. G. Wells didn't set a good example and his influence led to what in the book I have called Julian's *"Fugue."* The escapade: Julian fell in love with a charming American girl on a boat, between Marseilles and Port Said to be exact, and told me that he intended to have an affair with her. But I was no Mrs. Wells, and couldn't accept such an arrangement. We went through two years of hell, with frequent partings and reunions, as Julian kept going back and forth to America—what the French call *"un mauvais quart d'heure."* Finally Julian decided to break up the relationship and stay with the family. But marriages often go through stormy patches in mid-life. Nowadays couples seem too trigger-happy with divorce, to the detriment of their children who suffer terribly even if they

don't show it. It is better to weather the storm and come
out of it stronger. But then life is so much more difficult
for the young today, with all the pressures and threats of
the modern world.

INTERVIEWER

*Did you break your friendship with H.G. Wells because of
that episode?*

JULIETTE HUXLEY

No. I stayed friends with him till the end of his life. But
he broke with Julian over a slight matter: Julian cut his
speech short at a conference and he never forgave him.
Yet he had always been ruthless with *his* editing of Julian's
material. For example, Julian wrote an article on ants for
the *Science of Life* series and H. G. cut it down to a tenth
of its length, saying, "We don't want ants crawling all
over the page!"

INTERVIEWER

*At the time you also became great friends with D. H.
Lawrence and his wife Frieda. How did that develop?*

JULIETTE HUXLEY

Lawrence had few male friends, but Aldous was certainly
one of them. In the winter of 1928, we took a chalet in
Les Diablerets, in Switzerland, with Aldous and Maria, and
the Lawrences took a smaller one next door. We met
every day for tea, and went for long walks in the snow.
Lawrence argued with Julian about the theory of evolution
which he rejected instinctively and categorically: "God
created the world as it is and that is that!" he would say.
After a while Julian and Aldous gave up trying to persuade

him. Lawrence and Aldous talked about literature a great deal. He told Aldous that he should write about better, nicer women and men. Aldous's women were nearly always hard and scheming, and his attitude was rather misanthropic. Lawrence thought that human beings were better than that, or could be. This influenced Aldous greatly, and he did improve his women characters in his later novels.

INTERVIEWER
In the thirties, Julian became the director of the London Zoo. How did you like living above the shop, so to speak, in an apartment in the zoo?

JULIETTE HUXLEY
We loved it! We got used to hearing the lions roar at night and the monkeys shriek. We also had a camp at Whipsnade Zoo, at first a haystack in the middle of a field, then a couple of shacks which we arranged. We spent the summer weekends there with friends, sleeping in the hay, devoured by harvest bugs. We rode ponies at night to see the animals prowling in their enclosures, the big cats with their red eyes shining like torches in the dark. It was magical, like living in the Garden of Eden.

INTERVIEWER
That was the time when you discovered a new talent— sculpture. How did that happen?

JULIETTE HUXLEY
By a curious accident in 1934, my son Anthony, aged twelve, was knocked off his bicycle by a passing car, and suffered a concussion. He had to leave school for a term,

and to entertain him I began to make things with him, such as playing with clay. To my surprise I found myself enjoying modeling enormously. I did a striking portrait of a friend who kindly sat for me. Anthony recovered, mercifully, and I joined the Central School of Arts and learned sculpture under John Skeaping, a well-known sculptor and teacher. I carved in wood and chalk collected from the bottom of chalk cliffs in Dorset and made some quite creditable pieces. The large Red River hog you see behind you even got into the Royal Academy Show after the war; those hands in oak on the shelf and the few of the pieces in the garden are about all that is left of my work here; the rest was given to my sons and friends. Henry Moore was, among others, very encouraging.

Years ago I had bought a Henry Moore shelter drawing which I cherished. But a few years ago, I had to sell it. So with great sadness I rang him up and said: " 'I'm sorry Henry, I had to sell your picture." "I know," he replied, "I bought it." I was glad that it went to his own collection.

INTERVIEWER

Immediately after the war Julian became the first Director General of UNESCO, which he had helped to create. You went to live in Paris and met a whole set of new people. Did it help to be French-speaking?

JULIETTE HUXLEY

Very much. In France, if you speak French without a foreign accent you are accepted as French—although I was Swiss. But *quelles shambles!* There was nowhere to live and we put up at an hotel. Then Mini Gielgud (sister-in-law of Sir John Gielgud) rescued us in her large comfortable apartment. She had tame mice and I remember meeting

Josephine Baker at her house, with her hair wrapped in a turban and two mice running in and out of it all over her head, their eyes sparkling like little rubies. I went to fashion shows and bought designer clothes, as social life in France is much more formal than in England. At the center of that social life were Lady Diana Cooper and her husband Duff, then the British Ambassador. We met a number of French celebrities—André Malraux, Louise de Vilmorin, the poet Aragon and his wife Elsa Triolet, the sculptor Brancusi, and others. Julian was lionized everywhere on account of his energetic and idealistic championship of UNESCO as well as his own scientific achievements. I remember once at a reception seeing a woman wearing pearls as large as pieces of gravel. Someone admired them and asked where they came from. "*Oh, des restes!*" she said—just leftovers! Eventually I got tired of the formality and wrote to a friend in London that the more I lived among these "foreigners," the more I appreciated and loved the English. And I still do.

INTERVIEWER

Back in England in the fifties Julian retired and was knighted. You began to travel extensively in America, Asia and Africa. Were they working trips?

JULIETTE HUXLEY

Mostly on behalf of UNESCO. Or giving lectures. In East Africa Julian was one of the founders establishing National Parks and Conservation schemes.

INTERVIEWER

It was after a trip to East Africa that you wrote your first book: Wild Lives of Africa. It was highly praised for its

*poetic language and original style, as well as its acute
observation and sympathy for the land and its people. Were
you not tempted to carry on and write more books?*

JULIETTE HUXLEY

I wanted to do nothing else from then on. But Julian had
another severe breakdown and I felt it was my duty to
look after him. He got well again and wrote his memoirs,
which I had to help him with. He died more than ten
years ago at the age of eighty-seven. I went to pieces for
four years, then I began to sort out his papers. I put the
letters in order and sold them to Rice University together
with his scientific books. Then I decided to use the money
to set up a Julian Huxley Scholarship at Balliol, his old
college at Oxford. But Balliol told me that there were
enough scholarships already, and that it would be better
to have a research fellowship in a subject which was very
important to Julian—evolutionary studies. I accepted, little
realizing that it meant finding another £100,000. *Mon Dieu!*
Where to get it? We set up a committee with Andrew
Huxley, David Attenborough, and others, and wrote to
everyone likely to contribute. It took a long time but
eventually the money was found and the fellowship es-
tablished. There is still a lot to do—all those drawers are
full of letters and papers. The other day I found a letter
written by the great T. H. Huxley, in which he speaks
about *his* depression, and how he depends entirely on *his*
wife to make the decisions!

INTERVIEWER

*Julian Huxley was an agnostic, not to say an atheist, and
you yourself have said that you do not believe in organized*

religion. What are your religious beliefs, if any, and do you believe in an afterlife?

JULIETTE HUXLEY

I am not so sure that Julian was as irreligious as it is commonly believed. I think that both he and Aldous had a mystical temperament. That is why Julian was so interested in Teilhard de Chardin. As for me, I believe in Jesus Christ the Son of Man, and I believe in a life force which is in the living—you can call it God if you wish. But alas, unlike my friend Rosamond Lehmann, I do not believe in an afterlife. How can you see without eyes, or hear without ears? I think about death every day. The important thing is to be ready, as Hamlet says, and not to leave loose ends, a burden for others. But what is left after the flame of life has burnt out, except perhaps memories—*une petite fumée de souvenirs?*

Molly Keane

Molly Keane lives in a fairy-tale house perched atop a hill overlooking the bay of Ardmore on the Irish Channel. It is a small white edifice nestled amid well-kept gardens of scented shrubs and flowering hedges, with green slopes cascading down to the seashore below. Although aged eighty-five and recovering from a recent heart-attack, upon hearing my car she came up the steps to greet me: petite, neat, with short grey hair framing a viviacious face lit by a welcoming smile.

Inside, the house is furnished with taste and contains momentos that tell of a grander past: Sèvres china, Persian carpets, pictures by well-known artists. . . .

By contrast to the characters in her novel Good Behavior, whose perfect manners conceal deep resentments and nasty traits, Molly Keane's exquisite courtesy is based on genuine kindness and interest in others. Her hospitality is well-known, and unlike some of her peers she not only grants interviews, but invites their authors to stay with her—"My dear it's such a long way to come"—providing them with delicious and lavish meals. She has ample energy, an impish sense of humor, and eyes that see through you with tolerance. She speaks with a patrician accent and is as generous in her praise as candid in her strictures of other writers' works.

She was born at Kilnamora, Co. Kildare, in 1904. Her
father, Walter Skrine, was an Englishman and her mother,
Agnes Shakespeare Higginson, wrote poetry under the name
of Moira O'Neil. Both families belonged to the landed gentry
class, whose chief occupations were riding, fox-hunting, fishing
and shooting—a milieu she would later depict in her novels
and plays. She herself was passionately interested in these
activities. She was educated at home by a series of governesses
until fifteen, then sent to a boarding school in Dublin for
two years.

Her first novel, The Knight of Cheerful Countenance,
a romance, was published in 1928 under the pseudonym
M.J. Farrell. It was followed a year later by Young Entry.
Between 1929 and 1952 she produced seven more novels in
regular intervals: Devoted Ladies, The Rising Tide, The
Mad Puppetstown, Two Days in Aragon, etcetera . . .
which won her critical and popular acclaim. Though not
overtly political, they depict an accurate and witty picture
of the Irish Raj in its twilight, the beauty and poetry of the
great Irish houses before they were burnt down in the uprising
of 1922 or abandoned by their impoverished owners. (Both
Ballyrankin, where Molly Keane grew up, and Woodrooff,
the house of her friends the Perrys, in Tipperary, where she
spent long periods in her formative years, were torched during
the Troubles.)

In the 1930s she was encouraged by her friend John Perry
to write plays and created the following: Spring Meeting
(1938), Ducks and Drakes (1941), Treasure Hunt, and
Dazzling Prospect (1958), some of which had successful runs
in the West End.

In 1932, Molly met Bobbie Keane, five years her junior.
They married in 1938 and moved to Belleville, a ravishing
house in County Waterford. Their union was idyllically

*happy and produced two daughters, Sally and Virginia.
Bobbie died suddenly in 1946 at the age of thirty-six. Bereft
and her financial resources depleted, Molly eventually had
to sell Belleville. For a while she lived in London; in 1960
she returned to Ireland and bought the house in which she
has lived ever since.*

*In 1981, at the age of seventy-six and after over twenty
years of silence, she published* Good Behavior *under her
own name. It was an immediate best-seller and was short-
listed for the Booker Prize. It was followed by* Time After
Time, *three years later. Both books were later adapted for
television, the latter starring John Gielgud, who had produced
her most successful plays in the 1940s and 1950s. Her last
novel,* Loving and Giving *retitled* Queen Lear *in the states,
appeared in 1988.*

*This interview took place at Ms. Keane's house in June
of 1989.*

INTERVIEWER

*All your books, novels and plays, are about the Anglo-Irish
landed gentry, a class of moneyed, leisured aristocrats living
in beautiful desmenes in Ireland, whose main occupations
are hunting, fishing and shooting. Where did these people
come from originally?*

MOLLY KEANE

The Anglo-Irish, or The Ascendancy as they are sometimes
called, were English people who were planted in Ireland
as far back as Elizabethan times. Some, like the Knight of
Glynn, date back to the Normans. They were upper-class
Protestants, while the Irish were Catholics, which led
eventually to the Irish uprising in 1920. A few were
Catholics, but they fled to France before the Napoleonic

Wars when anti-Catholic laws were introduced. The relationship between the Ascendency and their tenants and work people was always good. There was gross error in government, such as the anti-Catholic laws under which no Roman Catholic could hold high office. That, and a justifiable desire to own land led to the Troubles. Enormous tracts of land, mostly mountain and bog, had been granted by Elizabeth and later by Cromwell in lieu of payment to the officer class in the regiments which had been sent to establish English rule in Ireland. For example, my mother's ancestor, Major Henry Higginson, settled in County Antrim until Gladstone's Irish Laws left so many well-meaning landlords financially more or less derelict.

INTERVIEWER

Surely religion was not the only reason for the uprising. Nationalism came into it. Didn't the English landlords have an imperialistic attitude towards the native Irish and treat them as inferiors?

MOLLY KEANE

That is what is said, but it isn't true, any more than anything else that is said is entirely true. They did send their sons to schools in England—my own brothers went to Rossall, and they did tend to marry English girls, which meant that the next generation was Anglo-Irish too. But it didn't stop them from being good landlords when they returned to Ireland.

INTERVIEWER

They lived in beautiful houses like your own, Ballyrankin, which you describe in your book The Mad Puppetstown. *Indeed the houses seem to be the real protagonists of the* stories, so great is their influence on the characters. Three-quarters of them were lost to their owners during your lifetime, through mismanagement, lack of money, etcetera. . . . Many were burnt down during the Troubles in the 1920s. Did you consciously take the great houses as a metaphor for the passing of an era?

MOLLY KEANE

Not quite consciously. But the houses did possess the people who lived in them because of the family tradition they embodied. You were born and went on living there till death. The house had an almost physical influence. And money was different in those days—it went much further. A good housemaid was paid £35 per year, an experienced butler £75, a Nanny, £100, and so on. We had a cook, a butler and two maids when I married in 1938, though we were not rich, my husband being the younger son. It is amazing how grandly we lived on very little money.

INTERVIEWER

This influenced the way people lived. I mean there was a lot more hospitality, as the chores were done by others and food was cheap. I know because the life you describe is similar to the one we lived in Persia when I was a child—grand without money, which is inconceivable today.

MOLLY KEANE

Exactly. You went and stayed with people for weeks, months, and you took your maid with you.

INTERVIEWER

Were the houses you describe in the books based on your own houses, and your friends', or did you invent them?

MOLLY KEANE

Very much based on the houses I knew. My own house, Belleville, where I lived with my husband until he died, I describe in *Loving and Giving*—my latest novel [American title: *Queen Lear*, published 1989]. Puppetstown was based on my parents' home, Ballyrankin, where I grew up. The house in *Two Days in Aragon* which is torched at the end of the story was based on Woodrooff, my friends the Perry's house, and so on. I didn't invent any of them.

INTERVIEWER

You saved Puppetstown in the book, whereas your own house, Ballyrankin, on which it was based, was burnt down in 1920. Can you remember the incident?

MOLLY KEANE

Very well, though I was away at the time. None of the children were there. They came one night, banged on the big door and burst into the house. My father had a bayonet and threatened to use it. They told him very politely: "Please don't, because we'll just *have* to shoot you." So he put it away. They stood my parents against a haystack in a field so that they could watch their house burn down to the ground. Pity! It was a lovely house. It stood on the banks of the River Slaney, surrounded with parkland. You reached it through a long avenue, with a gatelodge at either end. Between the river and the house was the Ladies Walk, flanked with beech groves and fields, with a picturesque waterfall at the end. There was an artificial pond which the previous owner had made, and whenever his agent came to worry him about the estate problems he got into a little rowboat and went out on the pond!

But at least they didn't kill my parents. There wasn't the senseless killing of today, when innocent people and children are murdered cold-bloodedly.

INTERVIEWER

You describe a torching in Two Days in Aragon, *which is your only overtly political novel. Whose house was Aragon?*

MOLLY KEANE

It belonged to some friends, and is still there. I substituted our house for it in the book.

INTERVIEWER

Your life was all about horses and hunting and fishing. Nothing destined you for a literary life. In fact, it was distinctly frowned upon for a woman to write. Yet your mother published poetry, albeit under a pseudonym. Was her work any good?

MOLLY KEANE

Good but not great. She came from County Antrim, in the North, and wrote love poems in the dialect of that area; being a lady she couldn't talk about love in her own voice. She was very popular and published her poems in top literary magazines, like *Blackwoods*. But she wouldn't have dreamed of writing a *novel!* That would have been quite wrong!

INTERVIEWER

Did she try to educate you?

MOLLY KEANE

Not in the least! She was very well-read, spoke French and Italian, but never bothered to impart any of it to us.

Similarly she was a good musician but never arranged for
us to have music lessons . . . I think because she adored
my father and didn't really want children. They were
happy together and had no need of anyone else. For years
they had no children and then out we tumbled, one after
another, five of us. She accepted us but never bothered
with us. I adored her as a child, but then in adolescence
I rebelled against her rigid Victorian habits and beliefs.
She didn't like any expression of freedom or *joie de vivre*.

INTERVIEWER

So how were you educated?

MOLLY KEANE

I wasn't! We had governesses who didn't teach us anything. They were usually daughters of clergymen with no money or future, so they became governesses. Then at fourteen or fifteen I went to a boarding school in Dublin for two years. We had a French mistress, Mademoiselle, whom we hated but who did teach us good French. I still read it, but the other day I was in France for the publication of my books, and had awful trouble at the press conference talking to the journalists.

INTERVIEWER

Did your mother at least read to you? Poetry and stories?

MOLLY KEANE

Never! Sometimes she made me read the novels of Sir Walter Scott to her aloud. I remember skipping all the passages about love. I did the same self-censoring with *Vanity Fair*. As a result I got into this awful habit of skipping. Nowadays most books are so overwritten that one can't help but skip.

INTERVIEWER

What about your father? Was he literary?

MOLLY KEANE

Not at all. When he got old he read Robert Smith Surtees and history, but in those days he hunted and fished and rode. He was a wonderful horseman and rode beautifully.

INTERVIEWER

You also had two old aunts living with you. Who were they?

MOLLY KEANE

They were my mother's sisters, and quite dotty. One of them, Aunt Bijou, had been briefly married and widowed; the other had never married. When I got married she said to me: "My dear I shall never forget *my* honeymoon; it was the most *horrible* time of my life!" They stayed with us till they died. After my parents my eldest brother had to look after them; that was how things were in those days.

INTERVIEWER

How did you set about "educating" yourself? Who did you read?

MOLLY KEANE

My first books were influenced by Dornford Yates, a very popular writer in the twenties. He is completely forgotten now, but then he was most popular. Recently they tried to revive him by publishing one of his books, but it was a flop. I thought he was wonderful. His heroes and heroines travelled all over Europe, while I hadn't even been to France! They were glamor itself!

INTERVIEWER

You mention Dornford Yates in your latest book, Loving and Giving, *as your heroine's favorite writer. But when did you start reading serious literature?*

MOLLY KEANE

Not until I was in my thirties. Then I read Jane Austen, George Eliot, Thackeray . . . . I read Proust, whom I

loved, in translation. I read the Russians, especially Chek-
hov, whose short stories I admired a great deal. I would
like to see him, have a nice chat with him over a glass
of vodka, wouldn't you?

INTERVIEWER

Indeed. What about Joyce. Did you read him?

MOLLY KEANE

Yes. I admired him, but disliked him. You see, I read
haphazardly. For example, I hadn't read Shakespeare's sonnets until I was twenty-five. As I said, I had no education.
I read Waugh with great pleasure; his novels are the
modern equivalent of Restoration comedies. I didn't care
for *Brideshead Revisited*, I thought it was selling the Catholic Church too hard, perhaps because he was a convert
and converts are usually more zealous. Now I like it more.

INTERVIEWER

What made you start writing?

MOLLY KEANE

Deep down I wrote because I resented my background. I
wanted to have fun, see people, go out. My mother never
let us see anyone who did not belong to our milieu.
Anyone remotely "fast" was out! And of course I broke
out into that set eventually.

INTERVIEWER

*But in your own milieu it was very mal vu to be clever,
especially if you were a woman. I mean the slightest hint
of blue in your stockings excluded any prospect of marriage.
So why did you do it?*

MOLLY KEANE

I was seventeen and fell ill, and they thought I had tuberculosis—which I didn't—and they put me to bed. I passed the time writing this novel about a handsome young Master of Hounds and a girl who falls in love with him— a picture of what I thought life should be, of what I wanted it to be. I took the name M.J. Farrell from a pub I saw one day as I was riding back home from a hunt.

After I wrote it I saw an advertisement for a literary agent in the *Times Literary Supplement* which my mother took, and I sent him my manuscript, written in longhand. They sold it to Mills & Boon for £70, which I spent giving a party for my friends at the Shelbourne Hotel in Dublin during the horse show week.

INTERVIEWER

That was The Knight of Cheerful Countenance. Then you wrote Young Entry, which was nearer real life than the fantasy world of the first novel. Did you send it to the publishers Mills & Boon?

MOLLY KEANE

Yes, but they rejected it. But William Collins who was a young dynamic and rather attractive publisher took it, and he went on publishing my books from then on. It was wonderful having a little money of my own and buying clothes. By then I had met the Perrys and moved to their circle.

INTERVIEWER

How did people find out that M.J. Farrell was you?

MOLLY KEANE

I told one friend, and of course soon enough my whole world knew.

INTERVIEWER

Did your mother read them?

MOLLY KEANE

I don't think she ever did. She was not remotely interested. She just said that I was being vulgar, which was a terrible accusation of non-Good Behaviour!

INTERVIEWER

Who were the Perrys? Obviously their friendship was of crucial importance to your development, since your life changed after you began to frequent their house.

MOLLY KEANE

I was lent a horse and for some reason I was prevented from riding it at a hunt. So I hid behind a fox covert to cry, and William Perry found me there. He took a great fancy to me and invited me to their house in County Tipperary. I was forbidden to go there, but went all the same, telling my parents that I was staying with a girl friend. One day there was a photograph in the paper, of a race-meeting I had been to with the Perrys; my parents saw it, and hell was let loose!

The Perrys had a tremendous social life, which we didn't have. Their son, John, was my contemporary and a charming playboy. He was a great friend of John Gielgud's, and the theater world of London.

INTERVIEWER

Did he take you to the theater, or encourage you to write plays?

MOLLY KEANE

Yes. He kept saying, Molly you should write plays. I said, Johnny how can I? He said write about yourself, just try.

So I wrote *Spring Meeting*, which starred Margaret Rutherford and became a hit.

INTERVIEWER

Your reviews included one from James Agate, then the most important drama critic in England, who compared you to Noël Coward. Did you meet Coward? Were you influenced by him?

MOLLY KEANE

That was a ridiculous comparison! Noël was an extraordinary dramatist. He invented a new language of comedy which other people copied afterwards. I did meet him later, and he liked my plays. Once he asked me: "What happened to that darling man who was a lover of yours and gave us lunch in Ireland?" I said that sadly he had died. "Oh dear! What a terrible change for him!" he said. Another time Lilli Palmer—Rex Harrison's German-Jewish wife—was starring in his latest play and they were great friends. One day at rehearsals she did something wrong, and Noël shouted: "And a great pity, darling, you didn't stay in Germany with Hitler. He would have burnt you up!"

INTERVIEWER

Overnight you were a star dramatist, met new people, a whole new world. Did you love it, or were you a bit bewildered by it?

MOLLY KEANE

Both. I was an alien and didn't belong to the theater world. I belonged here. After the success of the first play I rushed back to marry Bobbie in 1938 and to country

life, which I loved. But I also loved theater people—they
were warm and generous and full of gaiety. Many were
what you call today "gay," and, of course, being a success
helped.

The money was enormous compared to novels. I thought
I would never write anything except plays from then on.
Binkie Beaumont was the king of theater impresarios. He
produced them, and Johnny Gielgud directed them. I made
some life-long friends, like Peggy Ashcroft, Margaret Rutherford, Gielgud. . . .

INTERVIEWER

How much did John Perry help you with the plays?

MOLLY KEANE

He didn't help with the actual writing, but he had a great
experience of the theater in its mechanics and practicalities,
while I was ignorant of them. For example, in the *Spring
Meeting* the second act ended with a game of cards, and
I finished it with someone winning. Johnny Perry said:
"No, don't give it away. Bring the curtain down so that
no one knows who won." I did, and it worked much
better. In *Treasure Hunt* there was a scene between two
serious people, and the play dipped at that point. He said:
"write the same scene, but between two funny people."
Again he was right. So he helped me in that way—
technically.

INTERVIEWER

Your last play, Dazzling Prospects *was produced in 1959.
It was not a success. To what do you attribute its failure?*

MOLLY KEANE

The scene had changed. It was the time of the Kitchen-
Sink Drama and of the Angry Young Men. What they

called Drawing-Room Comedy was suddenly out of fashion.
The play was at fault too, but it happened to everyone
else as well: Terence Rattigan, Christopher Fry . . . all
successful playwrights of the day were silenced over night.
The press, led by Kenneth Tynan, started a crusade in
favor of a New Wave theater. He called Binkie Beaumont,
Gielgud, and Olivier "The Knights of Shaftesbury Avenue"
and ridiculed them. Olivier later redeemed himself by
playing in John Osborne's *The Entertainer*. There was an
organized gang of protesters who came to the first performance of my play and shouted it down. Tynan wrote:
"What is this irrelevant piece of nonsense doing in the
theater?"

Anyway, that finished me. I thought I would never write
again, for the theater or otherwise. And didn't for nearly
twenty years.

INTERVIEWER

*When you were writing for the theater did you read a lot
of plays?*

MOLLY KEANE

No. I read Maugham, but I didn't like his plays much.
He was a good writer of short stories and novels, but he
was not a natural writer; he taught himself to write and
went on until he became good. I read Shakespeare and
went to see the plays. I also read Restoration comedies.
Among the contemporaries I liked Rattigan because his
plays were so well-made and enjoyable. He was a delightful
man, kind, elegant, wonderful to his friends. Christopher
Fry wrote poetic plays, quite different from us. Beyond
me of course.

INTERVIEWER

Now that the climate has changed have you ever thought of reviving your plays?

MOLLY KEANE

No. They are *passé*. They belong to a world which doesn't exist any more.

INTERVIEWER

What about adapting your novels for the stage, or anybody else's? Now that they have proved so successful as television drama.

MOLLY KEANE

Once Binkie Beaumont gave me a French comedy by Marcel Aymé, *Say It With Flowers*, and asked me to translate it into English. It was hard, because French jokes don't translate, and you have to find substitutes for them. It was going to America first, but just before it was staged Albert Roussel's *The Little Hut* was a complete flop in New York, and Walter Chrysler, our backer, lost heart and withdrew. I was getting on the plane for New York, the cast was assembled there, and suddenly Chrysler said: "No more French plays!" Can you imagine?

INTERVIEWER

A case of the backer backing out! After the success of your first play you married Bobbie Keane. You said that you had "known" him for five years. Where did you meet him?

MOLLY KEANE

With the Perrys, in 1933. He was handsome and charming and I adored him. He was five years younger than me, and I didn't marry him straight away. But I had a relationship with him, which wasn't done in those days. Of course it *was* done, you just didn't talk about it to anyone, even to your best friend. The men of my generation had nearly all died in the First World War. There were so many women, and no men! Furthermore it was inconceivable marrying outside your own class. Nowadays you marry anyone you want—the Anglo-Irish gentry marry village girls.

Anyway, my sister Suzan was much better looking than me and rode better, yet she never married. She became a teacher and eventually had a nervous breakdown. They gave her electric shock treatment and put her in a hospital in Cork. I took her out and brought her here, and one night she sat by that bay window and said: "The sea that bares her bosom to the moon"—Wordsworth. I realised she had never had any fulfillment in her life! She died two years later, aged seventy-eight.

INTERVIEWER

What did Bobby do?

MOLLY KEANE

In those days people didn't *do* anything. You looked upon a day's fishing or hunting as serious work. His father had started a bacon factory in the village and Bobby was supposed to run that. We bought Belleville, which was a lovely house, and my daughters Sally and Virginia were born there in 1940 and 1945 respectively. Then suddenly in 1946 Bobby had an ulcer that burst. He was convalescing in the nursing home and I went to see him one morning as usual. The matron called me into her office and said:

"Now Mrs. Keane, you must be brave, your husband is dead."

INTERVIEWER

You said there followed "years of breadlining," so that lack of money was an added problem.

MOLLY KEANE

I kept the house for a while but eventually had to sell it. For a while I went back to London where my theater friends were very good to me—among others Adele Astaire (Fred Astaire's sister who married Lord Charles Cavendish, the second son of the Duke of Devonshire) who lived in Lismore Castle, in County Waterford, who became a friend of mine and used to give me her wonderful clothes. She was a great dancer, and forever witty and unspoilt. Later I met Fred Astaire, at Lismore. John Gielgud was a friend of his and thought very highly of him; he said, "Fred was such a good actor he could have played Hamlet if he had wanted to." I sent my eldest daughter to boarding school at thirteen, and later to a finishing school in Paris where she learnt very good French. But after *Dazzling Prospects* flopped I came back to Ireland and stopped writing.

INTERVIEWER

What made you write Good Behavior, *which many consider your masterpiece, after nearly twenty years?*

MOLLY KEANE

Just as the first time. To make a little money! I had an idea but didn't talk about it to anybody. I wrote the novel and put it under the mattress, so to speak. I only told my dear publisher, William Collins. You know how in the theater you want to shout to the protagonist: "Look out! Someone is going to push you over the precipice!" I said to Collins, suppose I wrote a novel about someone who behaves like that through out her life, who doesn't see what's coming to her. I had seen some of my contemporaries' lives being ruined by good behavior, and they had ended up closed and embittered. People hide behind good behavior and behave badly!

Collins said: "Wonderful idea. You go ahead and do it." So I did, and sent him the manuscript. To my staggering amazement he sent it back. Do you know what he said? "Molly, if you make half the characters in this book less unpleasant, of course we will publish it. But as it is there is not a single attractive character in it, and we shan't!" Well, I thought perhaps I should not have tried, and left it at that. I was seventy-six.

Then one day Peggy Ashcroft came to stay with me and she had a streaming cold. She asked me if I had anything unpublished for her to read, and I gave her the manuscript. She liked it, took it to London and gave it to the chairman of Chatto & Windus. He liked it too, but he was the old chairman and the young people in the firm didn't want it. Several other publishers turned it down, but my agents believed in it and persisted. Finally André Deutsch published it.

INTERVIEWER

The rest, as they say, is literary history. It was a huge success, and was short-listed for the Booker Prize, losing to Salman Rushdie's Midnight's Children. Were you surprised by the book's success? Did your friends think it was a roman à clef, since you published it under your own name?

MOLLY KEANE

Rather! It stayed on the best-seller list for a long time. It did well in America and France as well. Every one of my friends thought Aroon St. Charles was based on her, but she represents a *generation*: mine. So many of my contemporaries didn't get married because, as I said, the men weren't there—they had died in the war. The women came to terms with their lives; they were not happy, but they were not unhappy either—gardening and giving parties. You must read a book by McConville: *Ascendency to Oblivion*. It is the best on the subject of the Anglo-Irish, a history of the Establishment.

Then after *Good Behaviour* I wrote *Time After Time*, and that was successful too. Both books were adapted for television. The part of Jasper Swift, the elderly brother in the second novel was played by John Gielgud, and he was marvelous.

INTERVIEWER

All your novels are cinematographic; I'm thinking in particular of Two Days In Aragon, *with the Troubles as background, the torching scene, etcetera. . . . Have you thought of doing a filmscript of it?*

MOLLY KEANE

Funny you should say that, because several people have approached me for that book and bought options on it. But it hasn't materialized. John Osborne did a script of it, I believe, but the film wasn't done. Perhaps the question of the Irish Uprising has been answered, and that they fear the film may not be popular.

INTERVIEWER

I don't think that matters, because John Huston made The
Dead, *based on a story from Joyce's* The Dubliners, *and
it was very beautiful and moving. He made it as he was
dying, and it had a special grandeur, like sunset in the
desert. By the way, he made his Moby Dick in this area.
Did you meet him?*

MOLLY KEANE

Yes, I did. He was a friend of the communist journalist
Claud Cockburn who lived nearby and brought him to
see me one day. I liked him very much.

INTERVIEWER

*After the success of these two novels you wrote a cookery
book:* Nursery Cooking.

MOLLY KEANE

A title that killed it! It wasn't cookery, but reminiscences
and anecdotes. I was given a £20,000 advance for it, so I
thought I'd do it. I only started cooking in my forties,
when Bobby died; before we always had a cook. Then I
became a good cook. There is a lot in it about my childhood
and the cooks we had.

INTERVIEWER

After the success of Good Behaviour *Virago Press started
republishing your M.J. Farrell novels. Were you surprised
at their success?*

MOLLY KEANE

Rather! When Virago approached me I was apprehensive.
I thought they would be a bunch of lesbians. Not a bit!

They were delightful, all pretty and feminine, with husbands and lovers and babies.

INTERVIEWER

When Devoted Ladies *came out and was a best-seller, in 1934, you became a literary celebrity. Did you go to London and meet other writers and critics and journalists?*

MOLLY KEANE

I did go to some parties, but I didn't think of literary people as important, I mean they didn't ride or hunt or do anything glamorous like that. At a party someone introduced me to Elizabeth Bowen, who was very nice to me. She had a rather bad stammer and introduced me to David Cecil, who didn't impress me either! Can you believe it, I came from the bogs and didn't think these people were anybody! Later Elizabeth Bowen became a great friend. I think she was one of the best writers of her generation. She lived at Bowen's Court, her family home, and wrote a wonderful book about it.

Elizabeth wasn't particularly pretty; she rather looked like an Elizabethan pirate. But men adored her, and she loved them. Now that she is dead some people accuse her of having been a lesbian. An American woman—whose name I forget—has written a book about famous writers she has known, and in it she says she spent a night of love with Elizabeth Bowen! It is absurd, and I was appalled when I read it, not because I was shocked by lesbianism, but because it was untrue. She had a lover till the day she died. In fact, he came from America, where he was living, to be with her when she died.

INTERVIEWER

This kind of "biography" is appalling because the writers are no longer there to correct mistakes. There is a new book about George Eliot which apparently depicts her as a sex-maniac! What can one do?

MOLLY KEANE

A good biography is more than just gossip, malicious gossip at that. It certainly wouldn't be slanderous. I have been asked by various people if I would let them write mine, but I've said no. My daughter Sally is doing it, but after I'm gone, because while I'm alive I don't want to say anything that might hurt living people or their relatives.

INTERVIEWER

Did you meet any of the Bloomsbury people like Virginia Woolf?

MOLLY KEANE

No. As I said I was on the periphery of the literary world, living here and being busy with my family and animals and garden. I admired Virginia Woolf more than I liked her. Nowadays a lot of feminist writers emulate her, but she never talked nonsense, whereas they often do, a great deal! They don't have her substance, but imitate her style. She was a great writer, went mad every time she finished a book, which shows how intense the experience was for her. Of course, there are some young women writers who are awfully good. I'm thinking of Jennifer Johnson and Claire Boylan, both Irish, and there are others.

INTERVIEWER

Let's go back to your work and some of the recurrent themes in it. For example, that of "the Outsider": life goes on fairly

*smoothly, and then suddenly a stranger comes in and ruffles
the surface, revealing the turbulence beneath it. Usually it
is someone innocent that everybody uses, or someone who is
very cunning and preys on the innocent. In* The Rising
Tide, *Cynthia is the outsider, in* Devoted Ladies *it is George,
in* Loving and Giving, *it's Andrew, and so on . . .*

MOLLY KEANE

How clever to have detected that! I hadn't thought of it
that way, but now you mention it I can see the pattern.
You see I'm such an ignorant writer, totally uneducated!
That is why I find it hard to write book reviews, because
I neither have the knowledge nor the vocabulary. I have
written nothing invented, only what I knew. I only invented some of the plots, but the characters were based
on people I had known. For example, when I wrote *Devoted
Ladies* I hadn't the shadow of a notion of lesbianism. But
one day I was staying in London with a theater friend,
and a famous lesbian who is dead now came to stay with
her. She had a tiny hand bag, and I wondered what could
be in it. Do you know what it was? I had a peep: A
thousand cigarettes and a safety razor! And that put the
idea of *Devoted Ladies* into my head.

INTERVIEWER

*It was published in 1934, a period when it was very unusual
to talk about lesbianism. Did you have a* succès de scandal?

MOLLY KEANE

Not especially, but I had marvelous notices.

INTERVIEWER

*Another recurrent theme is that of power. One character
goes on exercizing power and then someone comes along*

and challenges it; the struggle for supremacy becomes the
focus of the plot. The person whose power is challenged is
usually an older character who has passed the sexual age,
like Lady Charlotte in The Rising Tide.

MOLLY KEANE

True. Lady Charlotte was based on one of my aunts. In
that sort of class the power the older women had was
terrifying. I saw that power struggle all around me. For
example, all my contemporaries struggled with their mothers to assert their freedom, as I did myself.

INTERVIEWER

Do you feel that the struggle for power is central in human
relationships? That in a way all relationships are based on
power, as some authors have maintained?

MOLLY KEANE

I wonder! My mother's generation wanted power to further
their idea of what was right. Some wanted power to push
their daughters into advantageous marriages, or prevent
"wrong" alliances. The power to rule was more in women
than in men.

But I don't think power enters into sexual relationships,
because men and women want different things. Women
want love and men want freedom. I mean that men can
have a perfectly happy marriage and at the same time a
little sex on the side. It is not so easy for women to
separate love from sex, or rarely.

INTERVIEWER

Do you mean that love transcends the desire for power?

MOLLY KEANE

Absolutely. But my aunt, who became Lady Charlotte in *The Rising Tide*, was the daughter of a titled family who lost it all and had to have something in its place. One uses the word snobbery as a shortcut, but for them it was much more. Their birth was almost a religion to them.

INTERVIEWER

You once said that the two great human motivations were sex and snobbery. Do you still believe that?

MOLLY KEANE

It was certainly true then. But I don't believe, as Freud does, that everything is related to early sexual experiences. For example, I had no Oedipus complex, as I adored my mother. And sexual drive is not the same in everybody. One of my brothers had no sexual urge at all. He was a gallant soldier in the war, a wonderful rider and sportsman, girls fancied him, but sex was not part of his life. Of course, if you are as sexy as I was, it becomes the most important part of your life, because as I said in women it is inseparable from love. I could be writing something very important, the best book of my life, and I would drop it without a thought to go off with a lover. Wouldn't you?

INTERVIEWER

Oh yes, like a shot, to the North Pole!

MOLLY KEANE

I do believe in love absolutely. Love means patience. It takes doing, and people today expect it to come out of

the blue and stay with them forever! But it isn't like that—
you have to work at it.

Class, or snobbery had to do with getting on in the
world and having fun. The way you spoke was important;
it opened or closed doors.

INTERVIEWER

*If sex was so important to you, what did you do after your
husband died? I mean you loved him and didn't want
anyone else, yet you were still a young woman?*

MOLLY KEANE

It was very hard. After a while I had a few lovers, but it
is not easy to take on a woman with two small children
and not much money. Some wouldn't and some didn't,
and nothing led to marriage. Then in my late fifties sex
gave me up, but I didn't mind, as the desire goes after a
certain age.

I could never write explicitly about sex, the way some
writers do. I think all this explicit sex in novels today is
a terrible mistake. I find it distasteful, particularly when
women write about it, and I dislike reading it. I think it
is much more potent if it is implied.

INTERVIEWER

What about the destructive power of love? In your last novel,
Loving and Giving (see p. 135) *Nicandra is completely
loving and trusting, and everyone takes advantage of it,
especially the man she loves.*

MOLLY KEANE

"Each man kills the thing he loves," as Oscar Wilde said.
There is that, and there is such a thing as loving too

much. I thought it would be interesting to have a woman who gave all and everyone failed her—or she failed them.

INTERVIEWER

In America the novel is being published soon under the title of Queen Lear. *Did you have* King Lear *in mind when you wrote it?*

MOLLY KEANE

Not really; it turned out like that. Nicandra is me. There is a lot of my childhood in the book. I always gave a lot, but unlike poor Nicandra I got something back. I was lucky.

INTERVIEWER

You said you didn't mind when "sex gave you up," as you put it. Did you find growing older very hard to bear?

MOLLY KEANE

I was never a great beauty, so it was easier for me than for women who are. It must be terrible losing your looks with age. But once I was looking through the kitchen window at dusk and I saw an old woman looking in. Suddenly the light changed and I realized that the old woman was myself. You see, it all happens on the outside, inside one doesn't change.

INTERVIEWER

Oscar Wilde said that the worst thing about getting old is feeling young!

MOLLY KEANE

How true! And you don't feel different, only other people's reactions change. I would like to write one more book,

about old age. Not a sad book, but a funny one, about
the small pleasures of old age; for example finding a
handkerchief in a pocket which you thought you had lost,
that sort of thing. You get on better with people when
you get older. I still like to entertain and amuse attractive
men. I love young people, and luckily they seem to enjoy
my company. I store up anecdotes to amuse them. It may
be a substitute for sex. Do you think if I wrote the book
it would be interesting, at least for older readers? I thought
the story would involve two sisters who have grown old.
One of them has lived in isolation and the other in the
world. Some years later the latter comes back to see her
sister, and the way they react to each other, each having
a secret and wanting to keep it, and the other trying to
find out!

I was once staying with a friend who was always stealing
to the sideboard and taking a surreptitious drink. Her
sister, a darling, who came to stay was on the booze too.
And they used to spy on each other! In fact, I wasn't
thinking of them when I got the idea, but now talking
to you I remembered them. I think old people can become
like naughty children.

There were a number of love-nests in Ireland where
men used to keep their mistresses. One of them looked
like a Swiss chalet, but full of chinoiseries inside. It had
a cellarful of good wine, and I thought that chalet might
make a nice setting for the story.

INTERVIEWER

*Perhaps it was Providence that sent me here, and I hope
you will start the book tomorrow!*

MOLLY KEANE

Not tomorrow, but soon!

INTERVIEWER

Did the success of Good Behaviour *change your life, after all those years? Does the fluctuation of fortune make a difference to an author like you, apart from the material gain I mean?*

MOLLY KEANE

Not at all. What affects me is what goes on in the world. When I read your book *The Blindfold Horse* and saw what was happening in Iran now, or what is happening in China, in Tiananmen Square, I feel wounded, devastated. I'm not political, but I'm horrified at what happens to *people.*

INTERVIEWER

Do you write regularly? Slowly or fast?

MOLLY KEANE

Slowly. I can't mix writing with other activities—nothing would get written. I have to start, keep regular hours, and go on until it is finished, then resume my life. Otherwise I can't do it. I used to write in bed, but now I'm told it is bad for the circulation, so I get up and sit at that table over there, and work three or four hours, then I stop. I can't go on for longer than that. Living has always been far more important to me than work. I write to live, not the other way around.

The other day I read somewhere about a writer saying that writing is like a prayer to her. That's schmaltz! Nonsense!

INTERVIEWER

Do you rewrite a lot?

MOLLY KEANE

Yes. I worry about grammar. At school I was hopeless at math and grammar. The teachers gave up on me. I write by eye: if it *looks* correct, I somehow know it is. I write in school notebooks which have two sides, and I write on one side and correct on the opposite page. After I have corrected it like that, I copy it so that the typist can read it. I do it all longhand.

INTERVIEWER

When your novels became successful in the 1930s, one critic wrote—I think it was Hugh Walpole—that you had brought style back into English novel. Do you consciously work on your style?

MOLLY KEANE

No. I think style comes from what you have to say. What I do like is clarity. V.S. Pritchett, for example, has wonderful clarity, not a word too many, not a word too few. When one has something to say one just says it as simply and straightforwardly as possible.

INTERVIEWER

Compton MacKenzie compared your descriptive powers to Corot's in his landscapes.

MOLLY KEANE

Oh my God! Did he? My description of hunting balls and landscape and people come from what I saw all around me. As I said I invent nothing—I have no imagination.

INTERVIEWER

What about dialogues? They are too witty and sharp not to be artfully constructed.

MOLLY KEANE

I used to have very good memory, and I listened and remembered what people said.

INTERVIEWER

Another critic recently compared you to Ivy Compton-Burnett. Do you feel any affinity with her?

MOLLY KEANE

Not at all! I don't like her a bit! She is considered a classical writer, but her dialogues are false, because everybody speaks the same way, that is to say like her! There is no characterization. I don't know why she has gained so much prestige.

INTERVIEWER

Is she much read now? Hilary Spurling's excellent biography rekindled interest in her, but I think it has now died down. But is writing easy for you, once you make a start?

MOLLY KEANE

No. I don't like the process of writing at all, only the result. Except for my first novel, writing has always been difficult for me. That first book was a miracle—I thought I was Shakespeare at seventeen! I realized I wasn't good enough!

INTERVIEWER

You said you start with an idea. Does the story develop as you go along?

MOLLY KEANE

Yes, and suddenly I get a little break with a character, and I can see the way forward.

INTERVIEWER

You have just recovered from a heart attack. It was a brush with death, did you think it was the end? How did you feel when you came to?

MOLLY KEANE

I had my first heart attack two years ago, when I was in the middle of writing *Loving and Giving*. This time they discovered a blood clot that could have killed me, but didn't. I never thought, oh dear I'm going to die.

INTERVIEWER

Do you ever think of death?

MOLLY KEANE

Not deeply. I'm not frightened of it. But while I'm alive I'd like to keep well and active.

INTERVIEWER

Do you think there is something after death?

MOLLY KEANE

I don't know. Sometimes I think it would be nice if there were. I would like to see Bobby again, but then we might have grown apart, developed differently. Rosamond Lehmann wrote the book *The Swan in the Evening* about her daughter Sally, who died young. She believes in life-after-death, but I thought it was romantical wishful thinking! How can we know? Sometimes I am conscious of life departing from me.

INTERVIEWER

But don't let's be sad. I'm excited about your new book.

MOLLY KEANE

I don't know if I'll ever be able to write it. A bird twittered in my head, and now it has flown away.

INTERVIEWER

Not so! It will return soon and sing! You will write the book about the joys of old age and give pleasure and comfort to your readers. Promise?

MOLLY KEANE

I promise!

Rosamond Lehmann

Rosamond Lehmann was born in 1901, in Bourne End, Buckinghamshire. Her father, Rudolph Lehmann, was the editor of Punch, as well as a well-known oarsman and fencer. He became a Liberal M.P. in 1906. Her mother, Alice Davis, was from Boston, Massachusetts. Rosamond was the second of their four children. One of her sisters, the late Beatrix Lehmann, became an actress. Her brother, John Lehmann, was a writer, editor, and publisher. The Lehmann family lived in grand Edwardian style in a large house on the river Thames, and the children were brought up by a staff of nannies, governesses, and tutors, only "coming down after tea" to see their parents.

In 1919, Lehmann went as a scholar to Girton College, Cambridge, and obtained an honors degree in English. In 1924, she met and married Leslie Runciman, now Lord Runciman. The marriage was not a success, and they parted three years later. Meanwhile, Lehmann had written her first novel, Dusty Answer, an account of a young girl's first encounter with love. After an initial mixed reception, the novel became a best-seller.

In 1928, Lehmann married Wogan Philipps, now Lord Milford, a Communist peer, and had a son and a daughter. Her second novel, A Note in Music, about two women locked in hopeless marriages in a northern town, was less warmly received. Undaunted, Lehmann went on to write Invitation to the Waltz, published in 1932, and The Weather in the Streets in 1936, both of which were instant best-sellers. In 1940, her private life was again shattered by the breakup of her second marriage.

During World War II, Lehmann lived in the country with her two children and started a long and happy relationship with the poet Cecil Day Lewis. During this time, she contributed a series of highly popular short stories to her brother's magazine, New Writing. The stories were collected in The Gypsy's Baby in 1946. Her next novel was The Ballad and the Source in 1945, which was also successful. Her relationship with Day Lewis ended in 1949, and in 1953 she wrote what is perhaps her most successful novel, The Echoing Grove. In 1958, tragedy struck, with the death of her young daughter Sally, who had married the poet J. P. Cavanagh. Shattered by grief, Lehmann thought she could never write again. She became interested in spiritualism, and in 1967 wrote The Swan in the Evening, fragments of autobiography in which she describes her psychic experiences following the death of her daughter. In 1977, she wrote A Sea-Grape Tree, a novel in which she introduces some of her new insights into psychic phenomena.

For years, Lehmann's novels were out of print, but now that both Penguin and Virago have republished them, her work has found a large and appreciative new readership. Several of the novels have become best-sellers again, and The Weather in the Streets recently was made into a film. In her last months she received letters every day from women who told her, "You have written my story."

Prior to her death in 1990, Lehmann lived alone in a small house in Kensington. Her great beauty—famous in *youth and middle age—seemed undiminished by age. Her ivory skin, silver-blond hair, and tall handsome figure still exuded dignified glamor. Then in her eighties, Lehmann was hardly idle. Her diary was filled with lunch and dinner dates, and a young BBC producer was at work on a documentary of her life and work. Lehmann was also vice-president of the College of Psychic Studies in London and edited their magazine, Light; in addition, she was active in PEN International. Lehmann wore pastel-colored clothes enlivened by touches of colored accessories. She spoke in a soft, firm voice and often used terms of endearment. The following interview took place in her small sitting room, in front of a log fire and a tray of tea.*

INTERVIEWER

When did you become aware of your vocation as a writer? Indeed, was it a vocation?

ROSAMOND LEHMANN

It was what you might call a vocation, insofar as I can't remember when I didn't have the sense that I was destined to write. The first time I actually wrote something was at the age of five or six. I was sitting in a walnut tree, eating toffee, and there was a scribbling block on my knees. Suddenly, I started to write a poem. It had three or four stanzas.

INTERVIEWER

Do you remember any of it?

ROSAMOND LEHMANN

Yes I do:

Out in the shady woodland glade,
Where the wind blows soft and sweet,

Where the leaves tell stories of sun and shade,
And the acorn drops at your feet,

I sigh as I wander amid the trees
And my sigh comes back on the wings of the breeze

. . . and so on. Well, I couldn't write it all down, so I
rushed to my father and said, "Daddy, what is this?" He
looked at it and said, "It is a poem. Where did you get
it from?" I said, "I made it up. *Is* it a poem?" and he said,
"Yes, well done!" Suddenly I had a sense of identity. As
you see, it was a sort of doggerel, but from that moment
on I never stopped writing.

INTERVIEWER
Did you write only poems?

ROSAMOND LEHMANN
Poetry and so-called poetry. Oh, it was so easy then!
Everything flowed. I wrote all about fairies, and moon-
beams, and nature, and it all poured out in rhymes. I
destroyed most of the poems when I was fourteen, because
I was ashamed of them, but I have kept a few. I think
they might amuse my grandchildren.

INTERVIEWER
Did your parents encourage you?

ROSAMOND LEHMANN
My mother was from New England. She was very puri-
tanical and upright, and she didn't want us to be conceited.
I remember—oh so vividly!—her saying to a guest, "Rosie
writes doggerel," which pierced me to the heart. But my

father was very encouraging, as he was a writer himself and came from a highly literary and artistic family.

INTERVIEWER

What was your father's family like?

ROSAMOND LEHMANN

The Lehmanns must have been Jewish in origin. My grandfather, Frederick Lehmann, came from Hamburg and married Nina Chambers, daughter of Robert Chambers, founder of *Chambers' Journal* and *Chambers' Encyclopaedia*. Robert was a famous literary figure in his day. One of his many works was a heretical book on evolution— *before* Darwin's—called *Vestiges of Creation*. It caused a great stir in orthodox Christian circles and he published it anonymously. Later, when he was asked why, he answered, "I have eleven good reasons." He had eleven children, you see, and he feared their chances in society would have been grievously affected. My grandparents, Frederick and Nina, had a literary and musical salon in mid-Victorian times. Nina was a brilliant pianist and had played with Clara Schumann and Joachim. Writers such as Robert Browning, Charles Dickens, and Wilkie Collins were their close friends. My great-uncle was the painter Henri Lehmann, who did that famous portrait of Liszt. His brother Rudolf painted most of the Victorian celebrities of the day. The two brothers' portraits hung in my father's library. I used to sit there and think of them as my ancestors; I feared I could never be worthy of my heritage. My father was a fine classical scholar as well as an athlete—an oarsman and a fencer. He was very beautiful and all my life I was in love with him. As a result, I have always been fatally attracted to good-looking men who

resemble him. I know nothing of his love life, except that
he remained a bachelor until he was over forty. Then, on
a trip to America to coach the Harvard crew, he met my
mother, a twenty-four-year-old New England girl, a grad-
uate of Radcliffe, and they fell in love. A year later he
married her and they came to live in England.

INTERVIEWER

In Invitation To The Waltz *you describe a wealthy Ed-*
wardian household. Was it based on your own home?

ROSAMOND LEHMANN

I suppose it was. My father was very well off, but he lost
half his capital by entrusting it to a friend who speculated
with it on the stock market. The poor man shot himself;
we became much less rich. We didn't have to leave our
home, but it meant the departure of our hated Belgian
governess, the loss of our horses and stables, and a much
smaller staff. Then came the First World War, and my
father began to develop Parkinson's disease. My mother,
who was a kind of Henry James heroine—in that she had
a formidable sense of duty—took it upon herself to nurse
him. Gradually he became a hopeless invalid and eventually
died in 1929.

INTERVIEWER

What kind of schooling did you have in those early years
before the First World War?

ROSAMOND LEHMANN

My parents didn't approve of girls' schools, and we were
educated at home. My enterprising mother had a pavilion
built at the end of the garden to house a kind of kinder-
garten for us and several little neighbors. Later we learned

excellent French from our governess, music from a lady
in the village, and a charming young woman came from
London once a week to teach us drawing. I had the run
of my father's library. I was allowed to read anything, and
did. I suppose such an education would be considered
hopelessly inadequate today, but the thought of being sent
away to boarding school was a nightmare to me.

INTERVIEWER

*What kind of books did you read in those early years, and
which ones, do you think, later influenced your writing?*

ROSAMOND LEHMANN

I read a great deal of poetry. Browning was my favorite.
I also read Matthew Arnold, Keats, Shelley, Byron. . . .
I didn't warm to Byron then, but later, when I read his
letters and his biography, I was fascinated by his personality.
I also read the great Victorian novelists: Dickens, Thackeray, the Brontës, Mrs. Gaskell, George Eliot, Jane Austen.
. . . Dickens was my passion. On the whole I was very
well read in Victorian literature. Amazingly enough, I can't
say that any of them influenced my writing, except perhaps
the poets. I read *Little Women*, by Louisa May Alcott, a
dozen times at least, and all E. Nesbit's wonderful books
as they came out. Later, when I went to Cambridge, I
read English, which meant all the greats. But I learned
more from reading on my own and discussing books with
my father than I ever did at Cambridge.

INTERVIEWER

*What about American literature? Did your mother introduce
you to American writers?*

ROSAMOND LEHMANN

She didn't introduce me to American authors, except Edith
Wharton, for whom she had a great reverence. She was
more interested in history than novels. I read Henry James,
and still do. He and Wharton are both giants, but at times
I almost prefer Wharton—she doesn't have the *longueurs*
or the convolution of Henry James. I have just reread her
novel *The Reef*, and I am amazed at her deep understanding
of the heart, of the relationships between men and women.
Wharton didn't have a happy marriage, did she? Bernard
Berenson told me that she had a great love affair with

Walter Barry, a well-known worldly figure in his day, whom she adored till the end.

INTERVIEWER
Did you write at Cambridge?

ROSAMOND LEHMANN

The flow became less and less and finally stopped. I mean poetry. Cambridge was a sort of explosion out of the cocoon. My father's family disapproved of my going to university, saying, "Poor girl! She is pretty, yet they send her away to become a bluestocking!" But my mother believed that girls should have the same education as boys. I was overjoyed! I thought I would be among the *finesfleurs* of the intelligentsia. But it wasn't so in my day. Most of my contemporaries came from a different background and were preparing to be teachers. That was a strange time. Most young men had been killed in the War and our circle was decimated. Those at Cambridge were the survivors, and they were older and more sophisticated than undergraduates usually are. The food and the cold were simply awful, and there was very strict *chaperonnage*. We were not allowed to visit young men in their rooms or ask them to a tête-à-tête tea in ours. A certain amount of climbing over the walls and dropping *billet-doux* took place; poems and letters were dropped for me, but we were not allowed to mix in any normal way. How different it is today! My granddaughter is having a happy relationship with a young man at Oxford who lives on the same hallway! I wonder if they get any work done. Apparently they do, because the standards are so high and the competition is so fierce.

INTERVIEWER

Did it worry you that you had stopped writing?

ROSAMOND LEHMANN

Not really. I wrote a few articles for *Granta*, which my father had started, and my essays were praised. It was generally assumed that I would be a writer. My ambition was twofold: to get married and have children, and to be a writer. After falling desperately and unrequitedly in love with a young man at Cambridge, I met Leslie Runciman in London and married him. We went to live in Newcastle, where he worked in his family's shipping business. I soon realized that I had made a terrible mistake, that the marriage was doomed. For one thing, he didn't want any children and I longed for them. I thought, "What have I done? What will become of my life?" Then Wogan Philipps came to work in my husband's firm and after a while I realized that I was going to fall in love with him. Instead of feeling hopelessly trapped, I suddenly saw a light, some hope. I dropped the rather boring novel I had started and began to write *Dusty Answer*. I went away to Dorset, rented a room in a farm house, and wrote and wrote for two or three months, until I finished it. Then I went back to Newcastle. I lived in a sort of trance and identified with Judith, the heroine, who is a lonely, romantic girl living in a dream. Now I find Judith far too sappy and overly romanticized. I can't bear her.

INTERVIEWER

At the time everybody assumed that Dusty Answer *was autobiographical and that you would not follow it up with anything of the same quality. How autobiographical is it?*

*Did you invent the two houses by the river, the children,
and the mysterious grandmother?*

ROSAMOND LEHMANN

People always assume that because my novels have real
locations that my characters are true portraits. They are
not. They were invented, but of course they were based
on fragments of children I had known. I invented entirely
the grandmother, and I put them all in the house next
door to ours in Bourne End.

INTERVIEWER

*The book has an atmosphere of poetic enchantment, a dream
quality, which reminded me of Alain Fournier's* Le Grand
Meaulnes.

ROSAMOND LEHMANN

Funny you should say that about *Le Grand Meaulnes,*
because that is what people said at the time in France.
Perhaps it explains the book's tremendous success with
the French, who still read it, even though they probably
think I have been dead for decades!

INTERVIEWER

Back in Newcastle, what did you do with your manuscript?

ROSAMOND LEHMANN

We had taken a house in Northumberland for the summer
and friends came to stay for weekends. Among them was
George Rylands, who had been the star of his generation
at Cambridge, both as a scholar and an actor. I told him
that I had written a novel and asked if he would mind
looking at it. Rather reluctantly, I think—judging by how

I feel when my friends ask me to do the same thing—he took it away to read. He must have been impressed, since he sent it to Harold Raymond, one of the directors of Chatto & Windus. Three weeks later I got a letter from Raymond saying that they would like to publish the book, though they did not expect to make any money out of it. I received a modest contract—very' modest—but I was overjoyed. By the time the book was published, I was separated from my husband and living in a cottage with my sister Beatrix. The first reviews of *Dusty Answer* were rather censorious. They said it was full of sex and that there was an intimation of lesbianism—you remember the two girls? My mother was loyal but upset. She wrote me some "never-mind-darling" letters, but I knew she was hurt. Then Alfred Noyes, who was a well-known poet and had been a protégé of my father's, wrote a long article in the *Sunday Times* in praise of the book, saying that it was the kind of novel Keats might have written if he were alive today.

INTERVIEWER

Your second novel, A Note In Music, *seems to be based on your unhappy life in Newcastle: two women trapped in hopeless marriages in a cold, northern provincial town. Yet you wrote it when you were happily remarried to Wogan Philipps. Did you need the distance from your first marriage to recount the experience in fictional terms?*

ROSAMOND LEHMANN

A writer works from the material she has, but it comes from the unconscious. Everything is stored up and one never knows what comes up to the surface at a given moment. A period of gestation is certainly needed, what

Wordsworth called "emotion recollected in tranquility." You cannot write about an experience when you are living it, suffering it. You are too busy surviving to look at it objectively. At least *I* can't.

INTERVIEWER

In A Note In Music, *the heroine, Grace Fairfax, never gets out of her marriage. Did you deliberately avoid the happy ending—which actually happened to you—because in those days most women never did escape their miserable marriages?*

ROSAMOND LEHMANN

I never do anything deliberately. It wasn't *my* story, it was the story of two women who didn't get out. I am amazed at writers who say that they know exactly what is going to happen and what a character is going to do. Perhaps that is the difference between a creative, imaginative writer and a reporter or journalist; once a character has been created it leads you rather than is led by you, although, I suppose, at the same time you have to control it. But the novel follows its own organic course.

INTERVIEWER

The reviews of your second book were less enthusiastic, though some writers liked it—E.M. Forster, for instance.

ROSAMOND LEHMANN

Perhaps that was partly because of the homosexual element. Homosexuality was never written about in novels in those days. E.M. Forster wrote *Maurice*, but never dared publish it—until many years later. Yet it was the beginning of the great homosexual wave; it was considered clever and so-phisticated and "being Greek." At Cambridge and Oxford,

it seemed everyone either was a homosexual or was pre-
tending to be. I remember my first husband wrote to a
Cambridge friend of his when we got married, "You might
think it degrading of me to settle for a woman, but she
is different—she has the mind of a *man*." *Me!*

INTERVIEWER

While you were married to Wogan Philipps, you wrote
Invitation to the Waltz, *and* The Weather in the Streets.
*Olivia is the heroine of both books. In the first she is a child
and an adolescent; in the second she is a young woman
who has been married and is now divorced. It seems that
once you had created Olivia as a child and an adolescent,
she refused to go until you told the rest of her story as an
adult.*

ROSAMOND LEHMANN

I think Olivia is a much more autobiographical figure than
Judith in *Dusty Answer*. As I said, I don't like Judith now.
Olivia is much more real, less romanticized. She is about
sixteen in *Invitation to the Waltz* when she meets Rollo
fleetingly at the ball. I thought Olivia would see Rollo
years later and fall in love with him. Some people were
scandalized by the back-street abortion scene in *The Weather
in the Streets*, yet abortions happened all the time. I had
friends who had been through it with my support, but
no one ever *talked* about it. To me, it seemed unthinkable
not to write the scene since it was part of the truth of
the story. Novelists worth their salt tell the truth as they
see it. My American publishers wanted me to remove the
abortion scene, but I refused.

INTERVIEWER

You were living in the country at the time, near Oxford. As a famous, best-selling writer, did you meet and make friends with other literary figures?

ROSAMOND LEHMANN

I did make a great many friends. Lytton Strachey and his wife Carrington lived within motoring distance and came over frequently. Others came and stayed for weekends— Vanessa Bell and Duncan Grant, George Rylands, Virginia and Leonard Woolf, Raymond Mortimer, and others from the Bloomsbury circle. I was rather shy and thought them all cleverer than I. We didn't talk much about our books but about writing and art in general, and there was a lot of laughter and gossip. As time went on we talked about what was inevitably to come—the war. They were all passionate anti-Fascists. My husband became more and more left-wing and eventually joined the International Brigade and went to Spain to drive an ambulance. Bloomsbury was the core of the literary world, but I never thought I belonged to them. In fact, I never belong to any group. I was completely engrossed with my children and my own writing. It was a bold and tragic gesture to go and fight in the Spanish Civil War, the last time that young Englishmen like Julian Bell and John Cornford—both of whom were killed—were ready to fight idealistically for what they believed to be human rights. Most, like George Orwell and Stephen Spender, were disillusioned, but Wogan held on. He had a Pauline conversion to communism and is still a believer, despite the Gulags and everything else that has come to light, much as a Christian holds on to his faith despite the bloody history of Christianity, or a Moslem *malgré* Khomeini. Anyway, at the time I was involved with them all—they were our friends. I read all of Virginia Woolf's books and thought them simply wonderful. Now I can't read them; I find her essays and journals infinitely better than her novels. Her heroines are not real women to me. She was an ardent feminist and argued the feminist case brilliantly in *Three Guineas* and *A Room of One's Own*. Both were clarion calls for women's equality. I never wrote anything like that, but then I wasn't that kind of writer. Woolf influenced people considerably, and for me that side of her work is far more important than her novels. Her journals remain her great masterpieces. I now find the Bloomsbury ethic a little parochial and intro-spective. They did not deal with universal aspects of things, and they always seem to be playing with meaning—"What is Truth?" "What is Love?"—forever *flirting* with truth. What they did and wrote about painting is their great contribution—people like Roger Fry and Clive Bell, who introduced the French impressionists to England. I made some lasting friendships. Elizabeth Bowen for instance, whose books I admire as much as ever. She said once that she was *envious* of my reputation, she was too great a person to be jealous. There were various complications in our lives which separated us for a while, but we became close later. I was with her a great deal during her last years. Ivy Compton-Burnett was another writer I admired. She was an extraordinary and unique woman, very witty and relaxing to be with. Her books wear well. I read one the other day and enjoyed it as much as I had in the fifties. Graham Greene and Evelyn Waugh were others I read and admired.

INTERVIEWER

When your second marriage broke up in 1940, you moved into a cottage and wrote the short stories which were later collected in The Gypsy's Baby. *What made you change genres, and what is the difference between a novel and a short story for you?*

ROSAMOND LEHMANN

The short story seems easier to me, perhaps because those particular ones were based on my childhood memories and I was creating from memory. My brother had started a literary magazine, *New Writing,* and asked me to contribute stories to it. Then one day I began what I thought would be a long short story and in walked Mrs. Jardine. As I wrote on, she kept growing and things began to happen around her and in her past, and the story became a novel, *The Ballad and the Source.* I think each work creates its own form and its own span and rhythm. Nowadays many novels seem to be padded short stories. But a good novel can't be conceived as a short story, because it couldn't be compressed into one.

INTERVIEWER

You once said that you were a privileged person with leisure and money, and could write without pressure. It corroborates Woolf's view in A Room of One's Own, *that women need five thousand a year and a private place to write. Do you still agree with that?*

ROSAMOND LEHMANN

That is nonsense! I don't know any writer today who has that kind of private income. A room, yes, one needs tranquility. But most women writers today work very hard to earn a living. Anita Brookner has a very taxing job as an art historian. In my case, although I started with a privileged life, I certainly had to make a living out of my writing after my separation from my second husband. I think the need to make a living can be a spur—it was in my case. I was lucky that by then I was well-known, since I can't write a book a year. I remember J.B. Priestley telling me, "You are good, but you are an amateur." He knew how professional and serious I was with my writing, and what he meant was that I didn't produce enough.

INTERVIEWER
Do you regret not having produced more books?

ROSAMOND LEHMANN
Not really. There were always so many other things I enjoyed—children, music, reading, friendship. I never thought my writing was the most important thing in my life and that I should withdraw from everything and everyone else in order to produce a book a year. Anyway, one waits for the creative flow to start. One cannot force it, and shouldn't. This is what I would like to make clear: that a creative novelist—or dramatist for that matter—*always* relates back to what he or she has stored up from the first two or three decades of life. Childhood and youth are the source. Certainly all that I have written—the voices, faces, places, and images—the whole creative thrust, comes from my early life. Of course, being older, I related all that to the present. I am not comparing myself to Dickens, but even he always went back to his childhood, or so we are told by his latest biographers. It doesn't matter how

late you start. George Eliot began to write after forty but her material came from her childhood.

INTERVIEWER

The critic Sydney Janet-Kaplan said that the story of Mrs. Jardine and the dead daughter in The Ballad and the Source *illustrated the myth of Demeter looking for her daughter Persephone. Do you agree?*

ROSAMOND LEHMANN

Who knows? I didn't think of it at the time, but with hindsight I can see that the myth is there. A creative writer is in touch with something much deeper which comes from the unconscious. I don't mean the Freudian *subconscious*—a wastepaper basket of unfulfilled sexual desires—but the Jungian *unconscious*—something deeper, belonging to the human race, whence myths spring. This is why so many critics and journalists are so boring; they don't see the deeper layers of things.

INTERVIEWER

In your last novel before your daughter Sally's death, The Echoing Grove, *the two sisters, Dinah and Madeleine, are in love with the same man, Madeleine's husband. Was it based on your own experience with Cecil Day Lewis, who was married?*

ROSAMOND LEHMANN

No. *Not at all.* Everyone seems to have assumed it was, and I was upset. My relationship with Lewis was very happy and its break-up was the biggest disaster of my life. I couldn't possibly have written about it. All my male characters are based on men I had known in my youth.

Madeleine and Dinah are *not* aspects of myself, whatever the critics say. Dinah is much more like my sister Beatrix. As I said, she is not a portrait. Neither is Madeleine.

INTERVIEWER

So it is a case of "Madame Bovary, c'est moi!" *and* "Madame Bovary, ce n'est pas moi!"

ROSAMOND LEHMANN

Exactly. The whole process in a nutshell.

INTERVIEWER

Your novels were almost forgotten for twenty years until Virago recently republished them and they became bestsellers again. It has been suggested that your novels depict an affluent upper-class milieu of Etonians and country houses which the Leftish sixties and seventies were not attuned to, and that now, with the revival of conservatism and the interest in our imperial past, they have become acceptable again. I am inclined to think that it has something to do with a distinct feminine sensibility which your work exemplifies. What do you think?

ROSAMOND LEHMANN

I think that's true, and also accounts for Virago's huge success. Virago novels are not feminist, in that awful, aggressive way which denies women their feminine identity. They are concerned with the understanding of feminine sensibility. Radical feminism denies the difference between men and women. My novels explore it. I do believe that women have a much richer emotional nature than men, and are more intuitive. They are as strong and intelligent as men, but in a different way. They often take the initiative; Judith in *Dusty Answer* and Rebecca in *A Sea-Grape Tree* both declare their love before the man makes the move. That used to be something quite unacceptable. Even today, women are supposed to wait for men to show interest, though I'm told this is no longer *de rigueur!* Similarly, my women don't play games. But then neither did Dorothea Brooke, George Eliot's heroine in *Middlemarch*. I love Dorothea, don't you? But if you don't play games you run the risk of being rejected and hurt, as Judith does. In *The Ballad and the Source* Rebecca says, "One day men and women will be able to speak the truth with each other." I remember Woolf saying, "Don't forget that we won this for you," referring to the ability to discuss sex frankly with our male friends. Generalizations are dangerous, but it seems to me that women tend to have higher emotional expectations than men; they are not content with a smaller-scale love or experience. I am always amazed at how little love and emotion men can get along with quite nicely! Women suffer much more when they are deprived of love.

INTERVIEWER

Do you think it is somewhat different today, when women have careers and responsible jobs?

ROSAMOND LEHMANN

I suppose they are not so dependent now, but think of the anguish of being a rejected Victorian girl. It wasn't considered correct to leave rejection behind and try again, it was once and for all, and you remained a rejected or widowed or abandoned woman forever. Even after the First World War, many young women remained old maids because they had lost their fiancés in the war. You don't mourn a faithless lover as Trollope's Lily Dale did, who never raised her head again, you just go and find yourself another one. This is why some contemporary novels are apt to be dull, because the concept of guilt about moral lapses doesn't exist any more. How can you write an interesting novel when there are no secrets, and nothing is sacred?

INTERVIEWER

The suffragette movement was before your time, but I believe your mother was active in it. Did it influence you?

ROSAMOND LEHMANN

As a Liberal M.P., my father was in favor of women having the right to vote. I don't think my mother would have stayed with him if he hadn't been, as she was an ardent suffragette. She wasn't militant. She deplored women tying themselves to railings and that kind of thing—she thought it was counterproductive to the cause. But she went to meetings and canvassed with my father in his constituency.

INTERVIEWER

What about the upsurge of feminism in the sixties and seventies, when many women writers became prominent by taking up the banner?

ROSAMOND LEHMANN

I'm afraid I didn't like that. I thought it was too aggressive and unfruitful. Now I am told some feminists advocate lesbianism as a matter of principle. That is what I feared might happen, a total breach. How can the majority of women go along with that? Even the Greenham Common women. Though I agree with their cause, that nuclear weapons should be banned. I couldn't be one of them, because the *way* they go about it seems to dehumanize them. On the whole anything that becomes a cult, or a mass movement, loses its moral and spiritual value. The crusade has to be personal, individual. As soon as it becomes collective it loses its purpose.

INTERVIEWER

It becomes what Jung called "a collective infection."

ROSAMOND LEHMANN

Absolutely. That is perhaps why my voice still may be "vibrant," because it is individual, whatever you may think of it. I think that the relationship between men and women is perhaps improving, that there is a dialogue, an understanding. Because men are beginning to realize that there is femininity in them and that there is a male ingredient in women which needs to be catered to. I think this is the greatest thing Jung bequeathed to us: the *anima*, or female in men, and the *animus*, or male in women, have to be recognized and dealt with. Few get the balance right, alas, but if one does there can be harmony.

INTERVIEWER

Painful as it is to talk about Sally's death, it seems to have changed your life and your work completely.

ROSAMOND LEHMANN

I described it as it happened in *The Swan in the Evening*. Yes, there was an omen. A blackbird hit against my window and dropped dead. It was like a hard thud in my heart, but I was quite happy at the time and brushed it aside, until the news arrived.

INTERVIEWER

I know you don't like the word "spiritualism" with its
connotation of charlatanism, but Sally's death did seem to
spark your interest in the spiritual life.

ROSAMOND LEHMANN

In the thirties, like most of my contemporaries, I was an
agnostic. I was never a staunch atheist, but I thought that
a spiritual life was a sort of gift that I didn't possess. I
rejected all orthodox religions: they seemed narrow and
dogmatically backward. I read with pleasure the great Christian mystics—Julian of Norwich, St. Teresa of Avila, St.
John of the Cross. . . . When Sally died I was completely
shattered; I didn't think of committing suicide, but I knew
I couldn't live without her. So what was I to do? Then
out of this appalling darkness came an extraordinary breakthrough: I had the conviction of her presence. I didn't
actually see her, but I heard her voice with my inner ear,
and I could touch her; I became convinced of the fundamental truth of "living on." I kept saying to people,
"But she is not dead!" and they thought I had gone round
the bend! I became a recluse, and listened to this inner
voice that kept telling me to go on and wait and grope.

INTERVIEWER

Didn't you get involved with some mediums, or "sensitives"
as you call them?

ROSAMOND LEHMANN

I went to one or two spiritualist séances but—without
wanting to be too critical—I found them cheap, elementary
and popular. Then I joined the College of Psychic Studies

and I met Lady Sandys who has become a close friend
and is a remarkable clairaudient. The College of Psychic
Studies is an intellectually based Jungian organization to
which many serious researchers, including doctors and
scientists, now belong. Through Lady Sandys I became in
touch with Sally and many others. I have written about
all this in *The Swan in the Evening.* I was lucky also to
meet Eileen Garrett, a celebrated medium and friend of
Aldous Huxley. Huxley was very much in touch with his
wife, Maria, through Eileen but was reluctant to admit it.
Eileen gives an account of it in her memoirs in which she
talks about how much he depended on her. Aldous came
to see me after he had heard of my mystical experiences;
he told me he had always longed for direct spiritual
perceptions. "You are very fortunate," he said, and added
very touchingly, "Perhaps I don't love enough." A rather
similar thing happened with Cyril Connolly. When I heard
that he was going to review *The Swan in the Evening* for
the *Sunday Times,* I was terrified; I thought he would
demolish it. Instead he gave it a marvelous review. I
couldn't believe it; obviously it had pierced through all
his defenses. Later when I met him he said, "You know
my mother believed in an afterlife. She died a few years
ago and I miss her terribly. She was a clairvoyant, but I
never mentioned it to anyone because I was ashamed of
it." So I said to him: "You do believe in an afterlife, don't
you?" He just turned away and didn't answer. You see,
because of the prevalent skepticism of our time many
people don't have the courage of their convictions. But I
received hundreds of letters—and still do—from people
who have lost someone and who have had spiritual experiences. More women than men write, and some say
that their husbands don't believe them, insisting it is just

their imagination. As if imagination were not the medium
by which this *super*-reality is perceived. What they mean
is "fancy," which is different. But for me God *is* imagination, the creative spirit is imagination. Women suffer
the loss of a child more acutely, because with them it is
a physical thing; men have not been through the process
of bearing and feeding the child. Yes, on the whole I am
very serene nowadays: I know that there is a life elsewhere,
in another dimension, and that wherever Sally is I shall
be soon.

INTERVIEWER

The Swan in the Evening *was very well received; you
seemed to be back in your excellent creative form. Why did
you wait another seven years before producing your last
novel,* A Sea-Grape Tree?

ROSAMOND LEHMANN

I was longing to write another novel, but my life was full
of such a different kind of learning and experiencing, and
I felt it would be impossible to incorporate it all into a
novel. I don't know of any novel that has achieved it
successfully. *A Sea-Grape Tree* was an attempt, and it was
meant to be more like a poem. I went back to Mrs. Jardine
because I had always longed to know what had happened
to her. The creation of a novel starts with a sort of
explosion: images appear and coalesce, people and landscapes come into focus, and you say, "Oh yes, it has come
back, now I can begin to write." Poets feel the same way.
After eleven years of total silence, Rilke wrote the glorious
Duino Elegies, as you may remember.

INTERVIEWER

The critics weren't very kind to your book. Were you hurt?

ROSAMOND LEHMANN

I don't know what to think of the critics. On the whole
they have been kind to my work. I was never so deeply
crushed and wounded as Virginia Woolf was when she
had a bad review. Leonard Woolf didn't allow her to see
them. I had no one to protect me, so I did read them.
Auberon Waugh, I believe, wrote a long, mocking review
of the book. My granddaughter rang me and said, "Please
don't read it!" And I didn't. The only thing I mind and
brood about is mockery. I had a few good reviews and
many letters—which are much more important for an
author. I think critics didn't understand the point of A
Sea-Grape Tree. I'm not comparing myself to Shakespeare,
but the island in the book is somewhat like Prospero's in
The Tempest. It is not a real island, but a place where
those who have been wounded go to be healed—an imaginary place. I would like to write another long novel
which would be a sequel to A Sea-Grape Tree. Perhaps
the story of Rebecca and Johnny after they leave the island.
Whether I shall ever finish it or not is another matter.

INTERVIEWER

Let's talk about your own technique. Once you have started
a novel, once, as you said, the explosion has taken place,
how do you work?

ROSAMOND LEHMANN

It's very straightforward. I write in longhand. The first
draft is the working draft, and no one can decipher it.
Then I rewrite it, and that second draft is the book in
its half-finished form. Finally I write it a third time—paring
down and trimming—and then I send it to be typed. I
never rewrite or touch the typescript; I simply send it to
the publishers and keep my fingers crossed.

INTERVIEWER

*How do you respond to people who say that the novel is a
dying form, that it has lasted three hundred years, which
is enough for any literary genre? Do you agree?*

ROSAMOND LEHMANN

People have been saying the novel is dead for as far back
as I can remember. The novel will never die, but it will
keep changing and evolving and taking different shapes.
Storytelling, which is the basis of the novel, has always
existed and always will. Nowadays, there are too many
books and not enough good ones. I find that the women
writers I most admire at the moment are biographers:
Hilary Spurling's biography of Ivy Compton-Burnett, Victoria Glendening's of Edith Sitwell, Marina Warner's Joan
of Arc. . . . I never wrote a biography, but today women
seem to be particularly good at it. The other novelists I
most admire and enjoy are Anita Brookner, Alice Thomas
Ellis, M.J. Farrell, William Trevor, and Sybil Bedford.

INTERVIEWER

So what is the future of the novel?

ROSAMOND LEHMANN

Who knows? Something will have to happen, but I don't
think it will come from Britain or America. Things have
gone too far in sophisticated countries; the intensity of
emotion, the moral conflicts, all that was the basis of great
novels has gone. The change will come from somewhere
quite unexpected. But it will happen—human beings have
infinite resources of renewal.

Diana Mosley

Diana Mosley, née Mitford, was born in London in 1910, the third of Lord Redesdale's six daughters. Endowed with beauty, talent and wit, the sisters and their brother Tom, a musician, were at the center of the social, artistic and political life of their time, and all achieved fame in various ways. Diana's eldest sister, Nancy, became the celebrated author of such best-selling novels as Love in a Cold Climate, The Pursuit of Love and Don't Tell Alfred, all based on her family and set in the upper-class bohemia of London before the war, and of highly praised biographies. Her younger sister, Jessica, married to an American and living in the United States, has written such acclaimed social commentaries as The American Way of Death and Kind and Usual Punishment: The Prison Business, and an autobiography, Hons and Rebels, later published in the United States as Daughters and Rebels, which depicts vividly the Mitford family life. Another sister, Unity, became a close friend of Adolf Hitler's, while the youngest, Deborah, married the Duke of Devonshire, and has also written books of memoirs and of family history.

Diana was considered the most beautiful of the "Mitford Sisters," indeed "the most beautiful girl of her generation." At eighteen she married Bryan Guinness (Lord Moyne) by *whom she had two sons in quick succession. Their marriage was dissolved after five years, and in 1936 Diana married Sir Oswald Mosley, formerly a Labour Member of Parliament, who in 1932 founded the British Union of Fascists. At the outbreak of World War II Mosley's Fascist Party was declared illegal and disbanded, and the Mosleys were put in prison, where they remained until the war ended.*

Already numerous books have been published about the various Mitfords. Unity is the subject of a perceptive but "hostile" biography by David Pryce Jones, while Sir Harold Acton and Selina Hastings have written respectively a book of memoirs and a biography of Nancy. The House of Mitford, *by Diana's son Jonathan Guinness, a chronicle of the family, and* Beyond The Pale *(published in the United States as* Rules of the Game*), by novelist Nicholas Mosley, a two volume biography of his father, Sir Oswald Mosley, notably tell the story of an era through the lives of these two families.*

In 1977 Lady Mosley wrote her own successful autobiography, A Life of Contrasts, *followed a few years later by* The Loved Ones, *a book of memoirs about some of the remarkable men and women she has known. Encouraged by the success of these books, she then wrote the biography of Wallis Simpson, the Duchess of Windsor, which was published in 1980. Since then she has contributed articles and reviews to a number of national and international publications.*

In 1950 the Mosleys moved to Paris and bought the house in which Diana still lives: Le Temple de la Gloire, designed by Vignon (the architect of the Madeleine, among other famous buildings in Paris), and built in 1800 in Orsay, twenty miles from Paris. It is set amid large gardens shaded by centenarian trees, with a pond in front and a canal at the side. *Swans and ducks build their nests amid the shrubs and willows, and glide over the water towards the lawn in front of the house. They are quite tame and often come up to the steps of the house to be fed or to bask in the sun.*

Inside, the house has been elegantly decorated by Lady Mosley and contains pictures and objets d'art that bespeak her extraordinary life. Tall, slim and elegantly dressed, Lady Mosley's beauty is unimpaired by age. Her famous blue eyes have retained their lustre, and her complexion its rosy hue. She speaks softly but often with passion, seasoning her arguments with anecdotes and quotations. Although I radically disagreed with some of her views, like most visitors I was seduced by her charm, courtesy and sincerity.

INTERVIEWER

So many books have been written by and about the Mitfords that already they would fill several library shelves. But before the Mitford Sisters became legendary your family were politicians and diplomats. The literary tradition goes back to your grandfather, the first Lord Redesdale. Can you tell us about him?

DIANA MOSLEY

He was a career diplomat and was sent to Japan as the First Secretary at the British Embassy in Tokyo. He fell in love with the country, learnt Japanese, and on his return wrote *Tales of Old Japan*. It became an immediate bestseller and is still in print. Japan had been completely isolated for more than a century, and he was one of the first Europeans to be presented to the Mikado. He describes the presentation ceremony in his two volume memoirs, *Memories*, which was also a bestseller. He was a remarkable gardener, passionate about bamboo, of all things, and wrote

a book about it called *The Bamboo Garden*. Later he wrote
Tragedy in Stone, a completely different book about the
Tower of London and its secrets. He was at the Office of
Works when excavations uncovered the bones of the Little
Princes. He died when I was six, but I remember him
vividly. His wife, my grandmother, lived longer and I was
twenty when she died.

INTERVIEWER

*Another literary vein comes to you from your maternal
grandfather, Thomas Gibson Bowles, who was a journalist
and founder of several publications, one of which, The Lady,
is still going strong. I remember putting an advertisement
in it for a Nanny once, when my children were small. I
think it is famous for that sort of thing.*

DIANA MOSLEY

Exactly! My maternal grandfather was an M.P.—Member
of Parliament—but his passion was the sea. He was a
Master Mariner and owned a yacht. He used to take my
mother and her brothers and sister on his voyages, because
their mother had died when they were small. He started
a magazine called *Vanity Fair*, named after Thackeray's
novel. It became the *Private Eye* of its day and he made
many enemies, but he engaged SPY, the famous cartoonist,
to do all the cartoons which were marvelous. He created
Lady for his girlfriend, and made her its editor, but he
himself didn't have the slightest interest in it. Politics and
above all the Navy were his interests.

INTERVIEWER

What about your parents. Was your father literary?

DIANA MOSLEY

Not a bit! He was a countryman who loved fishing and
shooting and hunting and so forth, not at all intellectual.
My mother told us that sometimes in the evening, when
she had nothing better to do, she would pick up a book,
but he loathed seeing her read, and so she would offer
to read aloud to him. She read him *Tess of the d'Urbevilles*,
and he got into a frightful state when it ended in tragedy.
My mother said: "Oh don't be upset! It's only fiction,
made up." "You mean it is not *true*? Oh that *damn* fellow
Hardy!" Nancy put this and similar stories in one of her
novels, in which the main character is supposed to be
based on our father. He says, *à propos* of *Romeo and Juliet*:
"The whole thing is the fault of that damned *Padre*!" He
was such a funny man; all Nancy's jokes came from him.
I adored him.

INTERVIEWER

*So the literary inclination in you and your sisters comes
from your mother? I believe she was a friend of Charles
Dodgson, author of* Alice in Wonderland?

DIANA MOSLEY

When she was tiny Dodgson wrote her a wonderful letter,
which he sent her with a copy of *Alice*. My mother left
it to my grand-daughter, Catherine Guinness. It is now
in a bank somewhere. My mother liked reading but not
as much as we did. Years later she wrote a book about
my sister Unity. My son Jonathan Guinness drew on it
when he wrote the family chronicle, *The House of Mitford*.
Before she died my mother told me that she would leave
all her papers to Jonathan because she believed that a new

generation should look at everything with a fresh eye, objectively.

INTERVIEWER

You lived in the country, in a large house called Asthall Manor. What was your daily life like there?

DIANA MOSLEY

We led a typical country life, with horses and dogs and other animals. We hunted and I went fishing with my father, and in summer we went to tennis parties and children's dances. On Sundays we went to Church, and all that was absolutely ordinary for children in those days. As we lived near Oxford we often went there, especially for music lessons.

INTERVIEWER

You were the loveliest of the six sisters from the start. The midwife who delivered you is supposed to have exclaimed: "Oh she won't live long, she's too beautiful!" Were your sisters jealous of you?

DIANA MOSLEY

I was probably a hideous lump of fat at three days! I don't think I was particularly pretty even as a little girl, but later they said I was considered good-looking. But no, we were not jealous of each other.

INTERVIEWER

But were you aware of your beauty?

DIANA MOSLEY

Sometimes artists wanted to paint me. When I was sixteen I was sent to Paris to learn French, and Helleu, who was

one of the most famous portrait painters at the time,
wanted to paint me, and he did. After him there were
others: Augustus John, Henry Lamb, Tchelitchew, and
William Acton. I didn't buy their pictures because I didn't
like the idea of having a houseful of my own portraits.
But my son Desmond has practically all of them now. The
guide who shows tourists round his house in Ireland keeps
saying: "Over the fireplace is the picture of Mr. Guinness's
mother," every time he opens the door to a new room.
I should think the visitors must get tired of it!

INTERVIEWER

*There was a good deal of age difference between you—
Nancy was six years older than you and sixteen years older
than Debo, your youngest sister. She was a great tease and
apparently teased and bullied you all mercilessly all the
time. How did you get on?*

DIANA MOSLEY

The one I really adored was my brother Tom. We were
like twins, very close and loving. Of course we all fought—
girls always do. Nancy didn't tease if you stood up to her.
My sister Debo remembered something the other day
which I had completely forgotten. Apparently one day
Nancy said to the three youngest ones: "Do you realize
that the middles of your names are Nit, Sick and Bore?
(Unity, Jessica, Deborah)! Even later in life if anything
funny happened I used to telephone Nancy at once and
tell her, and we would laugh. For example she didn't like
Violet Trefusis, and one day she learnt that Violet had
been saying nasty things about her behind her back. She
didn't get in touch with her, and after a while Violet rang
her up and asked if she could go and visit her. Nancy

said no, she could not. "Oh, have I given offence?" asked
Violet, "No, you have given an excuse," replied Nancy.
Violet was an inveterate liar, and lied compulsively. Nancy
said that when she died they should put on her tombstone:
"Here *lies* Violet!" At the end of her life Nancy was ill
with terminal cancer and it went on for four years, very
painfully. Yet she kept trying to be cheerful and funny.

INTERVIEWER

*As you said your family life was typical of that era and
milieu. In her autobiographical book, Hons and Rebels,
Jessica complains of your father's philistanism and says that
she saved every penny she had in order to be able to run
away from home as soon as she possibly could. You were
taught at home by governesses, normal in those days, but
apparently they were not much good though, and one of
them taught you shoplifting, is that true?*

DIANA MOSLEY

Of course not! *Really!* Jessica wants to amuse her readers
and she simply invents! The truth is that we were self-
taught. We had an excellent library, built in a barn set
aside from the house. It was full of marvelous books
collected by my grandfather, and we had the run of the
place. We were allowed to take any book we wanted
provided we put it back in its place. No one censored us.
There was a grand piano on which my brother Tom
practiced. Nancy read voraciously and so did I. In the
holidays we had French governesses who taught us the
language. I loved French literature and read a great deal
of it, and I still do.

INTERVIEWER

*What books did you read which have remained with you,
and have influenced you?*

DIANA MOSLEY

I read anything I could lay my hand on. At that age one
loves Scott and Dickens, though I don't think I could
read them now. But I still love Balzac and Proust, whom
I also read then. I remember Horace Walpole's *Letters*
making a great impression, and I love Saint Simon. Above
your head on the shelf you can see his Complete Works
in twenty-one volumes. I bought them from my father
who was always selling things. You open any volume at
random and you always find something amusing to read.

INTERVIEWER

*I picked one up the other day and read the following about
a difficult mother-daughter relationship: "Comme elle gran-
dit elle plut, et à mesure qu'elle plut, elle déplut à sa
mère!"*

DIANA MOSLEY

How true! I loved the bit about Louis XIV, whom he
took his hat off to and whom he didn't. Women, even
house-maids found favor with him, and he would bow to
them and take his hat off. But Cardinals he shunned,
turned his head and looked the other way!

INTERVIEWER

*At eighteen you married Bryan Guinness—Lord Moyne.
Lady Georgia Cavendish wrote that you were "the most*

*beautiful girl of your generation," just as Diana Cooper had
been of the previous one. Apparently you were the most
glamorous couple in London, at the centre of social and
artistic life. What was social life like in those days, when
people had a lot more money and leisure if they belonged
to a certain class? And at an age when life is just beginning
and one is eager for everything?*

DIANA MOSLEY

We went out a good deal—to parties and theaters and
operas. We had many friends, for example Emerald Cunard
who was at the center of London's musical life. We
travelled, went to Venice in the summer and to Paris in
the autumn; we had a wonderful life, really.

INTERVIEWER

Did you know Emerald's daughter, Nancy Cunard?

DIANA MOSLEY

Yes. But mother and daughter didn't get on. Nancy Cunard
had a black lover whom everybody knew about except
her mother. One day Lady Oxford [Margot Asquith, wife
of the Prime Minister] who was rather indiscreet, told
Emerald about it, and she minded terribly. There was an
awful row, and Nancy wrote a polemic called *Black Man
and White Ladyship*. She lived in Paris with him and
brought him over to England whenever she came to visit.
It was unheard of in those days.

INTERVIEWER

*You had a number of friends who became very famous as
writers and intellectuals and artists. How did you meet
them?*

DIANA MOSLEY

Some had been at Oxford with my husband, Bryan, others
we met later. At twenty one is constantly making new
friends: Harold and William Acton, Brian Howard, Evelyn
Waugh, John Betjeman, et cetera. . . . They all loved
Nancy who was funny and clever and every good company,
and, of course, so were they. Later we met Lytton Strachey
and Carrington.

INTERVIEWER

*Apparently your father couldn't stand them, especially the
aesthetes and homosexuals whom he considered effeminate
and namby-pamby.*

DIANA MOSLEY

Some he liked better than others. For example he liked
Mark Ogilvie-Grant, who was a great friend of Nancy's,
with whom she kept a correspondence all her life.

INTERVIEWER

*Apparently one early morning your father bumped into him
and said: "Brains for breakfast, Mark?" Whereupon Mark
got frightened and ran away!*

DIANA MOSLEY

Where did you read that? It's probably true! When we
were first married, Evelyn Waugh used to practically live
in our house, because his wife had left him and he was
lonely. I loved having him there; he was wonderful company, despite his unhappiness.

INTERVIEWER

So it was in appreciation that he dedicated his novel, Vile
Bodies, *to you?*

DIANA MOSLEY

I suppose so. And another one later was dedicated to me
as well. I don't think I was portrayed in *Vile Bodies*, but
Elizabeth Ponsonby was—she is the woman who takes
drugs. Diana Cooper was supposed to be Mrs. Stitch in
Scoop, but I don't think Evelyn knew her then; he met
her much later.

INTERVIEWER

*Reading Waugh's diaries and memoirs and letters, etcetera.
. . . and indeed speaking to some of his close friends, it
strikes one that he was a very disagreeable man, rather
snobbish and fastidious and bitchy. Is that true?*

DIANA MOSLEY

Oh dear! I do hope he doesn't come across like that,
because there were so many other sides to him. He was
extremely quick and witty, very knowledgeable, and marvelous company. Selina Hastings, who wrote Nancy's biography, is now working on yet another book on Evelyn.
But I suppose he is an inexhaustible subject, being so
complex and contradictory. Another close friend was Harold Action, who was and still is wonderful. His *The Last
Medici* and *The Bourbons of Naples* are remarkable books.
Have you read them?

INTERVIEWER

*I have. He makes history delectable, as well as instructive.
Where did you live as a young married couple?*

DIANA MOSLEY

Our first country house was Biddesden. Funnily enough
there is a lovely photograph of it in last week's *Figaro*,

but they don't give the name, they just say "An English Country House." Bryan [Lord Moyne] still lives there, quite rightly—it is too beautiful! We also had a house in London, in Buckingham Street, now called Buckingham Place, I think.

INTERVIEWER
In retrospect, your guest book—if you kept any—would read like a Who-Is-Who of that era: Cecil Beaton, the Sitwells, the Bloomsbury Set, et cetera . . . many of whom became famous later. Were they well-known at the time?

DIANA MOSLEY
Many of them already were. For example Kurt Weill and Lotte Lenya came, and Markevitch the conductor, and dozens of writers like Peter Quennell and Lord Berners, too many to mention.

INTERVIEWER
Kurt Weill was a fervent communist; did you clash over politics?

DIANA MOSLEY
Oh no! I never mixed politics with friendship. I was completely firm in my beliefs, but it never made any difference to me what other people's politics were.

INTERVIEWER
You were friendly with all the Sitwells, you told me, but I believe at one point fell out with Edith. Why?

DIANA MOSLEY
She wasn't pleased when Tchelitchew painted me. In fact the best picture painted of me, with my two first sons, is

by Tchelitchev. Edith adored him, you might say she was
in love with him. It was unfortunate, because he was years
younger than her and completely homosexual, so there
was no hope in her love. Tchelitchev was a Russian emigré
who had lived in Berlin after the Revolution of 1917 and
later in Paris. He ended up settling in the United States
and becoming an American citizen. When he died the
New York Herald Tribune wrote that an *American* painter
had died. There are a number of his pictures at the Museum
of Modern Art in New York, and his portrait of Edith
Sitwell is in the Tate Gallery in London. Anyway, I was
in Edith's black book because he painted me.

INTERVIEWER

*You said that among your closest friends were Lytton Strachey
and Carrington: "The light has gone out of my life," you
wrote when they died. They were part of the Bloomsbury
set, different from your social group?*

DIANA MOSLEY

Did I say that? I certainly loved them and missed them
terribly. The various social circles did mingle a good deal,
and I loved Lytton and Carrington. When Lytton died, I
knew Carrington couldn't bear living without him, and
she killed herself soon after. I missed her very much; it
is hard to describe her magic. I think her secret was that
she was genuinely interested in people and loved listening
to them talk about themselves. This was very flattering
for men, and they fell in love with her. But then she
would suddenly withdraw her attention which made them
worried and jealous. I think she only really loved Lytton,
and everyone else was just for fun. So many fell in

Bryan Guiness and Diana Mosley

love with her: Ralph Partridge, Mark Gertler, Gerald
Brenan. . . .

INTERVIEWER

Did Carrington ever paint you?

DIANA MOSLEY

No, but she painted a surprise for me: I was away having
my second son, Desmond, and she came over and painted
a window at Biddesden. In a letter she describes how she

did it. It was one of those blank windows you sometimes find in 18th century houses, and she used it as a canvas, painted the frame and the picture, as if you were looking through the window and seeing a woman and a cat and various objects. Bryan has put it under glass so that the weather doesn't damage it. There is a picture of it in my book, *The Loved Ones*.

INTERVIEWER

As you said many of your friends were Nancy's too. Where did she live and entertain?

DIANA MOSLEY

She had no home of her own and basically lived at our family house in the country, with an occasional bed-sitter in London. She married at thirty, and that didn't last long, but she had a house in Little Venice, by the Canal. Poor Nancy! She wasn't lucky in love. Selina Hastings makes her unhappy relationships with three men the pivot of her biography of Nancy: Hamish St. Clair-Erskine, Peter Rodd, and Gaston Palewski [De Gaulle's lieutenant during the war and later Directeur du Cabinet in his first Government]. At the end of her life, when Palewski married someone else and Nancy was dying of cancer, she never complained. If she had been an Italian she would have screamed and made scenes and got it off her chest. But she was incapable of it. However, she had in many ways a happy life: wonderful success with her books, which made money, and a great many devoted friends. She was loved by her friends, and having no children she could concentrate on them—one does get very taken up by one's children. She was a tremendous letter writer and kept in touch with her friends wherever they happened to be.

INTERVIEWER

Unlike you, Nancy didn't like the Bloomsbury Set—why was that?

DIANA MOSLEY

She couldn't bear them! But then she didn't really know them. I remember one day a French woman asked us, who do you think is the best living English novelist? I said Elizabeth Bowen, and Nancy was quite cross and dismissive of her. I only met Elizabeth Bowen once, but I think she had outstanding talent.

INTERVIEWER

Nancy once wrote that she started writing because she needed money. It seems strange for someone who is such a natural, wonderful writer.

DIANA MOSLEY

She did need money, because as a family we were poor. She was very elegant and later on she made beautiful homes for herself, here in Paris and in Versailles. Her first novel was *Highland Fling*, which was amusing but not as good as the ones she wrote in her forties, like *The Pursuit of Love* and *Love in a Cold Climate*. Those were more or less based on the family.

INTERVIEWER

You got up to some pranks with your husband and friends, didn't you? For example in 1930 you organized an exhibition of paintings by Bruno Hat, an allegedly German painter, and le tout London came to the opening and was taken in by the hoax. How did it happen?

DIANA MOSLEY

Brian Howard painted twenty pictures and we had an exhibition in our drawing-room. My brother Tom put on a beard and moustache and a German accent and pretended to be "Bruno Hat." Evelyn Waugh wrote the preface to the catalogue and Lytton Strachey actually bought a picture! He was the only one who did; it was done out of kindness. People didn't believe in Hat the artist.

INTERVIEWER

We now come to the main part of your life. When you were twenty-two, in 1932, four years after your marriage to Bryan Guinness, you left him to live with your two sons in Eaton Square, Chelsea. You had fallen in love with Oswald Mosley, who was then happily married to his first wife and had been a Labour M.P. It was very unusual for that time—or indeed any time—to accept living openly as someone's mistress without any hope of marrying him. What amazed me both in Nicholas Mosley's two volume biography of his father and in other books about the society of that period is the amount of extra-marital sex that went on, at least among the upper classes, in England. Far more than today, it seems.

DIANA MOSLEY

I think it is because people had more leisure. Everybody had servants, and people had nothing to think about except their lives and emotions and relationships. Nowadays they simply haven't got time. Women have to earn their living *and* look after their homes and children as well. It is too much for them, really.

INTERVIEWER

It seems to me that upper-class Englishmen were constantly hopping to bed with each other's wives. . . .

DIANA MOSLEY
Constantly! Don't they still? In England people didn't divorce; they had affairs and stayed married. Divorce came from America.

INTERVIEWER
Your love affair with Mosley broke this mold: you rocked the boat by being serious about it and leaving your husband. Why did you do it? I mean couldn't you have stayed married and been with him on the side, as everyone else did, and especially since he was happily married and there seemed to be no hope in it?

DIANA MOSLEY
I thought I needed my freedom. My husband wanted a real wife, which is what he got after me. In fact, we were both much happier with our second spouses. But apart from that I rocked the boat because politics came into it. Mosley was a star. He was marvelous looking, generous, a brilliant talker, an extraordinary speaker, a wonderful man in every way. He came from an old Staffordshire family, and when he was only fifteen he was the Public Schools' Champion of Fencing, and he fenced for England at international tournaments. So he was a great athlete as well as everything else. He did have endless affairs, but somehow it didn't matter, because he was so extraordinary.

INTERVIEWER
How and where did you meet him? I mean being in the same social milieu it is surprising that you didn't meet sooner.

DIANA MOSLEY
I was only twenty-one when we met, and he was thirty-five. We first met at a ball given by Philip Sassoon, then

a Tory Cabinet Minister. Later we met at Barbara Hutchinson's—later Lady Rothschild—twenty-first birthday party,
and she put us next to each other at dinner. Barbara's
mother, Mary Hutchinson, was a member of the Bloomsbury set, a friend of Virginia Woolf's and Vanessa Bell's.
After that party we seemed to see each other everywhere.
Mosley had left the Labour Party in 1930 because it had
refused to address the problem of unemployment. In 1931
there was a Tory landslide at the General Elections, followed by a National Government under Ramsay Mac-
Donald. It was hoped that it would solve the economic
crisis. Mosley knew that the Tory majority with a few
liberals thrown in would do nothing, and he decided to
form a new party from the grass roots, with the people,
not the politicians. So he founded the Fascist Party.

INTERVIEWER

*But until then you were not interested in politics. Apparently
you said to him, on that first dinner when he was expounding
on his ideas: "No use talking to me about these things, I'm
just an old-fashioned liberal!"*

DIANA MOSLEY

I think I did. But you see, so was he, in a way. In fact,
we agreed about almost everything. You have no idea what
it was like in the 1930s—it was impossible not to get
involved in politics. People were *starving!* Millions were
unemployed, and the dole [welfare] was totally inadequate,
about two *shillings* per week for each child. That was the
time when the King—Edward VIII, later the Duke of
Windsor—made his famous remark, "Something must be
done." The Conservatives were hopeless; once settled in

office they did nothing, while Labour had been a complete failure.

But why Fascism? The doctrine is per se repulsive, notwithstanding the conditions that might engender it. Was it because of Mussolini's success in Italy?

Mosley did admire Mussolini and what he had done in similar circumstances in Italy. The central idea of Fascism was that of the Corporate State, which is what we have now, in a way. It was a fashionable idea at the time. Mosley had a number of very interesting ideas relating specifically to Britain. A.J.P. Taylor, the left-wing historian, wrote in one of his books that Mosley had the cleverest ideas of any politician at the time. Richard Crossman, the Labour Minister, wrote in his memoirs that "Mosley was spurned by Whitehall, Fleet Street, and every party leader at Westminster, simply and solely because he was *right*." That was written two decades later, by a Labor Minister. So you see, it wasn't so unusual at the time.

I still can't see why he chose Fascism, and the Black Shirt and the implicit brutality—things which the British could never have swallowed.

Ah, but they did! They loved the Black Shirt because it had the double advantage of being very cheap and outside class distinctions. At demonstrations and marches they just joined hands as comrades, not as members of different

classes. Indeed the Black Shirt was so popular that an act
of parliament was passed forbidding it to be worn.

INTERVIEWER

*I know that Fascism "took" in Germany and that people
joined the Party en masse, but I feel that they wouldn't
have done in Britain, among other things because Fascism
is so dead-earnest and boring, and the British, rightly in
my view, are suspicious of too much earnestness and lack
of humor. They would have just laughed at Hitler's histrionics
and hysteria, don't you think?*

DIANA MOSLEY

But Hitler had a sense of humor. You should have seen
him mimic Mussolini! But I don't think that when you
are trying to save three million starving unemployed a
sense of humor matters very much. At the end of the
War Mosley said: "Fascism is finished." It was true, but
before the War it was the alternative to a hopeless situation.
Fascism came about partly because the Allies changed the
map of Europe after the First World War, leaving large
discontented German minorities in Eastern European countries. Economically they failed, with the burden of unemployment and consumption, they were unable to absorb
the power to produce. The American crash in 1929 made
the situation worse in Europe. But we needed the press
to put the policy of our Party to the people.

INTERVIEWER

*You did have the backing of the press at first: Lord Rothemere,
owner of the Daily Mail, and Beaverbrook, the most powerful
press baron, both gave their support to Mosley.*

DIANA MOSLEY

Rothemere did great harm with silly headlines like "Hurrah for the Black Shirt!" as if that was the point. It wasn't. The point was a very serious economic argument. Beaverbrook blew hot and cold, but we went on being friends with him, and after the war used to go and dine with him. As for the mainstream Tory press, like *The Telegraph* and the *Times*, they would never go for something as new as Mosley's party. But let me read you a paragraph from an article written after Mosley's speech at a meeting; it appeared in *The Guardian* (then the *Manchester Guardian*), a Liberal paper: "The audience, stirred as an audience rarely is, rose and swept a storm of applause towards the platform. Who could doubt that here was one of those root-and-branch men who have been thrown up from time to time in England? He said this: Better the great adventure, better the great attempt for England's sake, better defeat, disaster, better far the end of that trivial thing called the political career than strutting and posturing on the stage of Little England, amid the scenery of decadence until history, in turning over an heroic page of the human story, writes of us the contemptuous postscript: these were the men to whom was entrusted the Empire of Great Britain, and whose idleness, ignorance and cowardice left it a Spain." Mosley was far from sure he would win, but he thought he had to try.

INTERVIEWER

There is a controversy as to whether he converted you to Fascism or you had already been influenced by your sister, Unity. Which is true?

DIANA MOSLEY

It was my doing that Unity went to Germany. She was nineteen and I was twenty-three, and I suggested that we go to Germany to see what it was like. She fell in love with Germany completely and persuaded my parents to send her to a Baroness in Munich and learn German properly. I also learnt and later read a great deal of German literature, as I still do. There is my complete edition of Goethe as you see.

INTERVIEWER

Was it in Munich that you met Hitler and became friends?

DIANA MOSLEY

Yes. Hitler used to go to a small restaurant called Osteria Bavaria. One day he noticed Unity, who was often there by herself, and sent to ask her: "Would you like to have coffee with the Führer?" That was it! She wrote to me urging me to go and meet him too, and I did. We became friends and I grew very fond of him; he was a man of great fascination. From then on whenever I was in Berlin I let him know. His ADC might telephone me and say: "The Führer is by himself; would you like to come and see him?" When I arrived he would ask me if I had had dinner, and if I said yes we would just sit and talk—about politics, music which he loved passionately, and many other things.

INTERVIEWER

When we see Hitler in documentaries making speeches at rallies, he really does seem utterly demented. How could people not see that he was mad?

DIANA MOSLEY

You only see the peroration, the little bit at the end. But
when Hitler made important speeches at the Reichstag
nine-tenth of his argument was concerned with serious
economic problems, or foreign affairs, reasonably delivered.

INTERVIEWER

But in November 1938 the brutality of Hitler's regime was
brought to international attention on Kristalnacht, when his
troops went on a rampage and devastated Jewish shops and
burnt down Jewish homes, beating and killing people. Before
that even, he was killing homosexuals and communists and
brutally suppressing any dissent. Didn't you see all that?

DIANA MOSLEY

At that moment I was in London giving birth to my third
son. From June 1938 till March 1939 I did not go to
Germany. The Kristalnacht happened because a young Jew
walked into the German Embassy in Paris and shot a
diplomat, Von Rath, at close range. It caused anger in
Germany. The Jewish terrorists of the Stern Gang who
murdered my first husband's father in Cairo, where he
was Minister of State, chose their targets more carefully,
either British soldiers serving in Palestine or government
officials. Now, of course, any prominent person is a target
for terrorists, from Mrs. Thatcher to the Pope. What a
world! On Kristalnacht they went on a rampage, but I
don't think people got killed, because if they had there
would have been a terrible international outcry. The killing
took place during the war. One of the reasons why Mosley
was against the war was because he had fought in the
First World War and he knew the horror of it. He was

determined that it should not happen again. In war it is
not only one side who suffers. Think of Dresden and
Hamburg.

INTERVIEWER

But the Holocaust was a uniquely evil phenomenon . . .

DIANA MOSLEY

I agree, entirely. Nevertheless if I had been given the
choice for myself and my beloved children of being gassed
or of being burnt to death in one of the firestorms created
by Allied airmen in, for example Hamburg, I would have
chosen the former. Hitler's unforgivable crime for me was
starting the war, from which such horrors and cruelties
resulted. In England some said the only good German was
a dead German—Churchill said he hoped they would bleed
and burn. Perhaps in Germany some said the only good
Jew was a dead Jew. I can't see that one proposition is
different from the other. And the Czechs killed millions
of Germans at the end of the war. They just murdered
them in cold blood. Yet no one ever mentions that.

INTERVIEWER

*There have always been atrocities in wars. What makes the
Holocaust unique is the satanic nature of the enterprise,
worked out to the last detail, and the fact that it was based
on race, a notion which is offensive to human decency.*

DIANA MOSLEY

Yes, I agree. But what about the Gulag Archipelago? The
thirty million Chinese killed in the so-called Cultural
Revolution? What about Pol Pot? The fact is that we live
in a cruel world, and what I am saying is that it is not

only the Germans. While I do not forgive them for what they did, I feel that the brutality has something to do with our century. Now they speak of human rights conference in Moscow, which is extraordinary. It makes me happy to be still alive and see it happen, as the Cold War went on for four decades, causing so much misery and death around the world.

INTERVIEWER

Going back to your personal life, was it hard to be the official mistress of a public figure who was already happily married? What would have happened if his wife hadn't unexpectedly died of peritonitis?

DIANA MOSLEY

I suppose I would have just lived alongside him for ever. But we did marry and lived together forty-four years, perfectly happy.

INTERVIEWER

Did he go on womanizing and being unfaithful to you as he had been to his first wife?

DIANA MOSLEY

I'm sure he did! I don't think there was anything so special about me as to make him stop. But I really don't believe it matters. What is important is for two people to love each other and be friends as well as lovers. A good marriage is the greatest blessing in life, and very rare. Ours was one.

INTERVIEWER

You got married in Germany, and the reception was held in Goebbels' house. How did that happen?

DIANA MOSLEY

We decided to get married in Germany because in London
or Paris we would not have been able to keep the press
away. In those days you had to publish the application
three weeks in advance, and it was made public. So I
thought that if I asked Hitler he would tell the man at
the Registry Office in Berlin to put the certificate in a
drawer and forget it, which is exactly what happened. I
can still hear him saying to the Registrar: "Don't let anyone
see the marriage certificate, put it in a drawer." The
Goebbelses gave a lunch party for us and Hitler came and
it all went very smoothly. When we were arrested during
the War the British authorities opened our safe and took
all our papers, among them our marriage certificate. Years
later I needed it. Our lawyer asked the Home Office to
send it back, but they were in such a muddle that they
couldn't find it: "Oh please don't ask us to find it! We
haven't got the faintest idea where it is!" they said. It is
so English, really! Our lawyer suggested that the best course
of action was simply to get married again in London, and
we did. But by then we had two sons, grown up, and
they would have been considered illegitimate. In France
the *notaire* couldn't do anything without a piece of paper.
In desperation I wrote to Berlin's main Town Hall, saying
that I knew the city had been bombed and burnt down,
but was it at all possible to find out if my marriage certificate
was still there? To my amazement I received a letter, saying
that it would be in the Eastern part of Berlin, if anywhere
at all, and would I write to them. Again I did. Probably
the *notaire* thought I had invented the whole saga, and
every time he saw me he said: "*Alors*, any news from
Berlin?" sarcastically. But one day there was: a letter arrived

saying that if I sent nine francs to the German Embassy
in Paris they would forward me a copy of my marriage
certificate. I did, and the document arrived in due course.

INTERVIEWER

How did you and your husband react to Munich, and the
Chamberlain pact with Hitler in 1938?

DIANA MOSLEY

Six months after Munich, Czechoslovakia disintegrated.
The Slovaks hated the Czechs. Chamberlain gave a guar-
antee to Poland that if Germany attempted to change the
status quo Britain and France would go to war with
Germany. As a result the volatile Poles hardly negotiated
seriously with Germany. Yet there was nothing Britain
and France could do to help Poland, and they should
never have pledged themselves. Our blank check bounced.
Even now Poland is not a free country. Mosley thought
Hitler should have gone on negotiating, rather than start
a war.

INTERVIEWER

But the invasion of Poland was a pretext. We went to war
with Germany because Hitler had to be stopped, and because
Fascism meant the end of Western civilization, indeed civ-
ilization tout court.

DIANA MOSLEY

Quite so, because if the reason had been Germany's aggres-
sion we should have attacked Russia too, who had invaded
not only Poland but had also annexed the Baltic states
and fought Finland. So the invasion of Poland was an
excuse. Mosley maintained that if there was a European

war, it would have one of two outcomes: either England
would lose, which would be a tragedy for the whole world,
or she would win, in which case she would *have* to bring
in other countries, such as America or Russia or both,
because she couldn't win just with the French. He believed
that either way Britain would lose its position in the world,
and become a second-rate power, which is exactly what
we are now.

INTERVIEWER

*But Hitler wanted war, there was nothing anybody could
do. Unfortunately for human affairs, while it takes two to
make peace, only one can start a war. And there was his
behavior towards the Jews, and the Poles and the Slavs,
etcetera. It is the characteristic of the bully that he can't
be placated or argued with—he must be disarmed.*

DIANA MOSLEY

At the time the world was much bigger than now—it has
shrunk since then. We thought that there were plenty of
places where the Jews could go and have a country of
their own, and that they needn't stay in Germany where
they were killed by Hitler. But we were not anti-semitic.
Anti-semitism was not part of Fascism, it was an obsession
of Hitler's. Mussolini was not anti-semitic, and his own
mistress was Jewish. Only at the end he was bullied by
Hitler into introducing some restrictive measures against
the Jews. But my husband was not anti-semitic, while the
Jews were virulently anti-Mosley, and naturally sometimes
there were riposts to their violent tactics.

INTERVIEWER

But when you read in the papers what was happening in

*Germany against the Jews, events like Kristalnacht, didn't
you ask Hitler why he was doing these things?*

DIANA MOSLEY

I wish I had! But as I said I was not in Germany at the
time. People who are indignant today forget that no other
country wanted to accept the Jews. Yet there were still
plenty of places in the world they could have gone to,
but they stayed in Germany.

INTERVIEWER

Naturally, it was their country, their home . . .

DIANA MOSLEY

There should have been an international conference; the
League of Nations should have helped them. Personally I
was never anti-semitic; so many of my close friends were
Jewish: John Sutro, Oliver Messel, Brian Howard, etcetera.
We never argued about politics—you don't if you love
people, you accept them, and their opinions.

INTERVIEWER

*What about your husband? When he met Hitler, did he get
on with him? Did they talk politics?*

DIANA MOSLEY

Yes, of course they talked politics, but through an inter-
preter. They met only twice, and didn't like each other
very much—they were so different. I got on with Hitler
much better. Mosley blamed Hitler for the war and couldn't
forgive him. All the horrors, including the Holocaust,
stemmed from war.

INTERVIEWER

*When war broke out your sister Unity was in Germany,
and she tried to commit suicide, saying that she couldn't
bear seeing the two countries she loved fighting each other.
She was wounded but lived. What happened next?*

DIANA MOSLEY

The bullet lodged in her head and for a while she was
paralyzed. Later she recovered, but she had lost her sparkle
and her character changed. Eight years later the bullet
moved and killed her. After she shot herself she stayed
in a coma for six weeks. When she regained consciousness
Hitler went to see her in hospital and asked her what she
wanted to do: stay in Germany and be looked after, or
go back to England. She chose the latter. So he sent her
to Switzerland in an ambulance train and handed her over
to Swiss doctors. My mother went and brought her home,
and she was treated at Nuffield Hospital in Oxford. This
was in January, 1940.

INTERVIEWER

When the war broke out, how did your husband react?

DIANA MOSLEY

Years before Churchill, Mosley said we must be armed,
because one can't be unarmed in an armed world. His
theory was that since we already had a strong Navy, if we
built our air force to be as powerful as Germany's, then
no one could touch us, and we could just sit tight and
wait. Hitler had no intention of going to war with Britain;
he had no interest in the West, he wanted to go east.
This is all in *Mein Kampf* and I believe accepted now as

fact. But when Britain and France declared war on Germany, he had to fight. Then after many months of "the phony war" and Hitler's peace offers having been turned down, he attacked. When France fell quickly and our army got away at Dunkirk leaving all their tanks and amunitions behind, Hitler could have invaded Britain. But he didn't, which vindicated my husband's view that he had no desire to conquer Britain, and that if we had a strong air force as well as our navy we would be safe. People used to say to Mosley: "But you can't trust Hitler's word." And he would answer: "Of course you can't trust any foreign statesman's word; you must look after yourself."

INTERVIEWER

Is it true that after the War he would refer to Hitler as "that dreadful little man?"

DIANA MOSLEY

He never said that. Where did you hear it?

INTERVIEWER

I read it in Nicholas Mosley's biography of his father.

DIANA MOSLEY

Typical! He never greatly admired Hitler, and he thought he had made a terrible mistake starting the war, but he wouldn't have said that. It is an invention, like so much in Nicholas's absurd book.

INTERVIEWER

When the war did break out, you were arrested and put in different jails, Brixton, which was a male prison, for him

and Holloway, a women's prison, for you. Would your
husband have fought if he hadn't been arrested?

DIANA MOSLEY

We were not arrested at the outbreak of the war. For
eight months Mosley campaigned for a negotiated peace
settlement, as long as neither Britain nor the Empire was
attacked. But he wouldn't have been allowed to fight,
simply because he was a war veteran, with one leg shorter
than the other, and he would not have been considered
physically fit. There were other things he could have done.
My brother Tom, who was a member of our Party, joined
the Territorial Army and was killed. The first two bombers
shot down over Germany were piloted by members of our
Party. They were all very patriotic and joined immediately.

Mosley maintained that there was no reason for Britain
to fight over Poland. He published a statement in May
1940 saying that every member of the British Union of
Fascists would fight to drive the foreigner from our soil,
in the event of an invasion. He was arrested on May 23rd
by an Order in Council. He had never broken the law
in his life, and there was no charge against him. Anyway,
we were put in separate prisons. Then one day my brother
Tom came to see me and said: "I'm dining at Downing
Street tonight [with Churchill, the Prime Minister]; is there
anything you want me to say?" I said that if we had to
stay in prison, could we at least be together? And within
a month we were.

INTERVIEWER

What were your living conditions like? Did you have a
routine?

DIANA MOSLEY

There was a little house on its own next to a wing—it has since been pulled down—with bars on the windows. It had been the Preventive Detention Block. I asked the wardress what it meant, and she said that some women who had killed their babies would be put there in order to be protected from other prisoners who might attack them. Anyway, we had a double-cell as our bedroom and a little sitting-room with a barred window, and a small yard for exercise. We stayed there two years. Before that I was in Holloway for a year and a half on my own, and my husband was at Brixton.

INTERVIEWER

What did you do all day?

DIANA MOSLEY

We read a tremendous amount. Luckily we were allowed any number of books, a gramophone and masses of classical records. We read Goethe, Schiller, Racine, Corneille, Shakespeare. . . . We read them aloud to each other. My husband read masses of psychology, including Adler, Freud, and Jung. We read or re-read the Classics, Greek and Roman, and he read a great deal of philosophy. We really educated ourselves in prison.

INTERVIEWER

I read something he had written about Freud, saying that the worst influences on twentieth-century thought were Marx and Freud, the former because he reduced human motivation to economics, and the latter because he was deterministic and made man slave to his sordid childhood experiences. Did he talk to you about it?

DIANA MOSLEY

He thought that there was a lot of truth in Freud's theory, but that it was not the whole truth. Marx he had read years before, but as we now know Marxism has been a failure. I mean socialism has not worked anywhere, has it? Socialist countries now wish to get rid of it! Politically it has led to the most appalling dictatorships, and economically it has reduced socialist countries to such poverty that they can hardly feed themselves. In fact it is astonishing what a colossal failure socialism has been, isn't it?

INTERVIEWER

But when he was a member of the Labour Party wasn't your husband influenced by Marxism?

DIANA MOSLEY

Not really. The Labour Party in those days was based on the ideas of the Fabians, Shaw, and later Keynes. He thought Keynes was a genius, but his own great economic memorandum was written *before* Keynes wrote his book.

INTERVIEWER

So you stayed in prison till the end of the war?

DIANA MOSLEY

Just before the end of the war my husband got phlebitis and was very ill. The Home Office doctors preferred to release him in case he died in prison and became a martyr. So they let him out and me with him. The *Daily Worker*, a communist daily, published an article saying that it was alright to release Mosley on health grounds but not Lady

Mosley, "who is in rude health!" I was! Though I had become very thin.

INTERVIEWER

Apparently your sister Jessica wrote a letter to Churchill saying "You should leave them in prison where they belong!" Did you fall out with her?

DIANA MOSLEY

Oh no! I don't take what Jessica says seriously, though I'm quite fond of her. Even now she doesn't want to see me, I don't know why. My sister Deborah doesn't agree with me, nor do many of my friends, but we see each other. It's immaterial whether you share the same opinions, as long as you love each other. Nancy was anti-Fascist and Tom was a member of our party, but we always got on. When Nancy was dying in 1973, Jessica came from America to see her and say goodbye. We saw each other every day, were very friendly, and talked about her books. Then in 1981 there was a musical in London based on us, *The Mitford Sisters,* and in an interview Jessica said that she had not seen her "fascist sister" since 1937! You see, truth and lies don't mean anything to her!

Of course, she has reasons to be bitter about life. When she was twenty-two her husband Esmond Romilly, who was a bomber pilot, was shot down and killed. Two of her children have died. She married an American lawyer, her present husband, and their little boy had an accident and died. Jessica has suffered a lot; her silliness about me matters not in the least.

INTERVIEWER

When you came to live in Paris after the war, Diana and

Duff Cooper were at the British Embassy here, did you see them?

DIANA MOSLEY

No. They were friends of Nancy's and she saw them regularly. Later Diana lived in Chantilly for a while, but I didn't see her. Diplomats here were forbidden by the Foreign Office to see us. As Enoch Powell said the Foreign Office was a nest of spies and traitors at that time. We were proud of their enmity.

INTERVIEWER

What about French friends, did you make any?

DIANA MOSLEY

We had many French friends from before the war, and as you can imagine living here nearly forty years we made dozens more. But of course at my age many of our friends have died, which is very sad.

INTERVIEWER

Were you ostracized by some people because of your fascist background?

DIANA MOSLEY

Not at all. Practically the whole of the French nobility, what they call *le gratin*, were for Pétain. Later some of them sided with De Gaulle. But as I said I hardly think friendship depends on politics. My husband said, at the end of the war, that as we had obviously lost our Empire it was essential to make a United Europe in which England would have an important role to play. From 1945 until his death in 1980 he worked, wrote books, made speeches, appeared on television, saw people all over Europe, to promote this idea, which was to him of paramount importance. Fascism took seven years of his life, Europe thirty-five years.

INTERVIEWER

There were various intellectual coteries in Paris after the war. One centered around Sartre and Simone de Beauvoir, another around Aragon and Elsa Triolet. Did you know any of them?

DIANA MOSLEY

Both of those groups were on the Left, but many French intellectuals were not. Rather as in England, where great poets such as Yeats, Eliot, Pound, etcetera, were all on the Right. It was the second-rate who were communists and it helped them become famous as if they were of the first rank. I don't mean that the leaders, Sartre and Aragon, were mediocre—they were very much first class, but many of their followers were. Aragon's *La Semaine Sainte* is one of the great novels of our time. And Sartre was a wonderful playwright. We went to all his plays.

INTERVIEWER

Aragon's poetry too, is marvelous, especially some of the ones he wrote during the war: La Diane Française, Le Crève-Coeur, Les Yeux d'Elsa. *Anyway, how did you find this house,* Le Temple de la Gloire, *tucked away from Paris?*

DIANA MOSLEY

Through friends. It was built for General Moreau, who was the *Chef des Armée du Rhin* and more or less equal of Napoleon, who was made First Consul at the time the

Temple was built, around 1800. There had been a Château d'Orsay here before, belonging to the Comte d'Orsay, but was pulled down. Some of the large stones were used to build this house. There is a picture of it by Corot painted in 1840 which I once saw at the Biennale in Venice. But by then already some of the trees had gone. Still, in summer we are buried in greenery, and the pond has swans on it who come up the lawn to the steps. The architect was Vignon, who built the Madeleine. It is perhaps the last Palladian house. The boys grew up here, and my family come and stay. When my husband died in 1980 I decided to stay here and not go back to England. You see all my memories are here, and I love it.

INTERVIEWER

I would like to talk about your own writing. Did you have any literary ambition as a young girl? You told me that if you hadn't got married so soon and had children you would have written books.

DIANA MOSLEY

I wanted to be a writer. But I got involved with marriage and children, and later with politics as well. Then in the 1970s I started writing my memoirs, because I thought that if I didn't the children and grandchildren and great-grandchildren wouldn't know my side of the story. They would only know what others had written about us, which wasn't always true or accurate. The book was called *A Life of Contrasts*, and it was very well received.

INTERVIEWER

The reviewers said it was beautifully written and moving. Did it encourage you to write the next book, also memoirs,

but about some of the people you had known and loved:
The Loved Ones?

DIANA MOSLEY

In 1981 I had an operation for a brain tumor. Luckily it wasn't malignant. So I thought I would write about some of my friends: Lytton Strachey and Carrington, Lord Berners, and others. Lord Berners had a house in Rome and when I was twenty-three and he was forty-nine or fifty I used to go and stay with him and think of him as a very old man! He and Lytton taught me half what I know. He was a very loyal friend and came to see me in prison. Then after the war when he was ill, just before he died, he used to come and stay with us. We loved having him— he was so funny and brilliant. Mark Amorey—the Literary Editor of *The Spectator*—is writing his biography, and the other day he came to see me and talk about him.

INTERVIEWER

Your latest book is the biography of the Duchess of Windsor.
You and your husband were great friends with her and the
Duke, and saw each other regularly throughout the 1950s
and 1960s. Was it true that the Duke had pro-German
feelings?

DIANA MOSLEY

He was pro-British, and rather against the war. He thought it would be a great tragedy, and of course it was, for everybody.

INTERVIEWER

Were the Windsors really right-wing?

DIANA MOSLEY

Compared to us they were, because Mosley never considered himself right-wing, and he wasn't. In a way neither
was the Duke of Windsor. He had enormous compassion,
which *really* right-wing people lack. Anyway, Lord Long-
ford asked me to write the biography of the Duchess, and
just as I was about to say no a silly book came out in
America about the Windsors, and I thought I should write
a book and try to describe them as they were. Unfortunately she was already ill and couldn't help. Had I known
that one day I would be writing her biography I would
have asked all the right questions. She had a brain he-
morrage and foolishly the doctors brought her round, but
her brain was damaged. So I had to rely on written material.
A cousin of mine had been the Duke's Equerry when he
was the Prince of Wales, and I quoted him, as well as a
hundred other people who had known her. Everybody
had something to contribute.

INTERVIEWER

*What are you writing now? Would you like to do another
biography, since that one was so successful?*

DIANA MOSLEY

No, but I write articles. I have just written a long piece
on "1939," for *The Guardian*, and I am now wrestling
with a speech for the Historical Society of Trinity College,
Dublin. I do book reviews and used to write a regular
diary for a magazine called the *European*. Now an American
publisher wants to publish an anthology of those pieces
and has asked me to write a preface for it. I have also
been asked by the BBC to present a film in Paris.

INTERVIEWER

You have always been a great traveller. Do you still travel much?

DIANA MOSLEY

I go often to England, naturally, and I'm going to South Africa with my sister Pamela for the month of February, when it is so cold and grim here.

INTERVIEWER

What is your view on the situation there?

DIANA MOSLEY

I wrote an article about it the other day, saying that I go there for the sun, not the politics! So I think the West should help the South African government abolish apartheid as soon and as painlessly as possible, instead of knocking it. You know, twenty-five years ago I went to Mandela's trial. I was in Pretoria and read about it in the newspapers. I asked the hotel porter where the High Court was, and he said "round the corner from here." So every morning I walked there, sat down and listened. It was exactly like an English court. Apparently he had a fruit farm and all the boxes instead of being full of fruit were packed with dynamite. I thought he would get a death sentence for treason, but unlike Guy Fawkes, who tried to dynamite the Houses of Parliament in Britian in the seventeenth century, he didn't. Now they ask him to renounce violence and be free. I'm sure he wouldn't mind renouncing violence, that he doesn't want to blow things up with dynamite, but he can't bear going back to Winnie! She is such a frightful bore! But I may be wrong. Apartheid is absurd, but last time I was in South Africa I stayed in a big hotel where there were many black guests. Some of the best seats at the theater and the opera were taken by blacks too, so I think in practice petty apartheid is finished. But the blacks don't have the vote. Nor do I here, although I am a householder and taxpayer.

INTERVIEWER
Do you ever feel lonely? Or think of death?

DIANA MOSLEY
I like being alone; it is not a handicap to me, and Paris is full of friends. I am lucky to be mobile and able to walk everywhere. What I find hard to do is queuing. I missed the Van Gogh exhibition at the Musée d'Orsay because there was a queue three miles long. As for death, well it is about time I died, most of my friends have. I still have a happy life with my sisters and children and grandchildren and great-grandchildren, and I don't mind staying a bit longer, as long as I am healthy and no burden on others.

INTERVIEWER
Do you believe in an after-life?

DIANA MOSLEY
Oh no! I think death is like a candle being blown out; *pschut!* gone! Of course I may be surprised, but it is unlikely. I should be delighted if there was another life, because if it's anything like this one I should simply love it!

Frances Partridge

Frances Partridge is the last living member of the inner circle of that scintillating constellation of British artists and intellectuals of the 1920s and 30s we now know as "The Bloomsbury Group." She was born in 1900 the youngest of William C. Marshall's six children—four daughters and two sons. At the end of the First World War she went up to Newnham College, Cambridge, and read English, Philosophy and Psychology. David Garnett married one of her sisters, Ray, (who later became his Lady Into Fox) and started a bookshop in Bloomsbury, and when Frances finished at the university she went to work for him. Through Garnett she became involved with the Bloomsbury set and met her future husband, Ralph Partridge.

At the time of their meeting in 1922 Ralph Partridge was married to the artist Dora Carrington (known simply as Carrington in the annals of Bloomsbury), and the couple lived with Lytton Strachey in the country. Soon after Lytton Strachey's death in 1932 Carrington committed suicide, and some time later Frances married Ralph. Theirs was a perfectly happy union which lasted until Ralph's death in 1960. Three years later their only son, Burgo, died tragically young at the age of twenty-eight.

Although encouraged by Virginia Woolf to write, Frances

Partridge did not publish anything until she was in her seventies. In 1978 she published A Pacifist's War, a volume of her war journals. She and her husband had been active conscientious objectors and their house in Wiltshire, Ham Spray, was the refuge of friends and relatives, as well as assorted waifs and strays. Her vivid description of landscape and events, witty comments and lively conversation made the book an immediate success. It was followed three years later by Love in Bloomsbury, her autobiography and memoirs of the 1920s and 1930s. In 1983 she wrote Julia, a biography of her life-long friend Julia Strachey, who died in 1970, a famous beauty and author of two well-received novels. She followed it with Everything to Lose, another volume of memoirs which took her up to her husband's death. Finally, in 1988, she published a delightful photographic autobiography, a selection of photos from her albums in which not only members of the inner circle of the Bloomsbury Group, but more peripheral characters were portrayed.

At eighty-eight Frances Partridge is astonishing in her vivacity, energy and joie-de-vivre. Petite and slim, she is in full possession of all her faculties and enjoys robust health. She travels a good deal, both in Britain and abroad, and manages to do a considerable amount of literary journalism. She lives in Belgravia, London's grand residential area, in a spacious, light apartment in one of the few buildings still untouched by "developers." Her rooms are filled with the mementos of her long and fascinating life, and unique Bloomsburiana: pictures by Duncan Grant and Vanessa Bell, Carrington and other artists; first editions of various authors, photographs of family and friends. Above her sofa on the wall hangs Lytton Strachey's famous portrait by Carrington, recently reproduced on the cover of a new edition of his Eminent Victorians.

On the day of my first visit to her house—in 1988—
Frances Partridge had spent the morning with reporters,
giving interviews to radio and press about the Strachey book.
Then she had given lunch to a friend and her eight-year-
old son. After lunch she had done her best to amuse the
little boy with books, drawings and stories, but all in vain:
"All he wanted to do was to watch television, and I haven't
got the thing!"

The interview took place on two occasions, the second a
few days after the first.

INTERVIEWER

There is a letter from your husband to you in your book of
memoirs in which he tells you that he has seen Virginia
Woolf and that she had urged you to write, saying that she
was sure you were a writer. When your first book came out
decades later, it was obvious that she had been right, that
you have a natural gift for writing. Why didn't you start
earlier?

FRANCES PARTRIDGE

I was always aware of a desire to write, but I thought that
I lacked the vital ingredient, which is imagination. I have
only been able to write about what has happened. Another
reason was that I had to earn a living, and went to work
for my brother-in-law, Bunny (David) Garnett, in his bookshop, straight after Cambridge. Then I married and had
a child and a house to run. I look upon my writing as
part of my life, not as something in itself. I always wrote
an enormous number of letters. I don't always like it when
they come back to me! But I think of my writing in terms
of letters, which turned into a diary during the war. I had
absolutely no intention of one day publishing the diary,

though I kept it up for forty years. I still write as many letters as I can squash in, and still keep a diary.

INTERVIEWER

The last volume, Everything to Lose, *took you up to Ralph's death in 1960. Will you publish another volume, which would cover the years since then?*

FRANCES PARTRIDGE

I might publish one more, but it gets into difficult regions— sadness and loss. My son Burgo died of a heart-attack three years after his father, and afterwards I wrote a great deal in my diary. It makes very sad reading, because to groan into the diary was a relief to me. My agent thinks it is good and that people are interested in bereavement and how one copes with it. But publishers don't like sadness—they think it won't sell. I should have to cut and cut. When one is alone, people confide in one; there is a lot about other people's love affairs and lives which I would have to take out as well.

INTERVIEWER

It would be a pity to cut all of them out, wouldn't it?

FRANCES PARTRIDGE

Yes. So I shall have to use my judgment. I often make quite acid remarks about others, but I don't want to hurt living people. I have done so by mistake, when I thought somebody was dead when he or she *wasn't.*

INTERVIEWER

Let us go back to the beginning. Your father came from the Lake District, Wordsworth country. There is a great

feeling for nature in your writing which might come from
living in a beautiful countryside. Did you live there yourself?

FRANCES PARTRIDGE

We often spent holidays there. But my parents lived in
Bedford Square, in Bloomsbury, in one of those big houses
which are now all offices. My father was an architect and
had his office in the house, and we were six children and
six servants. We went to the Lake District for the summer
and loved it—it had a great and lasting influence on me.
My father used to take us for walks and infuse the love
of nature into us. Later I read the Lake poets. Again it
was my father who kindled the love of literature in me
by reading to us—Scott and Dickens and so on. I didn't
read a great deal of poetry at first, except Shakespeare's
sonnets, which had a tremendous effect on me and some
of which I learnt by heart. At Cambridge I started reading
English but later I changed to philosophy and psychology,
because for an English degree you had to study all that
horrible Norse and Old Anglo-Saxon. I adored the Eliz-
abethans and the Restoration writers, poetry and drama.

INTERVIEWER

When you were eight your father retired and you left London
for the country. Where did you go?

FRANCES PARTRIDGE

We had a house in Surrey, in a sort of beauty spot. Then
I was sent to Bedales. My mother was a Suffragist and
had a number of friends among the Strachey women of
the same persuasion. So I became great friends with Julia
Strachey, Lytton's niece, and when she went to Bedales
as a boarder I wanted to go too. Julia was less academic

Frances Partridge at age eighteen

than I was, and wanted to play the piano all day. But she was also more imaginative than I was, and very fascinating and beautiful. We remained each other's best friends till her death.

INTERVIEWER

Bedales was one of the first co-educational schools in this country. How did it work with boys and girls mixing together, rather unusually for the Edwardian period?

FRANCES PARTRIDGE

We had separate houses, but got together for lessons and for extracurricular activities like acting and music. Of course we fell in love, and everyone knew who was in love with whom, which meant that they met in the Quad and exchanged a few words. It never went beyond that. The occasional kiss on the cheek *maybe*. I had two brothers and was used to boys, but I fell in love more than once like everyone else. My last boyfriend turned up at Cambridge and I saw a bit of him there. But I made other friends at University, both men and women. One of them was Rosamond Lehmann, who was at Girton, and we went to the same English lectures.

INTERVIEWER

Was it not unusual for girls to go to University then?

FRANCES PARTRIDGE

It was, fairly. When I went up at the end of the First World War the rules were still prehistoric: If you had a bedsitting room you were not allowed to receive a young man to tea in it. I had a brother who had come back from the war, and I wasn't allowed to have him in my room either. So we staged a sort of rebellion; I remember one girl getting up and saying "Why is it that the rich girls who have two rooms—a sitting-room and a bedroom— are allowed male visitors? Is it because you are afraid of the temptation the presence of the bed would produce?" In the end freedom came and we were allowed to go dancing even. Everyone was *mad* on the new dances— Fox-trot I should think it was called—and soon after the Tango and the Charleston. I *loved* dancing.

INTERVIEWER

Did a lot of contemporaries get killed in the war?

FRANCES PARTRIDGE

They were just too young, most of them. One of my brothers was in Germany when war broke out. He was interned all through it, which probably saved his life but damaged him spiritually. Older boys from Bedales got killed whom we had known.

INTERVIEWER

When you came down from Cambridge, did you have to work? I mean families like yours didn't expect it of girls, or did they?

FRANCES PARTRIDGE

My family were liberal and rather advanced, my mother being a Suffragist. My father had retired—he died in my last term at Cambridge—and there were a lot of us to provide for. It was assumed that I would work, and I certainly wouldn't have wanted it otherwise. My father treated us very well: When I went up to University he made over $2000 to me, and out of the proceeds I had to pay for everything—college fees, clothes, pocket money, etcetera. . . . It taught me how to manage because every penny had to be counted. There was not enough for anything really—one pair of shoes per year perhaps. Once I could not go to a dance in London for not having the ten shilling train fare. That hurt! The young nowadays seem simply to go round hat in hand to their parents and to everybody else.

INTERVIEWER

Who were your teachers and mentors at Cambridge? I mean first in English and later among the philosophers?

FRANCES PARTRIDGE

By far the most inspiring was I.A. Richards. He thought as he spoke, and made strange marks on the blackboard which helped him to think. He was always stimulating. Another was Quiller-Couch. But some lecturers delivered their speeches with eyes glazed, and I used to think well I could have read that without seeing him. There was a little lady don who lectured on Shakespeare and took us for private tuition, which wasn't very common then. I have forgotten her name. Later I got very excited by philosophy and met several philosophers, in Cambridge first and then in London.

INTERVIEWER

G.E. Moore, Bertrand Russell, Wittgenstein, were still connected to Cambridge then. Did you meet them or work with them?

FRANCES PARTRIDGE

I met them all. G.E. Moore I saw only once: I went to some meetings of the Moral Sciences Club where everyone sat around and argued. To me it was most fascinating—I felt I was seeing *life!* G.E. Moore sat by the hearth and curled himself up into a knot—I can see him now. They discussed the maddest things: He would argue whether to say "The Present King of France is bald" is a meaningless statement, since there is no King in France . . . that sort of thing. Later I read his *Principia Ethica*, which was a very famous book at the time.

INTERVIEWER

Principia Ethica *was a sort of moral handbook for the Bloomsbury set. They based their attitudes on the principles it outlined. Did you share their admiration?*

FRANCES PARTRIDGE

It had a great influence on them, true. I used to argue
about it with Leonard Woolf. Moore was a very charming
man and sang Leider beautifully in a tenor voice. At the
end of his book he said that friendship and the Arts are
the best things in life, and the Bloomsbury people agreed.
But I was a thorough hedonist from my early days, and
Moore tried to demolish all other views than his own
including and especially hedonism. Hedonism means pursuing every action back to human happiness, and holds
that happiness is the only ultimate good. Some people
think it concerns only the happiness of the person who
holds this view, which is nonsense. The happiness of *all*
is the aim, the "happiness of the greatest number."

INTERVIEWER

*This is not the moment to profess hedonism, because it has
been vulgarized into the pursuit of personal pleasure, often
of the more superficial kind, so that it is held responsible
for a certain disintegration of moral values. It is believed
that such a view leads to excess, and all manner of an-
omalies. It is hard for any philosophy not to be reduced in
this way, but Hedonism more so than some other creeds,
because of what is happening in advanced societies. Even
AIDS is laid at its door.*

FRANCES PARTRIDGE

But hedonists distinguish between pleasure and happiness,
and say that one is temporary and superficial, and leads
to AIDS—jumping to bed with someone you don't even
know. That is an example of non-productive pleasure which
does not lead to happiness but to misery. But the pleasure

of music, poetry, friendship and true love, those are productive; they spring up and flourish like plants. Philosophers discuss things in a different way. Bentham was a great hedonist. His famous statement was something like: "Quantity of pleasure being equal, Houris and Hot Baths are as good as Poetry." I do not agree; you have to take into account not just the pleasure of the hot bath but what happens *afterwards*. The same is probably true of Houris! You can't go on having hot baths any more than Houris. I am a little rusty on this now. I had several friends who were declared hedonists: Clive Bell for example. But it wasn't very common in the philosophical sense.

INTERVIEWER

What about Wittgenstein and Russell? Did you know them?

FRANCES PARTRIDGE

I saw Wittgenstein fairly often when I went visiting friends in Cambridge. One of my Bedales friends had married to a brilliant young philosopher, Frank Ramsey, who died appallingly young, at twenty-seven, and who was a close friend of Wittgenstein's. Wittgenstein was deeply impressive, with the face of an ascetic monk, rather beautiful, and he loved music, as philosophers often do. In general company he put on a frivolous facade, made rather poor jokes, and spoke very slightingly of the Arts—unlike Moore who respected them. I can't remember his jokes, but sausages came into them somewhere.

INTERVIEWER

So if these contemporary philosophers didn't influence you, who did?

FRANCES PARTRIDGE

Mostly eighteenth century philosophers like Hume and Locke; also J.S. Mill and Bentham.

INTERVIEWER

When you came down from Cambridge, did you think of a career, or just earning a living?

FRANCES PARTRIDGE

The third year at college I studied Psychology and thought of becoming a psychologist. Applied Psychology was just beginning, and one professor offered me work doing intelligence tests on children, or finding out why Lyons' (a chain of tea-rooms) waitresses broke so much china, that sort of thing. He said he couldn't pay me because the department had no money as yet, but that they would have some later. I couldn't accept. That's when I went to work with my brother-in-law Bunny Garnett, who had started a bookshop in Bloomsbury.

He had married my sister Ray, who was an artist and illustrated his books. My father had died just before I came down from Cambridge and I lived with my mother. There was a great vogue for communal houses, in which we all had our own bedsitting-room where we received our friends, and my mother would ask how many there would be for dinner and provide it. She had a butler who helped and it was all very well organized. I lived there until I went to live with Ralph in Gordon Square.

INTERVIEWER

Was your mother very active as a Suffragette?

FRANCES PARTRIDGE

She called herself a Suffragist, which meant that she didn't fling herself at racehorses or carve a hole in the Romney

Venus, but believed in persuasion. As a little girl I went walking in a procession carrying a banner which said Vote For Women. That was as far as we went; we didn't tie ourselves to parliamentary railings, as the Suffragettes did. My mother had friends among the famous Suffragists: the Stracheys, Mrs. Fawcett, etcetera. Lots of men supported the Suffragists too. Others were dead against them and believed that women should remain thoroughly feminine and do women's things. What femininity had to do with voting I can't think.

INTERVIEWER

How did your mother's feminism influence you? Are you a feminist?

FRANCES PARTRIDGE

I think her non-violence was probably the source of my later pacifism. But I was never a real feminist, partly because I liked men too much. So did my mother. She once told me that all her life she was always in love with someone. Of course she would never have dreamed of being unfaithful to my father, but she was a very warm, loving person. I adored her. I think the radical feminism of today rather absurd. Men have a hard time too—having to shave every day and being conscripted in time of war. But it was very different then; women had a real grudge. I don't think it was the vote as such they wanted, but an end to the terrible condition of working women. But most of those battles have been won and women can do anything they want now. Of course there are still details to be worked out, such as equal pay for equal work and so on, but basically they can be anything they wish, except bishops. Who wants to be a bishop though? I think now feminism has an emotional basis, whereas in those days real battles had to be fought.

INTERVIEWER
While you worked at the bookshop you also helped indexing Freud's work. Can you tell me about it, because you once told me that your admiration for Freud dates from that time, when you read all twenty-two volumes of his work.

FRANCES PARTRIDGE
I did it to help James Strachey, Lytton's brother, and his wife. They were psychoanalysts and translated Freud.

INTERVIEWER
What do you think of Freud now? He is coming in for a lot of criticism these days, and grave doubts are cast over his theories, and even more on his practices.

FRANCES PARTRIDGE
I think he is one of the great geniuses of the age. Most of the effect he has had is a sort of underground seepage— it has crept everywhere. His notions about relationships between parents and children, brothers and sisters have affected everything. Even my son's nanny had got hold of the idea that you shouldn't put a child arbitrarily on his pot! But Freud himself doubted how much his theories worked as therapy. There is a new biography of him by an American, Peter Gay, which is excellent and gives you some idea of his stature—he was an intellectual giant. I didn't take to Jung much, but I haven't read him lately.

INTERVIEWER
But again some people think that the vulgarization of some of Freud's ideas—his pansexualism for example—play a part in today's excesses.

FRANCES PARTRIDGE

Oh yes, they do. But I think pan-violence is more terrible than pansexualism. Of course people want to sleep with one another, and so they should, but if they want to cut each other to pieces while doing so, then the world is in a very bad way indeed. Certainly Freud can't be held responsible for this state of affairs.

INTERVIEWER

When you were a child your godmother, Lady Prothero, took you to see Henry James in Rye. Do you remember the incident?

FRANCES PARTRIDGE

Yes. Henry James loved being surrounded by ladies and fussed about by them. He was a homosexual we are told today, but it wasn't known then. In those days there were what we called bachelors—men who never married. He was very thick with my Aunt Alice. You'll find her as Mrs. Dew-Smith in the index of his biography as one of his great friends. I think she took me to tea with him. I remember him picking me up—I must have been about six—my legs dangling, and starting a little speech: "My dear child . . .," he began, and I can't recall the rest of what he said. He looked like a stout butler, large and rosy faced. I've always adored his books.

Aunt Alice herself wrote in a modest way. She wrote short stories which were light and amusing, rather in the Rye School, frivolous but sophisticated. Her books are completely forgotten, but E.F. Benson, who was another Rye author, has recently been reprinted.

People said, "your Aunt Alice is going to marry Henry James," but of course it didn't happen. She talked to me about writing when I was a child, and how important it was to cut out adjectives. *Very important*, she said. She was aiming at admirable things like concision, in the French manner. Nowadays women write very long novels. Even some of the short ones are dull. I don't mind long books if they are good. At the moment I'm reading Trollope's *The Way We Live Now*, which is very long. And I must be one of the few people who has read all twenty-one volumes of Saint-Simon.

INTERVIEWER

I wonder if your Aunt Alice talked about concision to Henry James! Never use one word when six would do!

FRANCES PARTRIDGE

Henry James and Proust, two writers I most admire, but you can't call them concise.

INTERVIEWER

So you went to work at David Garnett's bookshop and stayed for some years. Where was it?

FRANCES PARTRIDGE

It was off Gordon Square which was the heart of Bloomsbury, in Taviton Street. My sister and David Garnett had rooms above the bookshop which was on the ground-floor of a terrace house. You had to ring the front door bell to get in, which intimidated people, so that strangers didn't come much—even though there was a window full of books. But all the Bloomsbury people bought their books there.

INTERVIEWER
Was it a kind of rendez-vous place for intellectuals?

FRANCES PARTRIDGE
It was, and that's how I got to know them well. I first met Ralph there; he was then working for the Hogarth Press with Virginia and Leonard Woolf, and he brought their books round. He invited me to stay with him, Carrington and Lytton in Tidmarsh, their first house, and later at Ham Spray. I was also invited to Charleston, to stay with Clive and Vanessa Bell and Duncan Grant. Virginia asked me to dinner and Leonard was most anxious to persuade us to fill the whole shop with copies of Vita Sackville-West's tiny *Seducers in Equador* which he had just published. His argument was that if you filled the window with this book then everybody would buy it. Leonard was very intelligent, he was always saying so himself: "I'm extraordinarily intelligent," or "I'm immensely intelligent," he would say, and I suppose he was. He had lovely blue eyes but in some ways he missed a lot. He became very mellow and charming in his old age, and of course he looked after Virginia devotedly. I went to their flat in Tavistock Square and to their country home too. There was a feeling of community in Bloomsbury, as we all lived close to each other. When I moved in with Ralph in 1926 there were others in the same house. James Strachey and his wife were both psychoanalysts and had their consulting rooms upstairs, while Lytton had a pied-á-terre on the ground-floor, and Dadie (George) Rylands and the Davidson brothers lived next door, etcetera. . . . Clive Bell took me out a lot; he loved girls and had love affairs with them, but with me he remained always a great friend. He would have liked to be more but it wasn't

on—I was rather proper in those days. Duncan Grant
lived at number thirty-six, I think, and Maynard and Lydia
Keynes lived nearby. They gave lovely parties which we
went to. Then there was the Gordon Square garden where
everybody met in good weather. We had a key to it, and
a lot of tennis went on. Arthur Waley was a keen player
and Ralph was very good at tennis; I was keen but not
so good.

INTERVIEWER

*When Ralph asked you to Tidmarsh where he lived with
his wife Carrington and Lytton Strachey, how did you feel
about their ménage-à-trois, being as you put it "proper?"
There seems to have been a lot of these civilized arrangements
among the Bloomsbury people: Vanessa Bell- Clive Bell-
Duncan Grant threesome, though from what you say about
Clive their menage was rather à plusieurs!*

FRANCES PARTRIDGE

But theirs wasn't really a ménage-à-trois, since there was
no sexual relation between Lytton and either of the other
two. Lytton had fallen for Ralph when he had arrived
from Oxford, a very handsome rowing man, but he soon
discovered that he was hopelessly heterosexual, and they
became tremendous friends. Then Ralph fell madly in love
with Carrington who was desperately in love with Lytton
who couldn't respond. It *is* rather involved! So the arrangement suited all three. It was consolidated by the fact
that they all really *liked* each other. Lytton depended on
Ralph for all practical matters. Ralph acted as his secretary
and business manager. When he also worked for the
Hogarth Press he only got £100 a year. So he did other
things beside to make money, like bookbinding and trans-

Frances and Ralph Partridge, 1929

lation and literary journalism—a lot of reviews. He wrote for the *New Statesman* which was quite a different paper then: it had Desmond MacCarthy as Literary Editor and was less political, though left-wing.

INTERVIEWER

Were most people in the Bloomsbury set left-wing? I know the Left was different then, but people like Julian Bell and John Cornford went to Spain and got themselves killed in the Civil War on the Republican side.

FRANCES PARTRIDGE

On the whole they had a tendency towards the Left. But
most didn't care greatly about politics. Vanessa Bell became
famous for her remark, when she sat next to Prime Minister
Asquith at dinner and turned to him to ask: "Are you at
all interested in politics, Mr. Asquith?"

INTERVIEWER

*Then you fell in love with Ralph, and Gerald Brenan with
Carrington. It all seems rather incestuous and muddlesome,
doesn't it?*

FRANCES PARTRIDGE

Do you think more than now? People get Carrington's
love life rather wrong. All her emotions were centered
around Lytton Strachey. When Ralph fell in love with
her she felt sorry for him and wrote a wonderful letter
to Lytton, saying, You know the man I have always wanted
to marry is you, "but I shall never have my moon"—that
was her phrase. "Ralph is a good man and I'm fond of
him, and he is so unhappy."

INTERVIEWER

*It is hard for us, the subsequent generations, to understand
her obsession, since Lytton was so very unprepossessive and
unmanly, with his castrato voice and funny beard! Where
was his charm?*

FRANCES PARTRIDGE

He had great elegance and tremendous style. He was very
amusing and charmed people. He wanted to fall in love
with women and become normal, and he was attracted to

Carrington because she was rather boyish. He had even proposed to Virginia. It hadn't worked, but to the end of their lives Lytton and Carrington were very close friends; they were no longer anxious that Ralph might abandon them. That was Lytton's great fear when he knew that Ralph was going to live with me.

INTERVIEWER

One way or another Carrington seems to have given Ralph a rough time, because there was the affair with Gerald Brenan, Ralph's best friend. What happened there?

FRANCES PARTRIDGE

Ralph and Gerald had fought in the First World War together. He was happy to see that his wife whom he adored was getting on very well with his friend, not realizing that they had fallen for each other. But you must realize that in those days people didn't immediately jump to bed with each other; there was a lot of "necking" as it was called, but it stopped short of copulation. For Carrington sex was high jinks, fun, light-hearted. And she was a bit lesbian too. But Ralph minded terribly when he found out about her affair with Brenan, because he valued truth highly and loathed deception. There was a big row. Carrington was not highly sexed anyway, and her lesbian affairs didn't go far either. She was keen on Julia Strachey who did not respond, and later on, the daughter of the American Ambassador, Henrietta Bingham, who was a famous lesbian. But as I said the sexual side of things wasn't so important in those days. Perhaps people didn't drink so much. You had *vin ordinaire* with dinner, but you didn't sit swigging whiskey and vodka all the time.

There was more dancing, though older people didn't dance,
they sat and talked.

INTERVIEWER
*The friendship between Ralph and Brenan seems to have
survived the row. Did it really?*

FRANCES PARTRIDGE
Xan Fielding has edited their correspondence which is
very interesting. It shows that these two young men who
were not yet thirty and had been through the ghastly
experience of the Great War were very mature compared
to people today. Gerald went back to live in Spain and
he and Carrington wrote quantities of letters which show
that they had a great affinity. They were both marvelous
letter-writers and their correspondence contains some of
the best either ever wrote. But when Ralph said alright,
let's be civilized; everybody can go to bed with whomever
they wish, Gerald realized that Carrington didn't really
love him and found every excuse *not* to go to bed with
him.

INTERVIEWER
*Again it is difficult for us to understand what made Car-
rington such a femme fatale that every man fell in love
with her. There was also Mark Gertler, the artist.*

FRANCES PARTRIDGE
She was extremely attractive in her vitality and originality.
She had a touch of genius which showed in the things
she did, her art in particular. She was not a beauty in the
classical sense, but had amazing big blue eyes and straight
cropped hair, and great charm. At the Slade she had a

circle of admirers, Mark Gertler among them. He later
married and had children. He died of tuberculosis. Or was
it suicide? I can't remember which.

INTERVIEWER

*Yes, I believe it was suicide. As an innocent young girl were
you shocked by all this promiscuity, even though it didn't
always go as far as today?*

FRANCES PARTRIDGE

No. The aristocracy were far more fickle than the Bloomsbury set. The very rich married and divorced more often
still, because they could afford to. There was hardly any
divorce in Bloomsbury. They were civilized about it all.
Boris Anrep, a Russian artist who became a great friend
of ours, and whose wife Helen went off with Roger Fry
in the end, was another one who put up with the situation.
Carrington encouraged Ralph to have affairs, but when he
became serious with me she was terrified of losing Lytton
if there was an absolute breach. We had a discussion about
it, and sorted it out.

INTERVIEWER

*I have to admit being shocked by Lytton Strachey's cynicism,
saying to Carrington who had loved him desperately and
unrequitedly all her life, well if your husband goes, you go!
His biographer, Michael Holroyd, maintains that he would
not have abandoned Carrington even if Ralph had left with
you.*

FRANCES PARTRIDGE

Lytton had an interview with me at his club, The Oriental,
and said that although he was fond of Carrington he

depended on Ralph for practical matters, and that he
couldn't promise to live alone with Carrington if Ralph
went away. He was rather selfish, but you can't promise
to go on living with somebody whom you never asked to
live with you in the first place. It was awful for me, as I
didn't want to hurt Carrington. So I said that there was
no question of disrupting their relationship. I said Ralph
is devoted to you both, as I am, and you needn't worry
on that score. So nothing changed. We found a flat in
the same house as his brother, and both of us went down
to Ham Spray every weekend. Ralph and I didn't marry
until Carrington died shortly after Lytton. We were rather
in advance on the times. Nowadays everybody lives together
without being married, but in those days it was very rare.

INTERVIEWER

*After their deaths you moved to Ham Spray with Ralph
and your home became once again the focus of the Bloomsbury friends. But you had younger, new friends too. Who
were they?*

FRANCES PARTRIDGE

Ralph was six years younger than Carrington and I was
six years younger than him, hence the younger friends.
Among them were Julia Strachey, David Cecil and his
wife, Desmond and Molly Macarthy, Julia's two husbands,
etcetera. In those days it was easier to feed people; Ralph
was good at cultivation and we had fruit and vegetables
all the year round. We kept hens for eggs and during the
war we had rabbits as well. Then people brought their
own rations—coupons and matchboxes full of butter.

INTERVIEWER
There was another focal point for Bloomsbury in the country—
Ottoline Morrell's house, Garsington Hall, near Oxford. Did
you ever go there?

FRANCES PARTRIDGE
Yes, I did. And to her house in London. I liked her,
though I thought her appearance grotesque, which made
people laugh at her. But then if she didn't like that, why
did she dress in that pure fancy-dress way? Everything
looked as if it had come out of a dressing-up box in the
attic. She talked in a strange way which everyone always
imitated, a slow drone: "Oooh, I was just giving Bertie a
little aaaaspirin," she said when she was caught in Bertrand
Russell's bed.

INTERVIEWER
What did you do when your husband died and you sold
Ham Spray in 1961?

FRANCES PARTRIDGE
I stayed on for a year to sort everything out, then sold
it for nine thousand pounds—it's worth probably half a
million now. It didn't have much land but was in the
middle of lovely country with fields stretching all around.
We put in a swimming pool and had a good orchard and
vegetable garden. We played bowls on the lawn and had
a great many friends to stay. Now a young couple and
their children live there.

INTERVIEWER
To go back to your writing. Apart from your diaries, there
are your letters. It seems that the lovely epistolary art is

disappearing, perhaps partly because of the telephone. It is
a great pity when you think that such masterpieces as Les
Liaisons Dangereuses, *or* Clarissa, *written entirely as letters,*
could not happen today, could they?

FRANCES PARTRIDGE

Television is a pest! People stop talking to listen to their
favorite program, or say I can't come to dinner on Tuesday
because it's "Upstairs Downstairs," and that sort of thing.
I won't have it here! It would be fatal living alone as I
do—one would get hooked.

INTERVIEWER

But being very popular, you do have a busy social life. Do
you go to many parties, literary events?

FRANCES PARTRIDGE

I sometimes go to literary parties and enjoy them, but on
the whole the idea of people standing up yelling at each
other doesn't appeal to me. For the young there should
be dancing, or something energetic.

INTERVIEWER

During the war you became pacifists. Ralph wrote somewhere
he believed that war does not lead to peace but to other
wars. Were you ostracized by people around you?

FRANCES PARTRIDGE

Not really. When I selected from my journals for the
book, A *Pacifist's War*, the publishers asked me to put in
episodes in which people were nasty to us. At the end of
the War Ralph was called up, not for the Army but for
the Home Guard. Every conscientious objector had to

attend a Tribunal to be judged, and to be given total
exemption or not. Ralph thought a great deal whether he
should do his Tribunal or not, and finally decided it would
be honorable to do it. Ralph didn't get total exemption
the first time. But he could and did appeal, and was given
exemption. It got into a local paper. There were one or
two people who would not speak to us. One man came
to the door and was rather disagreeable, but it was nothing.
As for our friends, they argued endlessly, because we were
all great arguers. Having eaten all our food—homemade
butter and honey, etcetera—they would say: "Well, of
course if I had my way I'd drop you over the North Sea!"

INTERVIEWER

*Everyone did their war effort: women drove ambulances and
knitted socks or served in canteens, that sort of things. Did
you do anything, or was it against your pacifist principles?*

FRANCES PARTRIDGE

I wasn't called up because I had a small child. But Julia
was called up and got very muddled over it, whether to
serve or not. I would not have made munitions, but done
nursing or something of that kind. I am still a strong
pacifist; it is my firmest belief.

INTERVIEWER

*In one entry in your war diaries in 1941 you write that
you have just received the news of Virginia Woolf's suicide.
How did the group react to it?*

FRANCES PARTRIDGE

Horror and sorrow, and much sympathy for Leonard who
had looked after her so splendidly. She had tried it several

times before, which if you are mad you do. I never met
her when she was in the slightest degree mad, but she
knew when a bout of madness was threatening her.

INTERVIEWER

*Did she ever talk about it to you? I mean when you had
dinner together or stayed with her in the country?*

FRANCES PARTRIDGE

No. It would have been unthinkable. She loved asking
young people about their lives, their love stories, the dances
they went to. She was very charming to Ralph and me
when we went there after Lytton and Carrington had died,
which had been ghastly for us. Ralph had done everything
to prevent Carrington killing herself, but failed in the end.
Virginia was most sympathetic to all that. She had a very
perceptive side. I don't suppose you can be a real writer
unless you do.

INTERVIEWER

*Nowadays she is considered one of the pioneers of Modernism.
There was a series recently on television about the ten most
important Modernists in literature—Eliot, Kafka, Joyce, . . .
and Virginia Woolf. How did the contemporaries receive
her work? I don't mean just reviewers, but friends.*

FRANCES PARTRIDGE

I heard her first book, The Voyage Out, discussed by my
Aunt Alice, Henry James's friend, and my mother with
great interest. It was discussed seriously by very intelligent
people. Then she became much more famous with subsequent books.

INTERVIEWER

*Michael Holroyd's huge biography of Lytton Strachey covers
the whole Bloomsbury period and dramatis personae. What
do you think of his assessments, having been at the very
center of it all, and now the last first-hand witness?*

FRANCES PARTRIDGE

Funnily enough I've been reading it again. It is an extraordinary achievement and on the whole gives a good
picture of the scene.

INTERVIEWER

*Lytton Strachey became famous with the publication of his
Eminent Victorians. Subsequently his reputation seemed to
rest on the central role he played in Bloomsbury, and
nowadays he is better known as Holroyd's subject and the
whole Bloomsbury myth.*

FRANCES PARTRIDGE

That is true. He was almost unknown until *Eminent
Victorians*. We had just had a war and few books had
been published when it appeared. Lytton was attacking
the old two-volume biographies by Victorian writers in
his book. He was aiming for something which had concision, this French quality. His provocative remarks that
historians should prune and leave things out made a big
impression and created controversy.

INTERVIEWER

*Little did he know that his own biography would be two
hefty volumes! But did people think that his book was
shockingly iconoclastic?*

FRANCES PARTRIDGE

It wasn't as iconoclastic as people thought at the time. Take the one I like best: Florence Nightingale, who I'm sure reminded him of his own sisters. He says enormously admiring things about her—her tact, efficiency, the way she moved mountains and got everything going. He describes the nightmares she was dealing with very vividly. So to say that it is complete debunking is absurd. It's perfectly true that she became gaga when she was a very old lady—she wore herself out in the Crimean War and lived far too long.

The section on the two cardinals—Newman and Manning—is a masterpiece. He has a lot of sympathy for Newman, the artist of the two. Then the one on General Gordon, who was an eccentric, and according to Lytton a little mad, not representative of the Army in general. But it was taken as an attack on the Army. He did attack Victorian values in Dr. Arnold. He was against his ideas on schools, and he was very anti-Church. But Lytton was an innovator, though people don't realize it because he has so many imitators today; writers who copy his style and the rhythm of his words. The two-volume Victorian biography consisted of uninterpreted *facts*—a mass of them.

INTERVIEWER

Soon after you sold Ham Spray and moved to London, your only son Burgo died. I wonder how you found the courage to go on living?

FRANCES PARTRIDGE

One realizes that going on living is something one has to do. I wasn't brave enough to take my life, and I have

always had a very strong feeling for life—I love it! I adore
nature, wild flowers, the country, which is a great solace.
I do admire the courage of those who prefer death to
grief and loss, but I cling to life. And by the time my
son died I was so battered by life that I had developed a
sort of pugnacity. Nevertheless I was totally devastated.
Burgo's wife, Henrietta, is the daughter of David Garnett
by his second wife, Angelica Bell—Vanessa Bell's daughter
by Duncan Grant, whom he had married after my sister
Ray had died young. Henrietta tried to commit suicide
and was saved by a miracle. It was partly my responsibility
to her and her little baby daughter, my granddaughter,
which kept me going. Now my granddaughter is herself
married and has children, and I love them.

INTERVIEWER

So you had all this mass of writing which was unpublished.
Who persuaded you to publish some of it?

FRANCES PARTRIDGE

I think because pacifism was so important to me I thought
I ought to bring out the book. So I looked at the diaries
and sorted them out, took the manuscript to Chatto and
to my surprise they agreed to publish it. I was encouraged
and wrote my autobiography, which the Americans have
called *Love in Bloomsbury*, but here was simply called
Memories. So far, all my books have been published in
America. The third one was *Julia*, which was partly what
Julia Strachey herself had written and partly from my
diaries, and the whole made a portrait of her. Julia wrote
two novels, *Cheerful Weather for the Wedding*, which
Virginia Woolf liked and published, and another one. Both
were rather short. Julia was constitutionally unhappy, per-

haps because she was separated from her mother whom she adored at a very early age. She took ages to write anything; that's why she wrote very little. After that book I edited the next section of my diaries, up to Ralph's death in 1960.

INTERVIEWER

You have such vitality and youthfulness that one feels you can go on working without it being detrimental to your excellent health. Will you produce another book?

FRANCES PARTRIDGE

I have been asked to do another volume about the period when I was on my own. It needs an awful lot of cutting as I said.

INTERVIEWER

You also do a lot of literary journalisms, reviews and prefaces and that sort of thing. In fact you are very busy, aren't you?

FRANCES PARTRIDGE

I *am* rather, for an eighty-eight year old! I also give lectures and things of that sort, mostly about Bloomsbury I'm afraid, because I am one of the last survivors and people want to know about that time and those people. I'm not sure why.

Kathleen Raine

Kathleen Raine has long been considered one of the most distinguished poets writing in English today. Besides her poetry, translated into several European and Far Eastern languages, her three-volume autobiography (a best-seller in France) and her scholarly studies of William Blake and W.B. Yeats have won her international fame. At the age of eighty-two (she was born in 1908) she has phenomenal energy and continues to travel widely in Europe, America and India.

Kathleen Raine was born in Ilford, Essex, to an English father and a Scottish mother, but spent much of her childhood with her mother's family on the Scottish border. She attended the local school in Ilford where her father was the English Master, and later won an Exhibition to Girton College, Cambridge. She read Natural Sciences and Psychology, wrote poetry and met other budding writers and artists—William Empson, Humphrey Jennings, Jacob Bronowski, Malcolm Lowry, Julian Trevelyan. . . . At that time she was famous as much for her beauty as her poetry: "A society of young men formed merely to watch her pass in the street," wrote her contemporary Professor Muriel Bradbrook (later Mistress of Girton). She married, briefly, a fellow student, and later Charles Madge, poet and sociologist, by whom she had two

children. Her second marriage broke up at the beginning
of the Second World War, and for a while she returned to
Cumberland, near her mother's family home where she had
spent long formative periods in her childhood, and where
she began seriously writing poetry.

Her first book of poetry, Stone and Flower, was published
in 1943 by Editions Poetry London, the journal edited by
the Ceylonese Tamil, Tambimuttu, a poet, editor and publisher of poetry who had published many leading poets long
before they became famous, among them Dylan Thomas,
Vernon Watkins and David Gascoyne. (Tambimuttu was
the nephew of the distinguished Ceylonnese aesthetician, A.K.
Coomaraswamy.)

Back in London after the war, she eked out a living from
translation and reviewing, and for a while went back to
Girton as a Research Fellow where her high standards
inspired equal measures of devotion and fear in her students.
In 1948 she met Gavin Maxwell, the naturalist author of
Ring of Bright Water and other best-selling books. The story
of their tempestuous involvement is poignantly described in
The Lion's Mouth, the third volume of her autobiography.
She worked for ten years on her seminal work, Blake and
Tradition (the basis of her Andrew Mellon Lectures, Wash-
ington 1962) published in the prestigious Bollingen Series.
Other scholarly and critical works followed, including De-
fending Ancient Springs, a collection of essays on poetry
and poets.

In 1981, with three friends, she founded Temenos, a
Review of the Arts of the Imagination, which she has been
editing ever since. At the time of this interview she was
preparing the eleventh and penultimate issue. The last volume
will appear this year.

All through the years she has produced volumes of poetry,
and her collected poems were published in 1981, Selected

Poems in 1988. She has just completed a fourth volume of autobiography, India Seen Afar *which has yet to be published.*

Kathleen Raine lives in a leafy square in Chelsea, where she works looking over the square on one side and her own overgrown garden on the other. Her home has always been a refuge for writers and poets whom she has supported long before they became famous, among them David Gascoyne, Cecil Collins, Elias Canetti, St. John Perse, Rafael Nadal, et cetera. Writers and scholars come to see her from all over the world, and she is as generous with her hospitality as with her advice and guidance. Already several doctorate theses on her work have appeared in France, America, Egypt, Canada and elsewhere. She is the recipient of the W.H. Smith Literary Award for her book of poetry, The Lost Country, *and has received Honorary Doctorates from several universities, including Leiscester, Durham, and Caen (France).*

This interview took place over tea and petite madeleines, cooked by Dr. Raine, on two summer afternoons in 1989. She had just returned from India where she had attended a celebration of Yeats' half-centenary. She was soon off to America for three weeks, where she lectures regularly and where she has numerous friends and admirers.

Kathleen Raine speaks with a firm, beautifully modulated voice and expresses her views forcefully. Her candour is disarming, her originality at times startling. During the course of our conversation a wistful expression suffused her face at times and she looked exactly like the ravishing eight-year-old girl with long golden hair whose photograph is on the cover of her autobiography, Farewell Happy Fields.

INTERVIEWER

You were born in Ilford. Where exactly is it? I couldn't find it on my map.

KATHLEEN RAINE

Where indeed! It's a most obscure dormitory suburb just outside London, in Essex. It used to be the country, but now suburbia has spread and overwhelmed the fields where I gathered buttercups as a child.

My father was the English Master at the County High School, which was at the time newly founded. He had come from the North, County Durham, and to him coming to within the range of London was coming to the center of culture. He was a man who lived by high principles and regarded teaching as a vocation. He had a sort of missionary zeal, and the humbler the surroundings the more he would feel that he was bringing light and enlightenment into dark places. He was a Christian Socialist.

My mother didn't feel it in quite the same way. She was Scottish, and I think she pined for the North and the places she had loved. Her love of poetry inspired me to be a poet, and from the start I was conscious of a vocation, of being "chosen," so to speak.

INTERVIEWER

Where had he found her?

KATHLEEN RAINE

They were both students at Durham University. She was training as a teacher, and he was reading English. He took his M.Lit. and wrote his thesis on Wordsworth, who was his great love at the time. My mother didn't aspire to higher degrees, after she finished her teacher's training she taught for a year, then married and gave up working. Women did in those days—I believe they lost their posts if they married. I was an only child.

INTERVIEWER

Only children have a different psychology from those who have been brought up with siblings. They are usually more self-sufficient. Were you?

KATHLEEN RAINE

I always had an imaginary, invisible playmate. In fact two playmates, a boy and a girl, who walked either side of me. Later there was my more enduring, permanent companion, my inspiring Daimon, who I suppose came from that early time when invisible companions were part of my daily life.

INTERVIEWER

Who was this Daimon? Could you describe him? Did you just imagine him?

KATHLEEN RAINE

Who knows what is imaginary and what is real? He had the reality of the Imagination. He had no visible, physical shape, but certainly personal presence. He was a sort of *puer eternus*. When recently I read about *al-Khidr* in Islamic philosophy I thought yes, I know that figure! *Khidr* was a confirmation to me that others had had the same experience of a personalized but invisible companion, and very much an inspirer of poetry—a messenger from the world of the Imagination.

INTERVIEWER

Isn't that what is usually called the Muse?

KATHLEEN RAINE

Yes, except that the Muse is female, mine was a male figure. Not a lover, but a youth.

INTERVIEWER

So you didn't feel lonely as a child?

KATHLEEN RAINE

Never as a child. Loneliness is a grown-up feeling. When
you are a child there are so many things in the world
that engage your attention: flowers and birds and trees.
Besides my parents were most devoted and loving. My
mother endlessly recited me poems and read me stories.
My father too was very much a near-at-hand father, perhaps
because he was a schoolmaster and not so remote as those
men who went away to an office. We were a close and
united family.

INTERVIEWER

The poetic vein came to you from both parents?

KATHLEEN RAINE

Yes. My mother was overflowing with poetry and poured
it into me in my earliest years. She knew endless Border
Ballads and Scottish songs by heart, which had come to
her through oral tradition, not education. My father knew
English Literature and was concerned with language. He
also knew Anglo-Saxon and Latin well. He gave me a solid
grounding in English Literature. To this day I can't make
a mistake in English grammar, because it was part of my
upbringing to know the language.

INTERVIEWER

*Is that why you chose to read Natural Sciences at Cam-
bridge—to learn something new?*

KATHLEEN RAINE

Precisely. I thought why should I read the literature of my own language; one should know that anyhow?

INTERVIEWER

What books did you read in those days?

KATHLEEN RAINE

The corpus of English Literature. Shakespeare—my father loved him and took me to see every one of his plays that was put on—the Romantic poets, Shelley and Keats and Wordsworth, et al. I loved Gray and Collins, but Pope and Dryden I read later. It was English Romanticism that was my spiritual home.

INTERVIEWER

And you have stayed with it?

KATHLEEN RAINE

Or rather I have returned to it, after a diversion through the Modern Movement.

INTERVIEWER

Goethe said, "Classicism in health, Romanticism in sickness," which didn't mean that he didn't enjoy the sickness himself! In some ways the Romantic Movement started with him in Germany, did it not?

KATHLEEN RAINE

It didn't entirely come from Germany, because after all one could say that Shakespeare was a Romantic, in the sense that I use the word. To me Romanticism means poetry that is grounded in the Imagination. That would take us back to Grey and Collins. Blake had no German influence, Coleridge of course did, but Shelley belonged to the Neoplatonic tradition. So Romanticism had many roots.

The question is: where does poetry come from? Poets like Pope and Dryden were technicians, admirable craftsmen. They were not concerned with higher levels of consciousness, with other, inner worlds. Whereas the Romantics had this extra dimension, which is the *poetry* in poetry. Otherwise why not write the same things in prose? Today people talk in psychological rather than metaphysical terms, so one might say that poetry comes from the soul, not from the mundane experiences of this world alone. Poetry speaks to and from the heart, and even more sublime regions.

INTERVIEWER

Your childhood was rich in poetry, songs and ballads. Then you went to Northumberland, which was a formative experience. What happened?

KATHLEEN RAINE

It was during the First World War and my parents wanted me to be safe. I was sent to my mother's family, on the border of Scotland, in Northumberland, and I got my roots back in the soil of the Border culture, the beauty of Nature. It was a wild little hamlet, but I loved it.

INTERVIEWER

The landscape and atmosphere are beautifully described in Farewell Happy Fields, *the first volume of your autobiography, and one of your most popular works here and abroad.*

KATHLEEN RAINE

When I went back in later life it looked like nothing. But in my memory it was paradise. One should never go back.

INTERVIEWER

If it is not "lost," then it is not Paradise! Perhaps the past can only be recaptured through the imagination, as Proust demonstrated. Did you go to school there?

KATHLEEN RAINE

My aunt was the village school mistress. Then when I came back after the war, aged eleven, I went to the girls' division of my father's school. The boys were downstairs and we were upstairs. We were not allowed to walk home with the boys. If any girl was seen walking with a boy, even her brother, there would be trouble with our fierce Head-Mistress. However, in the end I did fall in love with a young man, but by then he had left school. He was my first source of inspiration.

INTERVIEWER

You have told me how important that first love was to you. What happened?

KATHLEEN RAINE

He had been a pupil of my father's and his family attended the same non-conformist church as we did. My mother was Presbyterian and hated the service, as indeed I did. There was no poetry in it. But my mother had a wonderful gift for thinking of something else when she was in church! Anyway, this young man was the assistant-organist, a very good musician and highly cultured—for Ilford. He took

me to concerts of Debussy and Ravel, and introduced me
to unknown regions of poetry and music. My father didn't
approve at all—he liked his poets and composers to be
safely dead! He broke us up by forbidding me to see him.
I obeyed him with tears and much grief. I never felt that
kind of love again—strangely deep it went. The young
man's reaction was to become an Anglo-Catholic and to
seek for a time to become a monk.

In those days people didn't have sexual relationships;
we just held hands and kissed. We thought we would
marry in seven year's time, and go to the coast of Cornwall
for our honeymoon. It was all mixed with Tristan and
Isolde, Pelleas and Mélisande, the Celtic Twilight, that sort
of thing. Nothing physical. Perhaps that is why it was so
lasting.

INTERVIEWER

*You went to Cambridge to read Natural Sciences. Were
you good at them?*

KATHLEEN RAINE

I was good at botany. Perhaps because I loved the Botany
Mistress and it was fun doing botany and zoology with
her. To this day I haven't sorted out the difference between
the scientific and the poetic love of nature. In those days
you could see the things you studied, whereas today it is
more microbiology and has to do more with math and
physics.

INTERVIEWER

*Reading from the sciences, how did you get involved with
literary Cambridge?*

KATHLEEN RAINE

I had formed a long and important friendship with a French friend of my father's who was a *Professeur* at the Lyceé Condorcet in Paris. He took me in hand, taught me French and formed my mind. He had a little house in Brittany where we spent many happy summer holidays. Unfortunately he fell in love with me, and again my father forbade me to see him. So when I arrived at Cambridge I was doubly heart-broken and felt I had lost everything, my love and my mentor. I threw off all my upbringing and plunged into the Modern Movement, which had just begun—*The Waste Land* was published in 1922. You know how the young like being in the current with their contemporaries. Besides the whole cultural milieu was theirs. It was half a life time later that I discovered what I have called "the Excluded Knowledge," and "the learning of the Imagination": the tradition of Platonism which was the inspiration of the great Romantic poets of England, and of Yeats. But at the time I was living in the superficila world of "The Latest Thing." The whole basis of the Modern Movement was throwing off the past, not carrying *"le cadavre de mon père,"* which fitted in with my rebellious mood at the time.

INTERVIEWER

Were you thunderstruck by The Waste Land, *like so many people? Did you like it?*

KATHLEEN RAINE

"Like" is not perhaps the right word. One day I picked up in the office of a provincial newspaper a copy of *The Criterion*. I opened it and read a poem starting with the line, "*Lady, three white leopards sat under a juniper tree/ In the heat of the day.*" My hair stood up, and I thought "This is it!." Something new and wonderful! I went back to Cambridge for my second term and the future Mrs. Q.D. Leavis poured scorn on me for not having read *The Waste Land* already, which I proceeded to do. But I had the joy of discovering Eliot for myself and of feeling the tremendous frisson my generation felt with his new voice. I read *The Waste Land* at a time when, like so many others, I was lost, and I felt that Eliot spoke for my own unspoken grief. Reading it now I see what a personal poem it is, but at the time it spoke for a whole generation.

INTERVIEWER

It had an extraordinary collective power, and still does. But all those other budding writers and poets who were with you at Cambridge, what did you think of their work?

KATHLEEN RAINE

I tried hard to like it. William Empson I knew very well and strove to admire his poetry, but it was awfully difficult. Vernon Watkins, who was a Cambridge contemporary, I met only many years later. He came up for a term, realized that this was no place for a poet of the Imagination and fled back to Wales! He took a job in a bank in Swansea, where he lived for the rest of his life, writing, I think, some of the finest poetry of our time. Watkins is a poet's poet, and made a complete statement of an Imaginative universe into which he saw deeply. Dylan Thomas had a wonderful imaginative genius and a gift for words, but Vernon's statement was more total. Eliot published nine volumes of his verse and admired him greatly, as did Yeats. He then went out of print for years, but two years ago his *Collected Poems* were published—beautifully I might add—by the Golgonoza Press. Vernon saw at once, but it took me half a lifetime to recover from Cambridge and to discover the roots of this learning of the Imagination and the Platonic tradition. Later I found the poetry of Edwin Muir, which I admired, and whom I later came to know. He came from the Orkneys, and was steeped in Scottish poetry and oral tradition, and was uncorrupted by the ideologies of the Modern Movement.

INTERVIEWER

What about David Jones?

KATHLEEN RAINE

I knew David Jones during my Catholic phase. He was a friend of Helen Sutherland, who was a great patron of the arts, and who lived in Cumberland and with whom I often stayed during the war years, and after. She was deeply Christian and certainly influenced my mistaken decision to join the Catholic Church. For what I sought had nothing to do with churches. She had a beautiful collection of works by David Jones, Ben and Winifred Nicholson, Barbara Hepworth, Gabo, Christopher Wood, even two Picassos, which she didn't like and kept in a cupboard. These were also her friends, but David Jones she loved and admired above all, and she was surely right— he was a very great artist, both as a writer and as a painter. *In Parenthesis* is outstandingly the greatest novel of the First World War.

INTERVIEWER

When and where did you publish your own poetry first?

KATHLEEN RAINE

A group of students in Cambridge including William Empson and Jacob Bronowski started an undergraduate magazine, *Experiment*. There was another one, *The Venture*,
edited by Michael Redgrave, I think, and T.H. White who
later wrote *The Sword in the Stone*. *Experiment* published
some of my poems, but I think they only accepted them
because they thought I was pretty. I remember my surprise
when young Lord Ennismore wrote me a letter saying he
thought them good and that I should "let my friends'
advice go to the devil!"

A close friend of mine in Cambridge years and after
was Humphrey Jennings. He talked marvelously and was
our link with France and the Surrealists. He later produced
remarkable war documentary films, of which *Fires Were
Started/I Was a Fireman*, about fire-fighting in the London
docks, was the most famous. His *magnum opus* was a
collage on the Industrial Revolution, *Pandemonium*, published only two years ago and already a classic, as an
amazing record of that time. Humphrey had the magical
touch of genius, and was always unexpected. Just as you
thought you had "outgrown" the Victorians, Humphrey
would come back from the Long Vacation extolling the
wonderful poetry of Rosetti!

INTERVIEWER

*What about the Oxford poets, Auden, Spender, C. Day
Lewis and Louis MacNeice? Did you know them?*

KATHLEEN RAINE

Barely. They were political left-wing poets—so was my
husband Charles Madge. That was not my world. The
one I knew best was Louis MacNeice, who was redeemed

by being essentially an Irish poet. He had a true lyrical
gift. Auden will always be read as having given expression
to the mood and mentality of his time in a brilliant way.
He held a mirror to his time and place but he is not a
poet of the Imagination. Spender translated with Leish-
mann the works of Rilke, and that was a great contribution.
Through those translations I came to know Rilke, whom
I read constantly at that time.

INTERVIEWER

*There was a third current. Surrealism, which came from
France. Who were the English surrealists?*

KATHLEEN RAINE

The outstanding surrealist poet in English was, and still
is David Gascoyne—a truly great poet though he writes
little now. He is the one English poet of my generation
whom the French venerate and regard almost as their own.
The radio program, *Mass Observation* was an English
version of surrealism, one might say. Cecil Collins the
painter was also for a short time influenced by surrealism.

Charles Madge, Humphrey Jennings and the sociologist
Tom Harrisson had the idea of discovering and observing
the unconscious themes and dreams of the collective unconscious mind of the masses. There were "day-surveys"
and other attempts to tap unconscious currents. Julian
Trevelyan the painter and David Gascoyne also played a
part.

INTERVIEWER

*Eliot's influence was not only through his own poetry but
as editor, when he published younger poets in* The Criterion
and at Faber, poets whose works we have been discussing.

KATHLEEN RAINE

True. He was in this country the doyen of the Modern
Movement and of a new idiom in poetry.

INTERVIEWER

*In that respect he was very much influenced by French
poetry, especially by Apollinaire. I was struck by it, reading
him and Apollinaire last summer.*

KATHLEEN RAINE

It is not merely that Eliot was influenced by this or that
poet or movement, he had a sense of tradition as a whole,
and his own poems resonate within that totality. His view
of tradition was a historical one and nearly all his allusions
fall within the great structure of the European tradition,
from Dante to the French Symbolists, if you like. Whereas
Yeats saw tradition in relation to the timeless. His sources
were less literary, more metaphysical-Platonic, Hindu, Bud-
dhist, Islamic . . . He explored horizons beyond European
civilization. Eliot saw the end of European civilization and
the advent of a new Dark Age; Yeats was seeking to
reverse the premises of an age and find a credible alternative
to the materialism of what he called "the three provincial
centuries"—provincial in relation to *Sophia Perennis* common to all spiritual traditions including Christendom.

Prophesies of great poets are self-fulfilling. In my youth
we didn't see it in that way—Eliot as a critic was deeply
respected, whereas Yeats was dismissed as not knowing
anything of modern ideas and "dabbling" in spiritualism,
"seeing fairies."

Eliot deepened personal suffering into wisdom and wrote
Four Quartets, but for me he is the poet of *The Waste*

Land. That was totally unprecedented, while *Four Quartets* came from the long process of transmutation of the material life had given him. They are great poems, but they don't make my hair rise as *The Waste Land* did. It is difficult to describe to another generation the effect on us of Eliot's early poetry.

INTERVIEWER

When you came down to London and had to earn a living, how did you set about it?

KATHLEEN RAINE

I didn't! The war came and I was given shelter by friends in Penrith, with my children; later I moved to a vicarage not far from the remembered places of my childhood. I don't know how I lived! Some journalism, a little reviewing, a little money from my husband . . . I had fallen desperately in love with a young Scotsman—perhaps because he came from my mother's country—who almost immediately went to War. It was pure fantasy, but it broke my marriage. By the time he came back I had converted to Catholicism.

INTERVIEWER

Why Catholicism? Graham Greene said he was attracted to it intellectually, Evelyn Waugh more emotionally, but what was the attraction for you?

KATHLEEN RAINE

Perhaps the hope of bringing some order into my life. I realised that I could not go on drifting, and as a Catholic I could not, of course, remarry, so by that step I closed the door on such a possibility. Closed it rather untidily,

but still, it was in some sense a deep choice, to which I
have adhered. Not to the Catholic Church, but to the
decision not to involve myself in any sexual relationship.
I wonder if I made a mistake and would have done better
to entrust myself to Bohemia! But by temperament I am
not Bohemian. I was always torn between the knowledge
that I ought to live a more ordered life and my terrible
incapacity to do so. Besides, I saw "love" as something as
sacred as religion itself—another fallacy of my generation!
We took love very seriously and would endure lifelong
chastity in its name if need were. By its very intensity
love was a kind of misguided path to mystical realization.
It must seem odd to the present generation.

INTERVIEWER

*To return to your literary life, did you not think of going
to see Eliot, or Yeats and asking their advice? They would
have helped you, surely?*

KATHLEEN RAINE

I sent my early poems to Eliot and he advised me to wait
two more years. But I was young and impatient, and
Tambimuttu wanted them, and published them. He understood the poetry of the Imagination and loved my work
from the outset until his death. He produced books of
great beauty, poets illustrated by artists. For example, my
first book, *Stone and Flower* was illustrated by Barbara
Hepworth. I didn't appreciate Tambimuttu then, being an
intellectual snob, and having wanted to be published by
Eliot among the Faber poets. Yet it was Tambi who saw
and understood who I was. The Faber Poets, with the
exception of Vernon Watkins, were not poets of the
imagination, but something else altogether.

INTERVIEWER

When did you go back to Girton to teach?

KATHLEEN RAINE

I was invited to go back as a Research Fellow by Professor Muriel Bradbrook. At the time I was working on *Blake and Tradition*, with a fellowship from the Bollingen Foundation.

INTERVIEWER

Why did you give up teaching? I mean it is a good way of earning a living while leaving enough time for one's own work?

KATHLEEN RAINE

Being a poet is not a job or a profession but a way of life. I don't mean a bohemian "life-style" as it is called today, but a total dedication and commitment. I endangered that integrity in becoming a Catholic convert, but had I remained in academia I would have abandoned it altogether. Academia is a graveyard of poets. I don't think any true poet could do other than I did, and escape from it. The values of the poet are at variance with those of modern Academe. Even my scholarship was different from that of other academics.

INTERVIEWER

When did you start work on Blake and Tradition?

KATHLEEN RAINE

In the middle of the war I came back to London, alone and penniless, leaving my children in the care of a friend

who, as I said had thrown her house open to several
evacuees. I eked out a living in various useless ways, and
also began to read Blake's Complete Works. I thought I
could write a book relating his *Four Zoas* to the four
Functions of Jung's psychology. I was not the first to see
the connection, I hasten to add, Kerrison Preston had
already done so, who was afterwards very kind to me.
Why I was so conceited as to imagine I could write such
a book I do not know! However, I thought I would first
read all the source-books Blake was known to have read.
I thought it wouldn't be much, since Blake was not a
learned man but, as we thought at the time, a more or
less ignorant craftsman—Eliot had said he had made his
poetry from "odds and ends about the house." Well those
"odds and ends" proved to compromise the body of learning of the Imagination whose very existence I had never
suspected, since it formed no part of our modern culture.
As I wound in the golden string Blake so disarmingly
offers, I discovered Plotinus and Porphyry, the Hermetica,
the Bhagavad-Gita, the works of Boehme and Swedenborg,
Paracelsus and Henry Vaughan and Berkeley and Thomas
Taylor the English Pagan, and many besides. I began to
realise how shallow are the foundations of a materialist
civilization and to discover that Blake's golden string is
nothing less than the mainstream of human wisdom from
time immemorial.

INTERVIEWER

*Which goes back to the Greeks and to the Sophia
Perennis.*

KATHLEEN RAINE

Exactly. So as I read I went back to my original roots,
the Romantics, whose sources of wisdom I was discovering.

This knowledge proved so rich that I quickly abandoned my early intention of writing a book about Blake in the light of Jungian psychology and wrote instead of his sources within the Perennial Philosophy. Many of which, incidentally, were those to which Jung himself had returned in his own revolutionary reversal of materialist premises of the time.

INTERVIEWER

In a way your book on Yeats was a continuation of the same study, wasn't it?

KATHLEEN RAINE

Indeed, because all his life Yeats sought to establish this primacy of Imagination. He was Blake's first editor, and in a sense I was, in this respect, his sole successor at that time.

INTERVIEWER

The Platonic interpretation of Blake, it must be admitted, is not much favored today. For example Northrop Frye's famous book on Blake states that he invented the whole of his mythology.

KATHLEEN RAINE

My book came after Frye's, which is incidentally a very good book. But it is true that my view is not favored in academia. Perhaps because it would lead to questioning some of the fundamental premises of our culture as it stands at present. But then Blake's was a lonely voice too. Goethe had the stature in his lifetime to prevail. So did Yeats. I am a much humbler torch-carrier for that tradition.

INTERVIEWER
Blake & Tradition *took you twelve years to do. Did you publish lots of poetry in those years? How did you live?*

KATHLEEN RAINE
Unfortunately I have never been able to sit under a tree and write poetry. Besides, poetry grows out of life and study. I did a little reviewing, and Sir Herbert Read befriended me and was very good to me. He got me a fellowship from the Bollingen Foundation in America, and they renewed it three times. So for years I lived at the expense of the United States of America!

INTERVIEWER
When and how did you meet Gavin Maxwell?

KATHLEEN RAINE
Tambimuttu brought him to see me while I was working on my *Blake and Tradition*, living in a house on the other side of this same square. It was another of the long line of follies and disasters of my life. He came from Northumberland and it seemed that our childhood roots were entangled.

INTERVIEWER
If I may say so falling in love with someone who was not only homosexual but liked very young men, was asking for trouble. I mean it is hazardous enough when one falls in love in normal circumstances.

KATHLEEN RAINE
I knew he was homosexual but I thought a Platonic love was all I needed, because he would not want to possess

me physically. It was not so. I made terrible scenes of jealousy, tantrums, weeping, so much weeping . . .

INTERVIEWER

The third volume of your autobiography, The Lion's Mouth, *chronicles your relationship with Maxwell, and reads like a marvellous novel. Afterwards he wrote a book,* Raven Seek Thy Brother—*a best-seller like his other books—saying that you had cursed him on a rowan tree, and all the terrible things that happened to him as a result. Did you really put a curse on him?*

KATHLEEN RAINE

We parted in a final *déchirement.* Years later when he knew he was dying of cancer he wrote to me and said: "Accompany me in spirit."

INTERVIEWER

In a way you did, because On A Deserted Shore, *the elegy you wrote after his death, contains some of your most moving poems.*

KATHLEEN RAINE

Since then I have lived without any thought of a personal relationship with any man. Once when I organized a tableau in which we children acted as Greek Goddesses I chose Pallas Athene. Not only was she a virgin, but she made a shield that frightened men away! My shield was my vocation as a poet.

INTERVIEWER

In 1981 you started Temenos, *which means "sacred enclosure" in Greek. What was your purpose, since there are so many literary magazines already, many of them you write for?*

KATHLEEN RAINE

Our primary purpose and values are not literary; we wanted to publish work whose roots were in the Sophia Perennis, the Golden Thread that in the West runs through from Plato to Yeats. We hold that the primary function of the arts is to embody a vision of the Sacred. When not rooted in such a vision—*I don't mean religion as such*—they do not nourish the soul of any age.

INTERVIEWER

Why are you stopping with number twelve?

KATHLEEN RAINE

Because it has done its work, and I'm now working on number eleven. By the time the twelfth volume comes out I shall be old enough to stop.

INTERVIEWER

What about your own work?

KATHLEEN RAINE

That will continue for as long as I can. I have just completed a final autobiographical book, a book about India, the India of the Imagination, not a travel book.

INTERVIEWER

Do you rewrite your poems a lot, or do they come easily?

KATHLEEN RAINE

Oh no! It is hard, hard! I rewrite a poem ten or twenty times. In the end the poem is formally finished, but it never fully embodies the experience.

INTERVIEWER

Do you think about death?

KATHLEEN RAINE

I'm afraid of the judgment. The judge is within ourselves. The wrong we have done to others is so much harder to contemplate than the injuries we receive. But I hope I shall be ready when the time comes.

P.L. Travers

"*I am as anonymous as a beetle!*" *said P.L. Travers in response to my request for this interview. And indeed, although she lives within a hundred yards of my home, for a long time I did not know that the tall, elegant lady I sometimes saw walking down the street, with a queenly gait, was the creator of Mary Poppins, one of the most original and universally loved characters in modern fiction.*

"*As C.S. Lewis said, 'I don't like the word creator. There is only one Creator, and we merely mix the ingredients He gives us.'*" *She went on to say that for the same reason she did not like biographies and autobiographies: "What porridge Keats had does not really matter. Mary Poppins and my other books say enough about me. Besides I am Irish, and the Irish don't like direct questions, which you have to ask in an interview. If you ask an Irishman 'Is it raining?', he will perhaps answer 'Maybe!'*"

Later she relented and invited me to tea. She lives in a small Georgian house in Chelsea. Her sitting room, where she received me, is light, airy and sparsely furnished. She sits on the corner of a long sofa the rest of which is covered with stacks of books, letters, various publications. On the creamy walls hang a Paul Klee, portraits of great grandmothers and aunts, a drawing of P.L. Travers by AE (George

279

Russell), a Tree of Life by one of her students. . . . The mantlepiece is covered with photographs of family and friends, including many children.

Mary Poppins *was published in 1934 and was an instant success. The "Cosmic Nanny" who appeared out of the blue in Cherry Tree Lane to look after Jane and Michael, the Banks' children, was overnight a favorite with children and adults alike all over the world and was later turned into a film by Walt Disney.* Mary Poppins Comes Back *appeared a year later, followed by* Mary Poppins Opens the Door *(1944),* Mary Poppins in the Park *(1952),* Mary Poppins in Cherry Tree Lane *(1982), and just last year* Mary Poppins and The House Next Door.

In the intervening years she published The Fox in the Manger, *based on a Christmas carol in which the Fox makes an offering of his cunning to the infant Jesus, thus uniting intelligence and goodness, wildness and tameness, in cosmic harmony. Her unfairly neglected novel,* Friend Monkey, *the story of the Linnet family and their loving friend Monkey, was published in 1971. She has also written two companion books to* Mary Poppins' *canon:* Mary Poppins A. to Z. *(1962) and* Mary Poppins in the Kitchen, *a cookbook (1975).*

Over the years P.L. Travers has written essays and lectured extensively on her favorite subjects of fairy tales and myths, legends and nursery rhymes, parables and proverbs. What the Bee Knows: Reflections on Myth, Symbol and Story, *a collection of these, was published in 1989. Thoughtful and beautifully written, these pieces illuminate the connections between their various subjects and the depth of the psyche from whence they emerge. She has been writer-in-residence at various American universities and has received honorary degrees from universities in the United States and Britain.*

Pamela Lyndon Travers was born in Queensland, Australia, in 1906 to an Irish father and a mother of Scottish origin. She was educated at home by governesses, and as a young girl worked in turns as secretary, dancer, actress and journalist. She started writing poetry in childhood and published some of her poems while still a teenager. She left Australia in her early twenties and settled in London, where she worked as a free-lance journalist. On a trip to Ireland she met George Russell, AE, who became her friend and mentor. She went to Ireland frequently to see him, and met Yeats and other poets and writers of his circle.

P.L. Travers speaks with a soft but firm voice. Her deep blue eyes light up when she remembers or hears something that ignites her enthusiasm. She smiles often, especially when she does not wish to answer a question—which reminds you that Mary Poppins never explains!

INTERVIEWER

I have been re-reading your Mary Poppins books with great pleasure. They have lost none of their freshness.

P.L. TRAVERS

It all comes from Above. I didn't do it; it was given to me.

INTERVIEWER

Your friend AE said nothing is a gift, you have to pay for everything.

P.L. TRAVERS

That is true, too. In the jumble of life it is all paid for, even if you don't know it.

INTERVIEWER

Augustus John said that if one has one gift, one has them all. You danced, acted and wrote. Did you draw as well?

P.L. TRAVERS

If I have a picture in my head I can draw it roughly, but I felt that drawing was not what I was meant to do, and so I never developed it.

INTERVIEWER

You once wrote that Mary Poppins had invented you, not the other way round. How do you mean? It reminded me of a story about Harold Macmillan, the British Prime Minister. Someone told him that Harold Wilson, who had just become the Leader of the Labour Party did not believe in God. He answered: "The question is whether God believes in Harold Wilson!"

P.L. TRAVERS

I didn't say that about Mary Poppins. William Hendrick Van Loon, a famous American artist, said it. People were always asking me how I came to think her up, and I didn't know what to say. I told Van Loon about it, and he said: "What is interesting to me is to know how Mary Poppins came to think up *you!*" That gave me a clue, and made me realise that she had used me for her purpose.

INTERVIEWER

You also said that the six books you wrote about her were the story of your life. Is she to some extent you? As Flaubert said: "Madame Bovary c'est moi!"

P.L. TRAVERS

Only in so far as we are both "servants." "We serve a
purpose. The purpose may be unknown. I think that if
I were in Homer's house I would be sweeping the stairs,
or saying to him: "Don't be sad Mr. Homer, I'll pour you
a cup of wine." I would have enjoyed serving him. Today
the word "servant" has menial connotations, but we all
serve something. It is who, or what, you choose to serve
that matters.

INTERVIEWER

*The first Mary Poppins book was written in 1934 when you
were already a mature woman who had lived and experienced a good deal. People compared her to Sophia, the
goddess of Wisdom, Mary Magdalen, and the Virgin Mary.
One could write a long essay about the figures to whom she
was related by various commentators. Did you have those
archetypes in mind?*

P.L. TRAVERS

They said it! I don't assert it, and I don't deny it either—
it was all totally unconscious. You remember in the first
book when she arrives at the Banks' house, she doesn't
give any references? Well, I didn't know why that was
until I had written the fourth book, *Mary Poppins in the
Park*. There is a story in it called "The children in the
story" in which Jane and Michael are reading a book called
The Silver Fairy Book, which has a picture of three princes
and a unicorn. The trees above them have fruit and
blossoms at the same time, just as in Yeats' poem, "The
Happy Townland":

> Boughs have their fruit and blossom
> At all times of the year;

Rivers are running over
With red beer and brown beer.

Then the Princes come out of the book to greet Jane and
Michael who say to them "But you are the children in
the story!", and they reply: "We've been looking at you
for a long time, *you* are the children in the story!" Then
you learn that Mary Poppins has been nanny to these
princes as well. Their names are: Florimond, Veritain, and
Amor (Beauty, Truth and Love), and when the policeman,
mistaking them for circus people, asks them who their
parents are, he is told Fidelio and Esperanza (Faith and
Hope). Well, somebody who has been Nanny to such a
family could hardly produce references, could she? So you
see, it took me four books to realise it. How could I
identify with such a person? No, she is not me.

INTERVIEWER

*When you wrote it you were convalescing in the country
after a long illness, and "she came to you" to amuse you.
Perhaps being weak you were more receptive and childlike,
and she came to nurse you, "staying long enough for you
to write her down," as you said. How did it happen?*

P.L. TRAVERS

Suddenly there she was—plain, vain, capricious, able to
perform miracles for the children. But despite her plainness,
she appeals to men. A friend once said to me: "Don't
expect me to read *Mary Poppins*, I hate children's books!"
Nevertheless I sent the book to him. "Why didn't you
tell me!" he wrote, "Mary Poppins with her cool, green
core of sex has enthralled me for ever!" Men do fall in
love with her, so perhaps behind her plainness there must
be some beauty.

INTERVIEWER

*You don't elaborate on her physical appearance, except at
the beginning: "Turned up nose, blue eyes,"* . . . *But you
quote AE saying: "Had she lived in another age.* . . . *she
would have had long golden tresses, a wreath of flowers in
one hand, and perhaps a spear in the other. Her eyes would
have been like the sea, her nose comely, and on her feet
winged sandals* . . . *but this being Kali Yuga—the Iron
Age—she comes in the habiliments suited to it." How did
you get your illustrator to translate your picture of her?*

P.L. TRAVERS

She struggled nobly with the text—she is the daughter of
Ernest Shepard, the illustrator of *Winnie the Pooh*—but
couldn't get her. Then I found a wooden Dutch doll in
an antique shop: tiny, turned up nose, black shiny hair,
thin legs. I had one when I was a child. There was nothing
cuddly about these Dutch wooden dolls; they were very
sure of themselves. Anyway, I gave it to her, and she got
what was needed.

INTERVIEWER

At first you wanted to publish the book anonymously. Why?

P.L. TRAVERS

I wanted the author to be called Anon, because if you
look at poetry anthologies you see that some of the best
poems are by Anon, and they read as though they were
written by the same person. They come from the same
source. But the publishers threw a fit at the idea and put
my name on it.

INTERVIEWER

*Mary Poppins talks to birds and animals. Did you have St.
Francis of Assisi in mind?*

P.L. TRAVERS

I hadn't thought of it, but now that you mention it . . .
I can never explain these things: "By indirections find
directions out," says Polonius in Hamlet. And Walt Whitman says—in *Child on a Beach at Night*— "I give thee
the first suggestion, the Problem and indirection." I have
always worked by indirection.

INTERVIEWER

*It could also imply that as children we know everything,
the language of plants and animals and the constellations
. . . and then we forget.*

P.L. TRAVERS

That is true, but certain things come back to certain people.
After the awful business of adolescence what was known
in childhood begins to seep through, gradually, if you are
lucky.

INTERVIEWER

*Children are more "connected," to use one of your expres-
sions. The Prophet Mohammad said we must love children,
for they come from God and have not yet forgotten Him,
while the Taoists believe that the infant is the Tao, the Way.*

P.L. TRAVERS

Absolutely. As a child I was astonished that God was
referred to as just god, without even "Mister" or "Duke
of." I asked my father what was His other name. He said
that He didn't have any, that He was plain God. But I
didn't think He was plain at all; I thought we were friends
from afar.

INTERVIEWER

*Talking about your childhood, Australia and Australians
are not usually associated with mysticism—except the Aborigines. You are the first Australian mystic I have encoun-
tered, doubtless there are many more, but we don't know
them.*

P.L. TRAVERS

But I am not really Australian, I'm Irish. I think I was
born saying: "Get me out of here as quickly as possible!"
Although I enjoyed it all thoroughly, and I love Australia,
I knew I was meant to go somewhere else. When quite
a young child I stood outside the camp of some gypsies
in the hope that they would snatch me away. But they
didn't. I took off my sandals and went to the man who
seemed to be their leader, and I thought that if he took
them from me, he would take me as well. But he looked
them over, politely put them back on my feet, and gently
turned me towards home. I was surprised that he could
refuse such a prize! We were always warned that gypsies
stole children, and here was one dying to be stolen, and
they wouldn't have her!

INTERVIEWER

*You were only second generation Australian. How did your
family come to settle in Australia? You refer to your parents
in various autobiographical articles as Irish and Scottish.*

P.L. TRAVERS

My father came from a very old Irish family. Although
he died when I was small, I remember him intimately,
and I adored him. He told me poems—Irish poetry—and

stories. Our house had a completely Irish ambiance—
servants, grooms, everybody was Irish, and everything was
brought over from Ireland. If I spoke with an Australian
accent I was severely reprimanded.

INTERVIEWER

*You had a maid, Bertha, whose parrot-headed umbrella you
have given to Mary Poppins. She must have made an
impression on you to remember her after so many years?*

P.L. TRAVERS

Yes, I remember her as if it were yesterday. She was Irish
too.

INTERVIEWER

*So when did you learn, and from whom, about the Australian
Aborigines and their mythology? The "dreaming," the an-
cestral map of Australia drawn in dreams and songs? Bruce
Chatwin's Songlines was about that, which is how the
general public here learned about it.*

P.L. TRAVERS

The ancestors of the Aborigines invented Australia by
walking across it. Further back than grandparents the
ancestors go into Dreamtime. If we were willing to think
that way it would be the same with us, because beyond
our grandparents we don't know about people; they become dreams. But I learned about it all much later. There
is a wonderful book by Daisy Bates, an Edwardian woman
who went and lived among the Aborigines with a white
high-necked cotton blouse, elegant shoes and a hat. I came
across Aborigines from time to time, and had a strong

feeling for them, though I didn't really communicate with them.

Why did your father go to Australia?

My father went first to plant tea in Ceylon and then to Australia, where he met my mother and they married. He was a younger son. And younger sons tend to explore the world! My mother was Scottish, as I said. Her grandfather was from an old Scottish family, and he was sent to Australia as a young man to stay with the Governor, a family friend. They thought he might have tuberculosis and that the climate would be good for him. He fell in love with the country and bought some tracts of land there. Then he came back to Britain and married the woman whose portrait you see on the wall above your head. They went back to Australia, taking some retainers with them, including a midwife. The voyage was very long then, the Suez Canal was not built yet; you took a ship to Egypt, crossed the isthmus on mule-back, and another ship for Australia. So my mother was already third generation Australian, but brought to England to be educated.

As a child you wrote poetry; did you show it to your parents?

I showed them to my mother who showed them to my father. He said: "Hardly W.B. Yeats!" My mother said: "Well I don't know . . . I think it is quite clever the way she has rhymed mother with smother!"

INTERVIEWER

It must have been traumatic losing a father you loved so much. I remember as a child worrying about my parents dying. I think children often worry about their parents as much as the other way round.

P.L. TRAVERS

That is true, and I was bereft when my father died. I remember the night before: I took a three-penny coin to his bed and said that in the morning I would go and buy him some pears. "Pears are just what I need," he said. He took the coin and put it under his pillow. You must remember that we lived in a world where money wasn't handled in cash—it was despised. Once in between governesses we were sent, my younger sister and myself, to the little village school. My sister found the lost brooch of the teacher and handed it back to her. As a reward the teacher gave her a two-shillingpiece, which was something enormous then. When my father heard of the incident he was outraged that we should have accepted the money. He said that it had to be given back at once. I said: "We can't!" "Why not, pray?" he asked. "Because we have spent it." "On what?" "On cigarettes." He exploded. Then my mother found the packet of cigarettes on which was written "Simpson's Sugar Smokes"—they were made of candy! However, my father gave the two shillings back. To take money was disreputable!

Well, the next morning after I gave him my three-penny bit my mother was resting on a sofa in the drawing-room and she told me that Father had gone to God. I was seven and a half. I wore a frilly white dress with a black sash for some time. And for years I expected him to return, as from a journey. When things went wrong I used to say to my mother "Don't worry, it will be alright when Father comes back from God." She would look at me and her gray eyes would turn black. Then at thirteen I was sent to an elegant boarding school. One night I stood by the window and looked at a particular star, and suddenly I realized that my father was dead and would never come back.

INTERVIEWER

As if he had become that star. Your family's situation changed after his death. Was life very difficult?

P.L. TRAVERS

Things became more difficult financially. I learnt to type and took a job in an office. I was brought up hearing rich great-aunts saying: "You must be good and help your mother." That seemed to be my role, and I wondered if there was anything else for me in life except helping my mother. Evidently there was, as it turned out later.

INTERVIEWER

How did you become a dancer while working full-time in an office?

P.L. TRAVERS

I always loved dancing, and went to dancing classes in the evenings. It was not classical ballet, but it was good dancing just the same. Eventually I was given a dancing part in a pantomime of *The Sleeping Beauty* that was touring Australia at the time.

INTERVIEWER

Dancing plays an important part in Mary Poppins books. In Mary Poppins in the Park there is a lovely scene in

which the children dance "in time with the heavenly tune."
It reminded me of the mystic dances of the Sufis, the Whirling
Dervishes as they are called in the West.

P.L. TRAVERS

Quite right. I have become interested in Sufism recently,
which shows how things connect. Dancing is a mystical
experience, or can be. James Stephens said: "The first and
last duty of man is to dance." As a child in moments of
joy or sadness I danced. In a way I still do. So dancing
was part of my life, but what I really wanted to do as
profession was to be a Shakespearean actress.

INTERVIEWER

You succeeded, but how did you go about it without training?

P.L. TRAVERS

I loved the theatre and went to every play that was staged.
Once, having seen one based on Napoleon's son, *L'Aiglon*,
I rehearsed with a friend the various parts in the basement
where the big baskets of scenery and costumes and props
for *The Sleeping Beauty* were kept. One night the ballet
mistress, who was a very fierce woman, burst in and said
to my friend: "Peggy, go away! I want to speak to Pamela."
Then she turned to me saying: "Where did you learn to
act?" I said I never had. "Never mind, you'll have a small
part in the play," she said. Someone was leaving the cast
and I replaced her. That spurred me on. Later I made
friends with a theater critic of a big newspaper, and he
said to me that if I let him kiss me he would take me to
see the actor-manager of a Shakespearean company. I gave
him a gentle kiss on the cheek, which evidently was not

what he had in mind, but he kept his word and introduced
me to the man.

It must have been Edmond Rostand's L'Aiglon, *judging by
the period. What did you audition in?*

The Actor-Manager said: "Let's see what you can do. You
see that chair in the middle of the stage? That's a fountain
in the Market Place of a village, and there is a great revelry
going on; you are a girl of the town running around it
being chased by a young man. Go ahead and do it." I
did, and one of the actors chased me and caught me and
kissed me violently on the lips. I was very young and
innocent, and I had never been kissed that way before.
So I slapped him very hard! He put his hand to his cheek
and said to the Actor-Manager: "Sir, don't take her, she
is dynamite!" The Chief replied: "On the contrary, that's
why I *shall* take her; we need a bit of dynamite around
here!"

So I stayed with the company for several seasons and
ended up playing Titania in *Midsummer Night's Dream.*
Eventually I was allowed by my mother to go on tour,
and that is when I started writing. There was a journalist
who had taken a fancy to me, and followed the company
from town to town on his motorcycle. I showed him a
piece I had written and he took it to his editor who
published it.

Was it a poem?

P.L. TRAVERS

Not exactly, but it was a poetic, imaginative piece. The editor asked me to write for him regularly—articles and poems. I was by then nineteen or twenty.

INTERVIEWER

Did your family approve of your going on the stage? I mean in those days it was rather mal-vu *for girls from "good" families to tread the planks, as they say.*

P.L. TRAVERS

At first they were shocked and deplored it. But I was successful, and as you know success softens people up.

INTERVIEWER

So you were a successful Shakespearean actress and a published writer. What made you chuck it all in and leave for Britain and uncertainty?

P.L. TRAVERS

As I said I always wanted to leave Australia. I saved every penny I could, and finally I told my mother I wanted to go away and be a writer. She, who had disapproved of my acting partly because it was precarious, now panicked because she thought writing was even more uncertain. I said: "Don't worry, I'll take care of you just the same, but I must go." I took a ship and arrived in England. I had ten pounds, five of which I promptly lost! On the ship I had met some English journalists who introduced me to others in London, and everybody was kind and helpful.

They took me to Editors and got me jobs, and so it went.
I wrote journalism for a living—reviews, interviews, but
also poems. Everything.

INTERVIEWER

*Meeting AE changed your life, as you said. How did it
happen?*

P.L. TRAVERS

AE was the Editor of *The Irish Stateman*. When I arrived
in England I sent him a few poems, enclosing a stamped
addressed envelope for him to send them back. To my
surprise he published them and sent me two guineas. He
said he knew I was Irish because the poems could not
have been written by anyone who was not, and he asked
me to go and see him when I went to Ireland. Soon after
I went to see my Irish relatives and called on him in
Dublin. He was very kind to me, and asked me to go and
see him on my way back through the city. I didn't dare,
thinking he was a busy man and had suggested it out of
courtesy.

Sometime later he was in London to see his friend
George Moore and came to see me unexpectedly: "You
are a faithless girl! You didn't keep your promise to come
and see me," he said. "I wanted to give you a copy of
my book." And he gave me all his books. We became
friends, and from then on I went to see him whenever I
was visiting my relatives in Ireland. Through him I met
Yeats and James Stephens and other poets. He always had
time for young poets, and I saw a lot of him till the end
of his life.

*In your essay "Only Connect" you talk about an encounter
with Yeats. Once you went to see him in Dublin unexpectedly.
How did he react?*

P.L. TRAVERS

I took a boat to the Lake Isle of Innisfree in pouring rain,
cut off a huge armful of rowan branches, travelled to
Dublin and arrived at his door. He opened it and panicked
at the sight of this drenched gypsy. He called for help
and I was taken downstairs by a maid, dried and given a
cup of cocoa. Afterwards I wanted to slip away quietly,
but a servant told me that he was waiting for me in the
drawing-room. He never said a word about my rowan
branches. Instead he proudly showed me an egg his canary
had just laid. But I noticed on his desk a lone branch of
rowan in a vase, and I learnt then that you can say more
with less.

Later he gave me a couple of his poems, one of which
was *The Song of Wandering Aengus*. I told him that I had
put some of his poems to music, and he asked me to sing
them to him, which I did. "Beautiful," he said, "Beautiful,
I couldn't have imagined anything more like them." I was
very pleased and the next day I told AE about it. "You
must sing them to me as well . . . but remember that
Yeats is tone-deaf!"

INTERVIEWER

*Did your interest in Hinduism and Buddhism start with
your friendship with AE and Yeats?*

P.L. TRAVERS

I don't think so. I was always interested in mysticism, even before I knew what it was called. Later I studied Zen Buddhism for a long time. My Zen Master told me that the Mary Poppins stories were in essence Zen stories. But I found a kindred spirit in Yeats and AE. The latter told me we belonged to "the same spiritual clan."

INTERVIEWER

Did you meet G.B. Shaw with AE?

P.L. TRAVERS

I was supposed to, but never did. AE told him a story about me which amused him, and he said: "Bring her to see me; then she can decide if she wants to be friends with me." Somehow it didn't happen. At the beginning, my Irish relatives were not at all pleased that I was going to be a writer and mix with people like AE and Yeats, "who saw fairies." They said "you are going to be living in London where you might meet even more frightful people . . . like the Irishman who used to live in a whitewashed cottage across the fields over there. He is a great boastful fellow with a big voice. Be courteous to him but do *not* pursue the acquaintance! He calls himself George Bernard Shaw!"

INTERVIEWER

Parallel to that literary circle in Ireland, centered around AE and Yeats, there was another one in London around T.S. Eliot. Did you meet him?

P.L. TRAVERS

Of course, I had many friends among writers and poets in those days. But I also had, and still have, a great number of friends outside the literary field. I would hate to be surrounded by writers only; it would be very sterile. Indeed I never believed I belonged to the literary world as such. I belonged to my friends and family, some of whom happened to be literary people. Another good friend in those days was A.R. Orage, who was a famous editor. He was English but pronounced his name in French, *orage*, because it means storm. He first edited *New Age*, which I didn't know, then *The New English Weekly*, for which I wrote poetry and articles.

Much has been written about Eliot recently, saying that he was cold and unfeeling. Far from it. He was warm and generous and loving, a true poet.

INTERVIEWER

What about the next generation of poets? Did you meet them, or read them?

P.L. TRAVERS

I knew and read Auden and MacNeice, and I liked them. Now there are others like Ted Hughes and Philip Larkin, but I no longer read much poetry. Nowadays I mostly read mythology and mysticism.

INTERVIEWER

This brings me to your reading generally. Your essays attest a deep erudition; it seems that like most auto-didacts you have read widely on a variety of subjects—philosophy, mysticism, poetry, et cetera. . . . As a child did you read what is usually referred to as "children's books?"

P.L. TRAVERS

I read and liked Beatrix Potter. But my favorite fairy tales were, and still are, Grimm's. My father had a two-volume

Grimm's which I still have on my shelf upstairs. One day
I wrote an article about them in the *New York Herald
Tribune*, and the same night I met W.H. Auden at a party:
"This is what we have wanted for ages!" he said to me,
waving the article. Next day the Pantheon Press came to
me and asked if I wished to edit the two volumes for a
new edition. I declined, and they did it themselves, beautifully, with an introduction by Padraic Colum, and a
commentary by the great mythologist Joseph Campbell.

But I wonder if the label "children's literature" is not
just a convenient way for publishers and booksellers to
classify their products. I am amazed that they even put
the age group on the cover. Three to five, or nine to
eleven, like the sizes of socks! Who knows when childhood
ends and adulthood begins? I don't think authors write
specifically for children. Lewis Carroll dedicated *Alice in
Wonderland* to a child, but only, I think, after he had
finished it, as an afterthought. Beatrix Potter said: "I write
to please myself." I think the same can be said for A.A.
Milne, Tolkien and others.

I didn't have a specific child in mind either. How could
I have written that Mary Poppins slides up the bannister
when a Japanese child who reads it lives in a house without
stairs? Or talk about her umbrella for a child in Africa,
who has never seen one? Life is a continuous flow, not
chopped up in sections.

INTERVIEWER

*Nevertheless children have a more acute perception of magic
and mystery, and they have appropriated some folk treasure
of our ancestors. We label it "children's literature" for the
sake of convenience.*

P.L. TRAVERS

I agree; that is why I am grateful to them for including Mary Poppins in that treasure trove. I receive wonderful letters from them which I cherish. One little boy wrote the other day saying: "Will you marry me when you grow up?"

INTERVIEWER

How do you like Tolkien? He created a whole new fairy-tale world, which hadn't been done for some time.

P.L. TRAVERS

I admire him, but he is not one of my heroes, because he *invented*. An invented story doesn't appeal to me so much, although I see its cleverness.

INTERVIEWER

Yet you admire Hans Christian Anderson, and wrote an essay on him, About the Sleeping Beauty?

P.L. TRAVERS

True, he was also an inventor. But the Grimms didn't invent; they took down their tales from old soldiers and crones who had heard them from others. It was all transmitted orally and went back to no one knew when or where. It is rather like a song written in the traditional form, a genuine folksong.

INTERVIEWER

What about literature generally? What did you read?

P.L. TRAVERS

I did pass the entrance exam to Sydney University, but I didn't go because I had to earn a living. I read a lot of

novels, right across the board, English, Russian, French.
But I no longer read novels—modern novels bore me.

INTERVIEWER

Who were your favourite writers, I mean the ones with
whom you felt a spiritual affinity?

P.L. TRAVERS

It is hard to say, because I am a born classicist. I loved
Shakespeare, Plato, Plotinus. . . . I read the Hindu epics,
Mahabharata and *Rāmāyana*, and I spent a long time on
the great Russians—a whole year on *War and Peace*. The
French Classics I read in translation, and I loved the
American classics, particularly Melville and Whitman. This
business of influence is a tricky one. Things are absorbed
and you don't know how, or when they will surface.

INTERVIEWER

This brings us back to Mary Poppins, and all the influences
that have been detected in them by various commentators.
For example someone suggested that when AE referred to
her appearance in the Age of Kali Yuga, he meant that
she was a literary avatar of the Goddess Kali. Do you agree
with that?

P.L. TRAVERS

He was giving me a clue. Though not a feminist, I've
always been interested in the Mother Goddess in all her
aspects. Not long ago a reader wrote and asked me if Mary
Poppins was the Mother Goddess. Remember that the
very first godhead we know of, Inanna of Sumeria, was a
female. I have often felt that the women's liberation movement in its positive aspect, is an attempt at realizing the

Divine Mother. I don't mean that all women-libbers are
goddesses, far from it, but that perhaps the feminine
principle must be on the ascendance. All I hope is that
they don't try to become like men. Of course if they want
to fulfill themselves through a profession they must be
allowed to do so, but I hope it does not mean becoming
the Managing Director of General Motors or some other
such company. Women belong in myth; they carry the
world. Beside we have to think of Yin and Yang, the most
important of all concepts, and their balance.

INTERVIEWER

*But you yourself chose a career, and found fulfillment partly
through work, did you not?*

P.L. TRAVERS

I have never had a career! I have lived a life. That has
meant doing certain things and earning a living. It would
be different for other women. Of course, I was lucky not
to be in a profession where women are paid less than
men. So, I never had to go and nobble the Government
about Women's Rights. Perhaps as a result I have been
perfectly happy to be a woman. Yin does not resent but
receives.

INTERVIEWER

*Shakespeare's influence might have come through the char-
acter of the Fool, which is what Mary Poppins as well as
Robinson Ay have been related to by various people.*

P.L. TRAVERS

Yes, perhaps. Otherwise why would Robinson Ay stay
with a family like the Banks? I love the Fools because

they are wiser. They don't know much, but knowledge is
not wisdom. The Fool is wise. Once a young man asked
me to promise never to be clever. "I have just been reading
Mary Poppins again, and it could only have been written
by a lunatic," he said. I *am* a bit of a fool, but not, alas,
with a capital F.

The first legendary Fools were women. The most famous
was Iambe. Zeus sent her with Demeter, who was wandering and searching for what was lost. Iambe told her
stories and poems and ballads to charm the time away,
make the waiting and searching pleasant. From these poems
come the iambic pentameter, or so the legend goes.

INTERVIEWER

After four Mary Poppins *books you wrote* Mary Poppins
from A. to Z. *and* Mary Poppins in the Kitchen, *a cookbook.
Then for many years you did not write anything about her.
But in 1982 you published* Mary Poppins in Cherry Tree
Lane. *What made you decide to bring her back?*

P.L. TRAVERS

I didn't bring her back, *she came back.* So did the other
characters. I wanted to call the third book *Goodbye Mary
Poppins,* because I thought it would probably be the last
one. But my first American publisher, who was a great
personal friend, said "Oh you must not! I beg you not
to! How does she go away this time?" I said that she just
opens the door and disappears. He said "So let's call it
Mary Poppins Opens the Door." And that's what we did.
It turned out that he was right, since she did come back,
years later.

A little boy wrote to me and said: "Why have you sent
her away? You have made children cry." So perhaps she

came back for the sake of that little boy, and other children
who missed her.

INTERVIEWER

In the meantime you wrote Friend Monkey, *which I find
an enchanting as well as a profound book. People have
compared Monkey to a Christ figure. Do you agree? There
is a lot in common between him and Mary Poppins.*

P.L. TRAVERS

Perhaps. *Friend Monkey* is really my own favorite of all
my books, because it is based on a Hindu myth of the
Monkey Lord who loved so much that he created chaos
wherever he went. If you read the *Rāmāyana* you will
come across the story of Hanuman on which I built my
version of that ancient myth. I don't know when I first
heard it, but it made a deep impression, and I knew it
would surface someday, in some form. Hanuman is someone who loves too much, but can't help it. The book
wasn't well-received; people wanted more Mary Poppins,
but I wanted to do something different, newer.

INTERVIEWER

*You said somewhere that children need more than just the
love of their parents. Both Mary Poppins and Friend Monkey
provide that love. But can one love too much? I think the
idea has been invented by those who don't know how to
receive it!*

P.L. TRAVERS

It is difficult to talk about love, because it is such a private
matter. All I can say is that is is a life-long discipline, the
greatest discipline in the world.

INTERVIEWER

Miss Brown-Potter in Friend Monkey *is said to be both related to Mary Poppins and to Beatrix Potter. You describe her as having lived in an attic as a child, and being "a shy child in a white dress, isolated, plain, dreaming of far-away places," which is a bit like Beatrix Potter's childhood. Did you have her in mind?*

P.L. TRAVERS

I did make a connection, but she is also related to Mary Kingsley, the explorer, who went to West Africa as an anthropologist, wearing elastic-sided boots, flowing skirts, and a cape and a bonnet. She lived happily among the tribes, and gave the tribeswomen her high-necked blouses. But the men wore them instead! One day a leopard came sniffling around her skirt; she gave it a little shove with her boot and said, "Get along, you idiot!" and it did, at once! This was to me marvelous. She was buried at sea, as she had wished. "Of her bones are coral made!"

INTERVIEWER

Friend Monkey *could be made into a wonderful film. Did you enjoy Walt Disney's film of* Mary Poppins?

P.L. TRAVERS

Oh dear! They turned Mrs. Banks into a Suffragette! And in a film set in Edwardian times they made her pull up her skirt and display her underwear! Can you imagine? At one point Mary Poppins dances a cancan on the roof with the sweeps and she whirls around until all her underwear shows. Of course, she would *know* how to dance the Cancan, but her skirt would also *know* how to behave! Anyway, people liked the film, so I can't complain.

INTERVIEWER

Did you ever think of publishing an anthology of your poetry?

P.L. TRAVERS

No. Partly because I never keep anything. Even letters, I have given most of them away to whoever asked for them over the years. The poems were like leaves, at the mercy of the wind. They go back to earth after having served their purpose.

There is also the fact that they were largely written in assonance. Assonance is an Irish device, no longer much used. It is the rhyme of the vowel rather than the consonant. Yeats used it a lot, and AE, James Stephens . . . but it is certainly not fashionable now.

But there is a Professor at the University of Alberta who is doing a book on my work, and she will put in a lot of poems.

INTERVIEWER

By contrast, you have made a selection of your essays, What the Bee Knows, *which has just been published. It is a profound and beautifully written book, and I'm sure the poems would be just as well received.*

P.L. TRAVERS

Most of the essays were published in *Parabola* over the years, and it was easy to make a selection. There is an English saying that goes: "Ask the wild bee what the Druids knew." I took the title from that, and I wanted my friend Cecil Collins to paint a bee for the cover, as I wanted an archetypal bee, not an ordinary one. Eventually

I found the picture of a bee in the *Encyclopaedia Britanica*
which is 3600 years old.

Have you seen Cecil Collins' great retrospective exhibition at the Tate Gallery? He died just after the opening,
his life's work done. How wonderful!

INTERVIEWER

Do you write regularly?

P.L. TRAVERS

No. I have never written regularly or to order. At the
same time I am always working. When I am out shopping,
or doing any chores, I am thinking about what I am
writing at the time. I don't sit around and wait for inspiration.

INTERVIEWER

Do you write in long-hand or directly on the typewriter?

P.L. TRAVERS

Both. It depends, but my handwriting is quite different
from what I see on the typewritten page. I wonder where
my ideas come from: from instinct or prior knowledge of
some sort, or what. I am not a mental or analytical person,
it is all a mystery to me, a question of listening. The great
treasure is the Unknown, as a Zen Master said; it is a
matter of being "summoned not created."

INTERVIEWER

Do you ever think of that supreme Unknown which is death?
Do you believe in an after-life?

P.L. TRAVERS

The Tao says "The Great Way is not difficult, only cease
to have opinions." So I try not to have any, even about
an after-life. I have always been aware of death and think
about it. But death, like love, is a very private affair and
can't be discussed.

Shusha Guppy is London Editor of *The Paris Review* and a regular contributor to *The Daily Telegraph*, British *Vogue*, and other periodicals. She is the author of *The Blindfold Horse*, an autobiographical work, which won two literary awards in England from the Royal Society of Literature, and the *Yorkshire Post* Best First Book Award.